SCRIPTURE
AS
STORY

Morris A. Inch

University Press of America
Lanham • New York • Oxford

Copyright © 2000 by
University Press of America,® Inc.

4720 Boston Way
Lanham, Maryland 20706

12 Hid's Copse Rd.
Cumnor Hill, Oxford OX2 9JJ

Library of Congress Cataloging-in-Publication Data

Inch, Morris A.
Scripture as story / Morris A. Inch.
p.   cm.
Includes bibliographical references and index.
1. Narration in the bible. I. Title
BS521.7.I53   2000   220.6'6—dc21   00—044326 CIP

ISBN 0-7618-1779-4 (pbk: alk. ppr.)

⊗™ The paper used in this publication meets the minimum
requirements of American National Standard for Information
Sciences—Permanence of Paper for Printed Library Materials,
ANSI Z39.48—1984

CONTENTS

Acknowledgment

In general, I am indebted to the grand company of story-tellers, who have both edified and entertained me over the years. Some of my earliest memories concern perching on a barrel in my father's country store while the village narrators practiced their considerable talents. Then, more in particular, I would express my appreciation to my cherished wife, Joan, for her help with editing and formatting the text.

PREFACE

It should not come as a surprise that the Bible *contains* stories. Some are *legendary* in the sense that they explain persisting mysteries by way of religious means. Others are *heroic* in describing the feats of some bold spirit out of our distant past. Still others are *mundane* in that they report routine events with which we can readily identify. All are instructive and potentially inspirational.

Conversely, we may not be primed to think of the Scripture *as* story. That is, we may overlook the fact that narrative provides its dominant literary genre. All else fits within its scope. All else derives from a primarily narrative format.

Jacob Licht elaborates concerning three story formats: fiction, history, and traditional narrative. Qualifications aside, *fiction* records imaginary events. In contrast, the "historian is not supposed to invent anything. He necessarily selects and arranges his material, his ideas do influence the presentation of events, but he must not, or should not, change the 'hard facts.'"[1]

As for the authors or *recounters* of traditional narrative, they "are not supposed to invent anything. In this they are like historians. But their material is a web of notions in their culture and therefore changes, slowly and constantly, with the culture itself." In this latter regard they are unlike historians. Such is the general character of Scripture, not in some particulars but when viewed as a whole. We encounter change but with such change the things that matter most remain constant.

The Scripture *as* story invites us to enter into the situation recorded, identify with its characters, and learn from their experiences. Its meaning can't be understood apart from the story because the story always conveys far more than what the reader can reduce to flat propositional statements. "Rather, the interpreter must learn to *work through* the story and state the meaning *in terms of the story*. This is no easy task, because it means entering into the world of the story."[2]

This in no way detracts from the inspiration of Sacred Writ. "Above all, you must understand that no prophecy of Scripture came about by the prophet's own interpretation. For prophecy never had its origin in the will of man, but men spoke from God as they were carried along by the Holy Spirit" (2 Peter 1:20-21). As a result, "All Scripture is God-breathed and is useful for teaching, rebuking, correcting and training in righteousness, so that the man of God may be thoroughly equipped for every good work" (2 Tim. 3:16).

Welcome to the Scripture *as* story. Imagine the narrative as it unfolds. Join in the experiences of those involved. Recast life in Biblical perspective. Let the venture begin.

AN OVERVIEW

"It is characteristic of stories that they do not end where they began. Change, growth, and development are the very essence of stories."[3] The Biblical account begins with creation, concludes with restoration, and pursues its course from one to the other. As a result, Biblical narrative consists of three components: the beginning, conclusion, and development.

What of the narrative's *beginning*? *In the beginning* corresponds to the Egyptian *times of the gods*. It was reserved for such supernatural beings as might be present, and before human kind came on the scene. Of similar intent, the Babylonian *Enuma Elish* commences: "When above, the heaven had not been named (and) below, the earth had not been called by name."

From Hebrew perspective, God created man and man created gods. As a case in point, "For great is the Lord and most worthy of praise; he is to be feared above all gods. For all the gods of the nations are idols, but the Lord made the heavens" (Psa. 96:4-5). As another, "The arrogance of man will be brought low and the pride of men humbled; the Lord alone will be exalted in that day, and the idols will totally disappear" (Isa. 2:17).

Many supernatural powers to which the generic term *god* is applied are believed self-created, should their origin and existence be questioned at all. "Their numbers within any given religious system may be large or small; occasionally there is only one. ...The term *high god* or *supreme god* is usually applied to the deity that outranks all others; the same terms are used in monotheism, where there is one god."[4] Consequently, the Bible qualifies as an extended *high god* narrative in a monotheistic mode.

The *high god* is characteristically inscrutable and unpredictable. So God confirms: "As the heavens are higher than the earth, so are my ways higher than your ways and my thoughts than your thoughts" (Isa. 55:9). So Job confesses: "Surely I spoke of things I did not understand, things too wonderful for me to know" (Job 42:3).

What of Sacred Writ's *conclusion*? "The grace of the Lord Jesus be with God's people" (Rev. 22:21). "John's benediction at the very least universalizes the book's address: even as God's grace is bestowed first upon the seven Asian congregations in his greeting (1:4), now at book's end God's grace is extended to all those congregations who might read it."[5] As Scripture begins with God's creation, it concludes with the blessing of his people.

This calls attention to a distinctive feature of the Biblical text. Whereas its pagan counterparts suggested that the gods created mankind to serve their needs, the Scripture asserts that God wishes to pour out his provision on them. As Paul succinctly puts it, God "is not served by human hands, as if he needed anything, because he himself gives all men life and breath and everything else" (Acts 17:25).

As for the conclusion per se, it implies an evaluation of what precedes it. Those who trust their way to God's leading are blessed. Those who fail to do so will have reason to regret it. God knows how to comfort the afflicted and afflict the comfortable.

What of the third component of Biblical narrative: its *development*? Scripture continues to make reference to the *high god*. On one occasion, Abram is returning from defeating an alliance which had pillaged Sodom and Gomorrah, and taken captive Abram's nephew Lot and his possessions. Whereupon, Melchizedek the king of Salem came out to welcome him. "He was a priest of God Most High, and he blessed Abram, saying, 'Blessed be Abram of God Most High, Creator of heaven and earth. And blessed be God Most High, who delivered your enemies into your hand.' Then Abram gave him a tenth of everything" (Gen. 14:18-20).

Later on Abram was greeted by the king of Sodom. "Give me the people and keep the goods for yourself," he suggested. "But Abram said to the king of Sodom, 'I have raised my hand to the Lord, God Most High, Creator of heaven and earth, and have taken an oath that I will accept nothing belonging to you, not even a thread or the thong of a sandal, so that you will never be able to say, 'I made Abram rich.'" Only with regard to those who went with him was Abram willing to make an exception.

Sodom makes a short, almost rude demand of just six words: "Give me people; take property yourself." "There is none of the customary courtesy here. The word order (note how he mentions 'giving' before 'taking') reflects Sodom's ungracious self-centeredness. As their rescuer, Abram presumably had a right to both the people and the property."[6] As a servant of the *Most High*, he chose not to press his rights in any way that might compromise his loyalty.

At a later juncture in salvation history, Paul was called upon to give an explanation of his teaching before the Areopagus. "Men of Athens!" he addressed them. "I see that in every way you are very religious. For as I walked around and looked carefully at your objects of worship, I even found an altar with the inscription: TO AN UNKNOWN GOD. Now what you worship as something unknown I am going to proclaim to you" (Acts 17:22-23). Having set his course, the apostle continued: "The God who made the world and everything in it is the Lord of heaven and earth and does not live in temples built by hands. ...In the past God overlooked such ignorance, but now he commands all people everywhere to repent."

Hitherto the *High God* had overlooked their ignorance, but no longer. "Behind the *but now* of verse 30 lies the familiar concept of the new age inaugurated by Christ. Through him God had dealt definitively with the problem of sin. But for that very reason, he had now laid humanity under a new accountability."[7]

Such is the character of *traditional narrative* that it extends the story at later times and on different occasions. This is accompanied by change, growth, and augmentation. The trail of the *High God* would be more obvious but for the fact that it merges with the account of *Yahweh* in delivering his people from their bondage. It is a matter for celebration that the *High God* and *Yahweh* are one and the same. Otherwise stated, the God of creation is also the God of salvation history. He moreover means to lavishly bless those who trust their ways to him.

Every story has a central character. He or she is called the *protagonist*. Those arrayed against him or her are designated as *antagonists*. The *High God* who reveals himself as *Yahweh* is the protagonist of the Biblical narrative. The *antagonists* are made up of evil spirits and rebellious humans. "Readers and interpreters of biblical stories would do much better with these stories than they often do if they followed a very simple rule: *pay attention to what happens to the protagonist in the story*. Stories are built around the protagonist."[8]

As a prime case in point, we turn our attention to the *Akeda* (binding of Isaac). On a certain occasion God called out "Abraham!" "Here I am," the latter replied (Gen. 22:1). Then the former said: "Take your son, your only son, Isaac, whom you love, and go the region of Moriah. Sacrifice him there as a burnt offering on one of the mountains I will tell you about."

Early the next morning Abraham got up and saddled his donkey. He took with him two of his servants and his beloved son Isaac. When he had cut enough wood for the burnt offering, he set out for the place God had designated. On the third day, Abraham looked up and saw the place in the distance. "Stay here with the donkey," he instructed his servants, "while I and the boy go over there. We will worship and then we will come back to you."

As the two went on together, Isaac inquired: "The fire and wood are here, but where is the lamb for the burnt offering?" Abraham replied: "God himself will provide the lamb for the burnt offering, my son." Then, the two pressed on.

When they reached the place God had told him about, Abraham built an altar there and arranged the wood on it. He bound his son Isaac and laid him on the altar. He thereupon reached out his hand and took the knife to slay his son. But the angel of the Lord called out to him from heaven: "Abraham! Abraham!" "Here I am," the patriarch responded. "Do not lay a hand on the boy," the voice from heaven mandated. "Now I know that you fear God, because you have not withheld from me your son, your only son."

Abraham looked up and there in a thicket he saw a ram caught by the horns. He went over, took the ram, and sacrificed it in place of his son. After this, he called the place *the Lord will provide*.

The angel of the Lord called to Abraham a second time, saying: "I swear by myself, declares the Lord, that because you have not withheld your son, your only son, I will surely bless you and make your descendants as numerous as the stars in the sky and as the sand on the seashore. Your descendants will take possession of the cities of their enemies, and through your offspring all nations on earth will be blessed, because you have obeyed me."

"The main message of the story is spelled out in the divine speech at the end. Its tensions and tenor, however, are conveyed by its actions only. Neither can this action be made too involved, for it must retain its character as a simple carrying out of God's command."[9] A command, it should be added, based on the premise that God makes no mistakes. In this connection, things are not always as they appear. Negatively, God disassociates himself from the pagan practice of child sacrifice. Positively, he affirms the sanctity of life. As for a general impression, he is thoroughly awesome.

According to a rabbinic account, God created people because he loves stories. Amusing? Perhaps. Still, it contains an element of truth. It pleased God to reveal his ways primarily in narrative form. It consequently encourages us to consider his revelation in that fashion.

If a story, what is its setting? Qualifications aside, creation. God created the world and everything within it. He intended that man would serve as a steward in whatever circumstances he found himself. Moreover, he was not to live with disregard for others or of nature. At an appointed time, he would be called upon to give an account of his faithfulness or lack thereof.

Otherwise expressed, the Biblical narrative is *realistic*. There are no dragons, ogres, or enchanted palaces in it; few great deeds of valor, no exploited love adventures, or richly embroidered plots. "The fights are not described in detail and the miracles are rather subdued. The ultimate theme of these miracles is, of course, the mighty deeds of God, but these remain most of the time in the background."[10] The actual passage by passage subject matter consists of the lesser deeds of mortals.

If a story, what is its plot? "The plot of a story is the arrangement of events. ...(It) is a coherent sequence of interrelated events, with a beginning, middle, and end. It is, in other words, a *whole* or complete action."[11] The plot consists of a conflict or set of conflicts moving toward a resolution. Some conflicts built on circumstances. Others develop personal attributes. Still others reflect a moral and/or spiritual dimension.

The Biblical plot can be expressed as a contrast between *two ways*: those of the righteous and the wicked. "Blessed is the man who does not walk in the counsel of the wicked or stand in the way of sinners or sit in the seat of mockers. But his delight is in the law of the Lord, and on his law he meditates day and night. He is like a tree planted by streams of water, which yields its fruit in season and whose leaf does not wither. Whatever he does prospers" (Psa. 1:1-3).

"Not so the wicked! They are like chaff that the wind blows away. Therefore the wicked will not stand in the judgment, nor sinners in the assembly of the righteous. For the Lord watches over the way of the righteous, but the way of the ungodly will perish." The terms *wicked* and *righteous* are important elements of the psalmist's vocabulary (and Scripture as a whole). "They are used to characterize individuals and groups. The particular discrimen in question will differ, but always the basic criterion is the rightness or wrongness of one's response to the reality and revelation of the Lord's sovereign rule over human affairs."[12]

If a story, what test is implied? "The test motif is pervasive in the stories of the Bible. Whenever it is present, it is a good framework for organizing the story. Usually it is also a key to the story's meaning."[13] Adam and Eve's defection provides not only the initial test but a characteristic expression of what is involved elsewhere. In particular, we should focus on what led up to their choice, the choice itself, and what follows by way of consequence. As for the antecedents to choice, God placed Adam "in the Garden of Eden to work it and take care of it" (Gen. 2:15). The Lord God subsequently instructed him: "You are free to eat from any tree in the garden; but you must not eat from the tree of the knowledge of good and evil, for when you eat of it you will surely die."

As for the choice, the serpent was more crafty than any of the wild animals the Lord God had made. He inquired of Eve: "Did God really say, 'You must not eat from any tree in the garden?" Eve said in response: "We may eat fruit from the trees in the garden, but God did say, 'You must not eat fruit from the tree that is in the middle of the garden, and you must not touch it, or you will die.'" "You will not surely die," the serpent replied. "For God knows that when you eat of it your eyes will be opened, and you will be like God, knowing good and evil." When Eve saw that the fruit was good for food and pleasing to the eye, and also desirable for gaining wisdom, she took some and ate it. She also gave some to her husband, and he ate as well.

As for the consequences, God cursed the serpent so that it would crawl on its stomach and eat dust all the days of its life. "And I will put enmity between you and the woman and between your offspring and hers; he will crush your head and you will strike his heel" (Gen. 3:15). Then, God said to Eve: "I will greatly increase your pains in childbearing; with pain you will give birth to children. Your desire will be for your husband, and he will rule over you." Then, God said to Adam: "Cursed is the ground because of you; through painful toil you will eat of it all the days of your life. It will produce thorns and thistle for you, and you will eat the plants of the field. By the sweat of your brow you will eat your food until you return to the ground, since from it you were taken; for dust you are and to dust you will return." So God banished them from the garden, and set cherubim with flaming swords to assure that they would not return to eat of the tree of life in their fallen condition.

Edgar Peters observes: Chaos theory has shown us that in natural systems "events can change the course of history, even if the total number of possible results is within a finite space. ...From a sociological point of view, we can say that certain events must have changed the course of history, even if society does not remember when those events occurred."[14] So Scripture assures us in the above connection.

If a story, what does it say about life? In the first place, what is really real? Life is brief. "As for man, his days are like grass, he flourishes like a flower of the field; the wind blows over it and it is gone, and its place remembers it no more" (Psa. 103:15). "The length of our days is seventy years--or eighty, if we have the strength; yet their span is but trouble and sorrow, for they quickly pass, and we fly away" (Psa. 90:10).

In the second place, what is genuinely worthwhile? "Do not store up for yourselves treasures on earth, where moth and rust destroy, and where thieves break in and steal. But store up for yourselves treasures in heaven, where moth and rust do not destroy, and where thieves do not break in and steal" (Matt. 6:19-20). "Those who assess their own worth and that of others in terms of acquired treasures render themselves exceedingly vulnerable to the vicissitudes of life. Jesus' followers are instructed to avoid such insecurity by accumulating an invulnerable treasure consisting of kindnesses performed for the glory of God."[15]

In the third place, wherein should we be encouraged? "And we know that in all things God works for the good of those who love him, who have been called according to his purpose" (Rom. 8:28). This does not mean that all things are good. Indeed, they are not, and to call evil good would be in error. It means that no evil can befall those who love God that he cannot employ for their benefit and his glory.

If a story, what of the details? "All of this leads to an important principle of narrative interpretation: *assume that the storyteller has included every detail for a purpose, and do not hesitate to reflect on how the story is affected by the inclusion of a detail as compared with the effect if the detail were omitted.*"[16] For instance, we read that as soon as Judas had taken the bread, he went out. "And it was night" (John 13:30). No doubt it was night, but what significance has this detail? Probably that it symbolizes his retreat into the darkness that characterizes this current, evil world. In this connection, John reasoned that this "is the verdict: Light has come into the world, but men loved darkness instead of light because their deeds are evil. Everyone who does evil hates the light, and will not come into the light for fear that his deeds will be exposed. But whoever lives by the truth comes into the light, so that it may be seen plainly that what he has done has been done through God" (John 3:19-21).

If a story, what of our response? Do we applaud when evil gets the upper hand? If so, we have missed the point. Do we sympathize with those who suffer for righteousness sake? If so, we have tuned into the narrative. A good story should leave us better persons. Understood in this connection, Scripture is the best of stories.

NARRATION

"All narrative is inevitably concerned with time of two kinds, the time of the action and the time of its telling. A hero's deeds have taken a lifetime to perform: they are told around the campfire in one long evening. ...Narrative is about action, which takes time; narration itself occurs in time."[17] Both alike are embodied within traditional narrative.

Telling time is characteristically shorter than *action* time. We speed up the action in order to maintain interest. We likewise exclude what seems insignificant. We may embellish so as to cultivate suspense. We employ a variety of techniques, such as the use of *foils* (something to heighten the point we wish to make, often by way of contrast), *irony* (where there is a marked difference between what is said and actual), and *poetic justice* (whereby persons get what they richly deserve).

As relates to Scripture, *telling time* originates in traditional perspective with the Mosaic era, although this would not rule out the use of prior sources. It is far removed from such action time as recorded in the Genesis' account of creation. It is much closer to God's deliverance of his people from bondage in Egypt. Herbert Wolf comments as concerns the latter that an epic contains numerous historical references and usually has a strong nationalistic thrust, "so with its description of the formation of the nation of Israel and its strong religious emphasis, 'the Epic of the Exodus' is quite characteristic in its development. Unlike some epics, however, the hero of the biblical epic is not a man but is God himself."[18] As for Moses, he comes across as a reluctant leader who is neither eloquent nor an imaginative military strategist. Such *greatness* as he exhibits consists in his obedience and service to God.

In opting for a traditional approach to the *telling time*, I am not unmindful of the controversy that continues to rage concerning the literary composition of the narrative. New approaches to the study of the Pentateuch continue to expand our understanding, "some by scholars as firmly committed to the non-Mosaic character of these books as Wellhausen was a century ago. Yet at the same time the case for the

Mosaic authorship has been strengthened by our increasing knowledge about the history, culture, and religion of the ancient Near East."[19]

In any case, Scripture associates *telling time* with the exodus experience, rather than something earlier or later on. Sinai is where our study properly begins, not in person "but vicariously through the sacred text of Scripture. As best we can, we shall have to recover from antiquity what happened here and how the saga of the Spirit got under way. There are no subsequent developments which can be understood apart from this original setting."[20]

Whereas Genesis closes with the Hebrew people secured by their Egyptian patrons, Exodus begins with a new king *who did not know Joseph*. "Look," he said to the people, "the Israelites have become much too numerous for us. Come, we must deal shrewdly with them or they will become even more numerous and, if war breaks out, will join our enemies, fight against us and leave the country."

So they put slave masters over them to supervise their forced labor. "But the more they were oppressed, the more they multiplied and spread; so the Egyptians came to dread the Israelites and worked them ruthlessly. They made their lives bitter with hard labor in brick and mortar and with all kinds of work in the field; in all their hard labor the Egyptians used them ruthlessly." By way of repetition (*ruthlessly, hard labor*), the writer emphasizes the malicious and abusive behavior of those in charge, and its oppressive results.

Not content, the Pharaoh instructed certain midwives: "When you help the Hebrew women in childbirth and observe them on the delivery stool, if it is a boy, kill him; but if it is a girl, let her live." The midwives, however, feared God and did not obey the king's directive. Then, when called to give an account for their failure, they explained: "Hebrew women are not like Egyptian women; they are vigorous and give birth before the midwives arrive." (So favorable a comparison would no doubt delight the storyteller's audience.) God moreover was gracious toward the midwives in giving them families of their own, and the people increased and became even more numerous.

Frustrated by this turn of events, Pharaoh issued a decree to all his people: "Every boy that is born you must throw into the Nile, but let every girl live." As for the boys, the threat was genuine, whether or not it was implemented to any great degree. As for the girls, they would presumably become slave wives, and absorbed into the Egyptian populace. As for the conspiracy, it would fail. "Jewish expositors have seen parallels to pharaoh's action in the attempted genocide of Israel by Hitler and others;

Christian expositors have sought such parallels in the persecutions suffered by the church throughout her history."[21]

Now there was a Levitical couple who gave birth to a son. The mother hid him for three months, but when she could hide him no longer, she placed the child in a papyrus basket coated with tar and pitch. She then put it among the reeds along the bank of the Nile, and had his sister keep watch as to what would happen. When Pharaoh's daughter went down to the water to wash, she discovered the basket with child inside. The child was crying, and she felt sorry for him. "This is one of the Hebrew babies," she concluded. At this, the infant's sister inquired: "Shall I go and get one of the Hebrew women to nurse the baby for you?" "Yes, go," she answered, and the girl went off to get her mother. At a proper age, his mother took him to Pharaoh's daughter and he became her son. She called him *Moses*, perhaps from the Hebrew meaning to *draw out* or the Egyptian term for *son.* Either might fit the context.

One day, after Moses was fully grown, he went out to where his people engaged in *hard labor* (mentioned for the third time). Whereupon, he observed an Egyptian beating a Hebrew, *one of his own people* (mentioned for a second time). "Glancing this way and that and seeing no one, he killed the Egyptian and hid him in the sand."

The next day Moses went out and saw two Hebrews fighting. He asked the one in the wrong: "Why are you hitting your fellow Hebrew?" The man replied: "Who made you ruler and judge over us? Are you thinking of killing me as you killed the Egyptian?" Then Moses was afraid since he supposed that what he had done was known to others. When Pharaoh heard of this, he tried to kill Moses, who fled for safety to Midian.

Sooner or later, the storyteller ponders how much time to commit to reporting an incident. He or she must decide "whether a year's journey is to be described in two hundred pages, or twenty pages, or one single page. All this is necessarily so, since narrative, like all representation selects the relevant features and reduces the scale of reality."[22] With such in mind, we pick up the story line.

It seems that Moses was tending the flock of Jethro his father-in-law and priest of Midian. This comes as the climax to a series of episodes beginning with Moses' early life in Egypt and subsequent sojourn. The episode takes place on the far side of Horeb, *the mountain of God.* Mountains often have religious connotations, and this seems to have served as a religious sanctuary. There appeared to him the angel of the Lord in flames of fire from within a bush. So reports the storyteller with his privileged insight. As for Moses, he thought to himself: "I will go over and see this strange sight--why the bush does not burn up" (3:3).

Given the modern mind-set, naturalistic explanations forge to the front. Perhaps the incident did not occur, or if it did the reference was to the flowering of the bush or sunlight reflected on its leaves. We need to caution ourselves in this regard, especially now that our contemporary cultural bias seems to be losing its appeal. As a case in point, *Modernity* rather than being regarded as the norm for human society toward which all history has been aiming and into which all societies should be ushered (forcibly if necessary) "is instead increasingly seen as an aberration. A new respect for the wisdom of traditional societies is growing as we realize that they have endured for thousands of years and that, by contrast, the existence of modern society for even another century seems doubtful."[23]

When the Lord saw that Moses had drawn near to the bush to observe more closely, he said called out to him: "Moses! Moses!" "Hear I am," Moses replied, as if to suggest his availability. "Do not come any closer," God commanded. "Take off your sandals, for the place where you are standing is holy ground." Then he explained: "I am the God of your father, the God of Abraham, the God of Isaac and the God of Jacob." At this, Moses hid his face, because he was afraid to look at God.

God expanded on his initial revelation to incorporate how he had heard the cry of his people in bondage, and was intent on delivering them to a land of promise. "So now, go," he concluded. "I am sending you to Pharaoh to bring my people the Israelites out of Egypt." Moses nonetheless replied: "Who am I, that I should go to Pharaoh and bring the Israelites out of Egypt?" He had quite missed the point: it was not *his* significance but *God's* that was at issue. Then God said, "I will be with you. And this will be the sign to you that it is I who have sent you: When you have brought the people out of Egypt, you will worship God on this mountain."

Moses was still unconvinced. "Suppose I go to the Israelites and say to them, 'The God of your fathers has sent me to you,' and they ask me, 'What is his name?' Then what shall I tell them?" God responded to Moses, "I am who I am. This is what you are to say to the Israelites: 'I am has sent me to you.'" *I am who I am*, or *I will be what I will be* is obviously a reference to God's covenant name *Yahweh*. God is or will be not in some abstract sense, but as actively engaged in life. It consequently might be interpreted as *I will be there for you*. Since that is the case, it calls for a confident response.

The scene shifts to Pharaoh's royal court. Moses and Aaron announce that this "is what the Lord, the God of Israel, says: 'Let my people go, so that they may hold a festival to me in the desert.'" Pharaoh inquired in response: "Who is the Lord, that I should obey him and let Israel go? I do not know the Lord and I will not let Israel go."

"At this time in history Egypt was one of the most powerful nations on earth and was proud of its heritage and religions. But by means of the ten plagues, Pharaoh and his people learned the hard way there was no one like the God of Israel, who was supreme in heaven and earth (cf. 7:5; 9:14)."[24] The Hebrew people likewise were reassured that God was sovereign (cf. 6:3, 7), and were instructed to inform their posterity what he had done on their behalf (10:2).

Moreover, the plagues appear directed against specific Egyptian deities to reveal their impotence. For example, the Nile River was worshiped as the god Hopi. In addition, the "plague on livestock may have been a direct rebuke against the bull-gods, Apis and Mnevis, and the ram-god, Khnum. In the ninth plague, 'total darkness covered all Egypt' (10:22).... . Where was Ra, the sun-god, who was revered as one of the main Egyptian deities?"[25] As a rule overlooked in the examples cited was the tenth plague concerning the death of the first-born son, which may have been directed against Pharaoh's claim to divinity and progenitor of those who would succeed him.

Most of the plagues begin with the request that Pharaoh let God's people go so that they may serve him in the wilderness. This is followed by a description of the plague. This, in return, solicits Pharaoh's response: sometimes seeking an accommodation and sometimes with categorical rejection. The plagues appear arranged in sets of three, the first in each set introduced with a warning to Pharaoh *in the morning*, and climaxing with the crushing final catastrophe.

In order to escape the last plague, the Israelite households were instructed to sacrifice a lamb and smear its blood on the doorposts of each house. Henceforth, the occasion of the *Passover* would be celebrated annually. Closely associated with the Passover was the Feast of Unleavened Bread, which began the next day and continued from the fifteenth to the twenty-first of the month Abib. In the latter connection, folk recalled their bitter experience in Egypt and God's deliverance. It became rabbinic custom to remind those observing these religious festivals that no one is genuinely free while anyone is enslaved.

The scene again shifts: this time to the people of Israel encamped between Migdol and the sea. The narration is exceptionally vivid: "As

Pharaoh approached, the Israelites looked up, and there were the Egyptians, marching after them. They were terrified and cried out to the Lord." They subsequently complained to Moses: "Was it because there were no graves in Egypt that you brought us to the desert to die? What have you done to us by bringing us out of Egypt? Didn't we say to you in Egypt, 'Leave us alone; let us serve the Egyptians?' It would have been better for us to serve the Egyptians than to die in the desert!" (14:11-12).

Moses answered the people: "Do not be afraid. Stand firm and you will see the deliverance the Lord will bring you today. The Egyptians you see today you will never see again. The Lord will fight for you; you need only to be still."

Then God instructed Moses: "Raise your staff and stretch out your hand over the sea to divide the water so that the Israelites can go through the sea on dry ground." Moses obediently stretched out his hand over the sea, and all that night the Lord drove the sea back with a strong east wind, so that the waters were divided and the Israelites went through on dry ground. Then when the Egyptians attempted to follow them, the water flowed back and covered both chariots and horsemen--*the entire army of Pharaoh that had followed the Israelites into the sea*. In response, Moses acclaimed: "I will sing to the Lord, for he is highly exalted. The horse and its rider he has hurled into the sea. The Lord is my strength and my song; he has become my salvation."

Three months later, the Israelites arrived at the Desert of Sinai, and encamped before the mountain. Then Moses went up before the Almighty, and God called to him from the mountain that this "is what you are to say to the house of Jacob and what you are to tell the people of Israel: 'You yourselves have seen what I did to Egypt, and how I carried you on eagles wings and brought you to myself. Now if you obey me fully and keep my covenant, then out of all nations you will be my treasured possession.'" (19:3-5).

So Moses went down and shared what God had revealed to him. Then all the people responded: "We will do everything the Lord has said." So Moses brought their answer back to the Almighty. So also with the passing of time God laid down the stipulations they must observe. The Mosaic Covenant consequently set forth the conditions by which the people's corporate identity could be forged, righteousness cultivated, and God's blessing assured.

Problems were already on the horizon. Thus when the people saw that Moses was so long in coming down from the mountain, they urged Aaron: "Come, make us gods who will go before us. As for this fellow Moses who brought us up out of Egypt, we don't know what has happened to him" (32:1). Aaron answered them: "Take off the gold earrings that your wives, your sons and your daughters are wearing, and bring them to me." So he made them an idol from their jewelry, fashioning it in the form of a calf. Thereupon, they declared: "These are your gods, O Israel, who brought you up out of Egypt."

When Aaron saw this, he built an altar in front of the calf and announced: "Tomorrow there will be a festival to the Lord." So the next day the people rose early and sacrificed before the image. "Afterward they sat down to eat and drink and got up to indulge in revelry."

When Joshua heard the noise of shouting in the encampment, he said to Moses: "There is the sound of war in the camp." Moses replied: "It is not the sound of victory, it is not the sound of defeat, it is the sound of singing that I hear." When Moses saw the calf and the dancing, his anger was kindled, and he broke the tablets that he was carrying. Subsequently he ground the calf to powder, scattered it on the water, and made the idolatrous Israelites to drink it. "The gold dust sprinkled on the water of the wady...reminds us of the 'water of bitterness' to be drunk by the wife suspected of unfaithfulness (Num. 5:18-22). As Israel has in fact been unfaithful to YHWH, her heavenly 'husband', so the curse will indeed fall upon her (32:35; cf. Num. 5:27)."[26]

On the twentieth day of the second month of the second year, the people took their leave from Sinai (Num. 10:11). They were bound for the promised land. In due time, the Lord instructed Moses to send out men to explore the land of Canaan, "which I am giving to the Israelites." Moses did as he was directed. When they returned, they gave Moses this report: "We went into the land to which you sent us, and it does flow with milk and honey! Here is its fruit. But the people who live there are powerful, and the cities are fortified and very large." At this, Caleb silenced the people and advised them: "We should go up and take possession of the land, for we can certainly do it." But those who went with him protested: "We can't attack those people; they are stronger than we are. ...We seemed like grasshoppers in our own eyes, and we looked the same to them." Once again the people complained against Moses-- God's representative, and a generation perished in the wilderness.

"It must have been an impressive ceremony when Moses stood before the Israelites on his last day with them. The song of witness had been orally delivered with Joshua standing by his side. After Moses had given his final words of admonition to the people assembled before him, he received divine instructions."[27] He was to ascend Mount Nebo, east of the

Dead Sea and Jordan River, over against Jericho. He would be privileged
to see the land of promise, although not permitted to enter. Shortly
thereafter, Moses died and was grieved by all the people for thirty days.
So is was told, one generation after another.

FROM THE BEGINNING

The creation account resembles a flashback to the beginning. A *flashback* is defined as an interruption in a narrative to relate events that have happened earlier. In this instance, it occurs at the outset in anticipation of what would follow. The interlocking key becomes the identification of the *High God Elohim* with his covenant name *Yahweh*. Frank Eakin, Jr. enthusiastically comments: "How does one account for the ordered universe and man's unique place therein? Yahweh! What was the basis for the Hebrew people's having been formed into the Israelite nation? Yahweh! Who rules the universe and enacts his will and purpose therein? Yahweh!"[28]

As alerted by its *High God* setting, we anticipate that *Yahweh* will work in mysterious ways his wonders to perform. Leland Ryken confirms our suspicion: "The supernatural slant of the Bible also produces a sense of mystery and wonder. By refusing to allow reality to be conceived solely in terms of known, observable reality, biblical literature continually transforms the mundane into something with sacred significance."[29]

Considered from a different perspective, *mystery* is truth in the process of being revealed. As a rule, it refers to God's involvement in the world to achieve his purposes. The more we know, the more we realize that we don't know. God shares with us what we need to know, but not to satisfy our idle curiosity. We are expected to act on the basis of what we know or could know, and trust God to guide us.

If the creation account is the answer, what is the question? Some suppose that it has to do with how things began. That is a part truth at best. Others suggest that it speaks to what life is all about. That helps to round out its significance. John Polkinghorne assures us: "God is not just there to start things off. He's not simply the answer to the question, 'Who lit the blue touch paper of the Big Bang?' ...He holds the universe in being and his mind and purpose are behind its evolving history."[30]

In particular, we note that in the beginning God stands alone in his solitary splendor. The Egyptian pantheon is noticeable for its absence.

It appears as a later invention meant to justify the political/social establishment, and to oppress the Hebrew people. By way of implication, man was born free, with the intent that he should remain free. Not free from obligation, which is license, but free to cultivate a relationship with God and one another.

In the beginning, God created the heavens and the earth. As for the earth, it was formless and empty. This combination of terms occurs only here and in Jeremiah 4:23, the former concerning physical conditions and the latter extended to incorporate the disintegration of the social order in the wake of the Babylonian invasion. As a rule, this imagery in *High God* tradition suggests a potter who casts his clay before fashioning a vessel from it. In an exceptional instance, the *High God* takes a stick from which to whittle an object.

If anything, initial chaos appears in a positive context, as a stage in God's creative venture. As such, it is a continuing reminder that God acts in creative fashion, bringing order out of chaos. "We cannot know what God intends to accomplish in spite of human failures; nor can we know how far God intends, within and through history, to change human nature. Prophetic hope must be absolutely open because it is based on the faith that God is absolutely powerful and good."[31]

Conversely, "This frightening disorganization (chaos) is the antithesis to the order that characterized the work of creation when it was complete... . The same point is made in another powerful image in the next clause, 'darkness covered the deep'."[32] Since God introduces light, darkness comes to represent all that is adverse--wickedness, self-deception, death, and judgment. All things considered, chaos is a continuing aspect of life. As a worse scenario, it results from man's repudiation of God's righteous design. At its best, chaos is a necessary step in the creative process. In any case, it ought not to be perpetuated unnecessarily.

Now, the spirit of God was hovering over the waters. Much as would a potter's hands hover over the formless clay, in preparation for the task ahead. So likewise to solicit the interest of the listener in what would follow. The pump is primed.

And God said: "Let there be light," and there was light. God saw that the light was good. And God said: "Let there be an expanse between the waters," ...and it was so. And God said: "Let the water under the sky be gathered to one place, and let dry ground appear." And it was so. Then God said: "Let the land produce vegetation," ...and it was so. And God said: "Let there be lights in the expanse of the sky to separate the day from the night," ...and it was so. And God saw that it was good. And God said: "Let the water teem with living creatures, and let birds fly above the earth across the expanse of the sky." And God saw that it was good. And God said: "Let the land produce living creatures according to their kinds," ...and it was so. And God saw that it was good. Then God said: "Let us make man in our image," ...and it was so. "God saw all that he had made, and it was very good" (Gen. 1:31).

God said and it was done, and it was good--indeed it was very good! One could imagine the text read to the accompaniment of a celestial orchestra and choir: the fanfare of the trumpets, rolling drums, and mixed voices. The listener or reader is ushered into a box seat, from which to enjoy the creation anthem. As a result, we are meant to conclude that qualifications aside, life is eminently good.

Milton Steinberg comments: "Wherefore a man should treasure it, not despise it; affirm and not deny it; have faith in it and never despair of its possibilities. For behind it is God. Life is good and man can find it such, provided--and this is the great condition to everything else--that it is properly lived."[33] Why ultimately is life good? Not because of circumstances, which change from moment to moment, but because of God who remains constant in his love and benevolence. How can we frustrate God's good intention? By not living life according to his direction.

So we saw in an earlier connection with the original couple. Offered the opportunity to live in communion with God and from his bounty, they *chose* to usurp life on their own. "The presence of the great spiritual conflict makes choice on the part of biblical characters necessary. Every area of human experience is claimed by God and counterclaimed by the forces of evil. There is no neutral ground."[34] So it was with Adam and Eve, and so it has been with their posterity.

Our choices either open new opportunities, or restrict further those we previously enjoyed. They moreover impact positively or negatively on those around us. Either we make progress or lose ground. Robert Seltzer agonizingly observes that we have a series of tales in which the world, created by God to be good and containing one creature in God's image, "turns out full of violent, murderous, and self-glorifying men. This...leads to the formation of people nurtured by God, capable of producing a few individuals of satisfactory spiritual nature, but in the main those who are obtuse, unfaithful, and frequently backsliding from the divinely given task."[35]

In the main, Scripture describes the devolution of mankind. Eve gave

birth to Cain and then Abel. Now Abel kept the flocks while Cain worked
the land. In the course of time, Abel offered fat portions from the
firstborn of his flock to the Lord, and Cain some of the fruits of the soil
as an offering. Whereupon, the Lord looked with favor on Abel's
offering, but disfavor on the offering of Cain. The reason being that the
firstborn is the most highly prized among the flocks, and the fat the richest
part of the animal, as contrasted to the nondescript offering Cain
managed.

Then the Lord said to Cain: "Why are you angry? Why is your face
downcast? If you do what is right, will you not be accepted? But if you
do not do what is right, sin is crouching at your door; it desires to have
you, but you must master it" (4:6-7). In this regard, *sin* resembles a
vicious animal positioned to spring upon its helpless victim.

Now Cain said to his brother Abel: "Let's go out to the field." Then,
while they were in the field, Cain attacked his brother Abel and killed
him. After this, God inquired of Cain: "Where is your brother Abel?" "I
don't know," he replied. "Am I my brother's keeper?" Indeed, he was!
Indeed, he knew he was! Indeed, those who listened to the story knew he
was! The Lord responded in astonishment: "What have you done?
Listen! Your brother's blood cries out to me from the ground. Now you
are under a curse and driven from the ground, which opened its mouth to
receive your brother's blood from your hand. When you work the ground,
it will no longer yield its crops for you. You will be a restless wanderer
on the earth."

Cain protested: "My punishment is more than I can bear. Today you
are driving me from the land, and I will be hidden from your presence; I
will be a restless wanderer on the earth, and whosoever finds me will kill
me." "Not so," God replied, "if anyone kills Cain, he will suffer
vengeance seven times over." Then, God put a mark on Cain so that no
one who found him would kill him. So Cain went out from the Lord's
presence and lived in the land of Nod, east of Eden.

Some generations later, Lamech said to his wives: "I have killed a man
for wounding me, a young man for injuring me. If Cain is avenged seven
times, then Lamech seventy-seven times." "Lamech's taunt-song reveals
the swift progress of sin. Where Cain had succumbed to it (7) Lamech
exults in it; where Cain has sought protection (14, 15) Lamech looks
round for provocation; the savage disproportion of killing a mere land for
a mere wound is the whole point of his boast (cf. 24)."[36]

Eve again bore a son, called *Seth.* Seth, in turn, had a son, named
Enosh. "At that time men began to call on the name of the Lord" (4:26).

In this regard, they resembled Abel, who Seth replaced. They moreover attest to the *few individuals of satisfactory spiritual nature* Seltzer allows in his earlier comment. Not that they could altogether escape the ravages of sin, but in that they were sensitive to the things of God.

Such was the state of affairs that set the scene for Noah to come on stage. The Lord saw how great the wickedness of man had become, how "that every inclination of the thoughts of his heart was only evil all the time" (Gen. 6:15). The Lord was grieved that he had made man, and his heart was filled with pain. So he said: "I will wipe mankind, whom I have created, from the face of the earth--men and animals, and creatures that move along the ground, and birds of the air--for I am grieved that I have made them." "Either the animals contributed to the depravity in the world, or else they are innocent victims. The form of judgment, a deluge, would of necessity kill all forms of life."[37] Thus are we alerted to the fact that the innocent may suffer with the guilty in a world shared by all.

Nevertheless, Noah found favor in the eyes of the Lord. "Noah was a righteous man, blameless among the people of his time, and he walked with God" (v. 9). He was not simply the best of a bad lot, but distinctive in his righteous ways. So God said to Noah: "I am going to bring floodwaters on the earth to destroy all life under the heavens, every creature that has the breath of life in it. ...But I will establish my covenant with you, and you will enter the ark--you and your sons and your wife and your sons' wives with you. You are to bring into the ark two of all living creatures, male and female, to keep them alive with you." Noah did as God commanded him, and God shut them in as evidence of his providential care.

The storyteller retraces his steps for dramatic effect. Having introduced the flood (7:6), he extends his discussion (10-12). Likewise, having detailed the entry into the ark (7-9), he amends it (13-16). The novel feature of the second account is the convergence of a vast tidal wave along with a steady downpour.

For forty days the flood *kept coming. The waters rose* and increased greatly on the earth, and the ark floated on the surface of the water. *They* rose greatly on the earth, and all the high mountains under the entire heavens were covered. *The waters rose* and covered the mountains to a depth of more than twenty feet. *Every living thing* that moved on the earth perished. *Everything* on dry land that had the breath of life in its nostrils died. *Every living thing* on the face of the earth was wiped out. *Only* Noah was left, and those with him in the ark.

Then, God *remembered* Noah and all that had survived with him. The term translated *remember* implies steadfast love and timely intervention. As for the former, God was as favorably disposed toward Noah as previously. As for the latter, it was time to rescue the faithful few. Whereupon, God sent a wind over the earth and the waters receded, the springs of the deep and the floodgates of the heavens having been closed. The ark came to rest on Ararat. (A play on words may be intended since we derive the name *Noah* from the verb meaning *coming to rest*.) The waters continued to recede until the top of the mountains could be seen.

After forty days, Noah released a raven, known for its great endurance. It continued to fly about until the water had dried sufficiently for it to be on its own. Then, he sent out a dove, a less rigorous and readily domesticated creature. After some time, the dove returned. Noah waited seven more days before sending the bird out again. This time it returned bearing a freshly plucked olive leaf! At this, Noah knew that the water had receded from the earth. He waited seven more days before sending the dove out once more, and this time it didn't return. According to a rabbinic saying, "Better bitter food (the olive leaf) that comes from God than the sweetest food at the hands of man."

We have the first explicit mention of a *covenant* with Noah. Then God said to Noah: "*I now establish my covenant* with you and with your descendants after you and with every living creature that was with you-- the birds, the livestock and all the wild animals, all those that came out of the ark with you--every living creature on earth. *I establish my covenant* with you. Never again will life be cut off by the waters of a flood; never again will there be a flood to destroy the earth" (9:8-11).

A *covenant* is a relationship implying mutual obligations. The covenant with Noah is universal in character. God promises never again to send such a flood in judgment on the world. The rainbow serves as a sign, since it resembles a bow held high over one's head as an expression of peace. Jewish tradition has elaborated on the covenant concerning seven laws pertaining to idolatry, blasphemy, murder, theft, sexual relations, eating the flesh of a living animal, and establishing courts of law. As a case in point, "If two litigants appear in court, one a great wise man and the other a simple person, the judge may not ask about the welfare of the great one nor express pleasure at being in his presence in any way, nor give him honor in any way. Otherwise, the arguments of the simple person would be stifled."[38]

"This is the account of Shem, Ham and Japheth, Noah's sons, who themselves had sons after the flood" (10:1). Not the first time we have encountered *genealogy*, it will not be the last. *Genealogy*, unless otherwise augmented, resembles narrative stripped of content. Such and such a person lived and died, leaving us no detailed information. It served a number of purposes in antiquity. For one, it established claims for inheritance. For another, it was evidence of ritual purity as with the priestly line. For still another, it confirmed alliances among diverse people.

In addition, this so-called *Table of the Nations* provided a theological and literary bridge between what it preceded and followed. As an extended unit, three conclusions can be derived. First, the human race is united by virtue of being one family. Such was already implied by the monotheistic orientation of Scripture. Polytheism in contrast tends to fragment the human society and invite conflict. The genealogical table thus makes explicit the human solidarity already implicit to Biblical monotheism.

Second, the human race is separated and dispersed as a result of its defiant effort in seeking to erect the tower of Babel. It has consequently failed in the attempt to usurp God's rightful place at life's center. As a result, it is inclined to cherish ethnic diversity, not for the contribution it can make to others, but to further selfish ends at the expense of others.

Third, the nations one and all stand within the divine structure of blessings and curses set forth in the covenant with Noah. As a consequence, it can be said that "righteousness exalts a nation, but sin is a disgrace to any people" (Prov. 14:34). It allows for no exceptions.

With such in mind, we turn our attention in conclusion to the story concerning the tower of Babel (11:1-9). Now the whole world had a common language. As men moved eastward, they found an inviting plain in Shinar and settled there. Whereupon, they said to one another: "Come, let's make bricks and bake them thoroughly." Then, they said: "Come, let us build ourselves a city, with a tower that reaches to the heavens, so that we may make a name for ourselves and not be scattered over the face of the whole earth."

Primeval history reaches its fruitless climax as man prepares to glorify and fortify himself by collective effort. "The elements of the story are timelessly characteristic of the spirit of the world. The project is typically grandiose; men describe it excitedly to one another as if it were the ultimate achievement--very much as modern man glorifies in his space projects."[39] At the same time, they reveal their insecurity by crowding together and endeavoring to control their own fortunes.

What must have seemed so impressive to the builders, appeared inconsequential to God. So we read in satirical fashion that the Lord *came down* to see the city and the tower that they had erected. As such, their idolatrous monument was so minute as to require a closer inspection. God subsequently confused their language so that they would not be able to understand one another, and be scattered abroad. So things would remain until a subsequent time, with the reversal of tongues at Pentecost, but this is another story that can wait its turn.

WITH THE PATRIARCHS

The call of Abraham constitutes a new phase in the Biblical narrative. In this era we encounter a succession of individuals who become God's appointed means for extending salvation history. In the process, God's character is increasingly revealed, as is his will for mankind. Likewise, the focus shifts from universal man to a select people. The latter take center stage as if to perform a religious morality drama for all to view and benefit from. As Jesus subsequently observed, "salvation is from the Jews" (John 4:22).

More in particular, this collection of stories would seem to qualify as *heroic narrative*. "Such stories spring from one of the most universal impulses of literature--the desire to embody accepted norms of behavior or representative struggles in the story of a character whose experience is typical of people in general."[40] In this instance, to draw from the precedence of the fathers for subsequent generations.

The prime task that confronts us in heroic narrative is to explore the character of the hero or heroine for its relevance to how we should negotiate life, both as individuals and in cooperation with others. This can be done by considering the person's character traits, actions, motivation, responses, relationships to others, and roles. The associated task is to consider the supportive cast, circumstances, and outcomes. Such are the matters to keep before us as the narrative unfolds.

At the outset, God directs Abram: "Leave your country, your people and your father's household and go to the land I will show you" (Gen. 12:1). This was coupled with an extended promise: "I will make you into a great nation and I will bless you. I will make your name great, and you will be a blessing. I will bless those who bless you, and whoever curses you I will curse, and all peoples on earth will be blessed through you."

The succession from *your country*, through *your people*, to *your household* solicits our initial attention. Each appears more stressful than the preceding. Worst of all, Abram must leave his extended family, from which he not only derived his personal identity but gained security. This was a classic instance of a fate said to be worse than death.

In response, God declared that he would honor Abram's faithfulness. *I will* show you the land of promise; *I will* make you a great nation; *I will* bless you; *I will* make your name great; *I will* bless those who bless you and curse those who curse you. As a result, all the peoples on earth will be blessed through you. On the one hand, God's blessing is focused on Abram. On the other, it extends to all who walk by faith. Paul consequently concluded that "the promise comes by faith, so that it may be by grace and may be guaranteed to all Abraham's offspring--not only to those who are of the law but also to those who are of the faith of Abraham" (Rom. 4:16).

All things considered, we are alerted to the *promise/fulfillment* motif that characterizes Biblical narrative. This is especially true contrasting the Old and New Testaments: *promise* as relates to the former and *fulfillment* as concerns the latter. However, the motif is more pervasive. So much so that if not explicit then implicit throughout Scripture. As a result, the person of faith lives between *promise* and *fulfillment*, even though he or she has experienced an earnest of things yet to come.

God subsequently assures Abram concerning the land of promise. First, as he traveled throughout the region and observed those currently living there (12:6-7). Second, when parting from his nephew Lot (13:14-17). Finally, in connection with the covenant (15:18). It is in the final connection that we pick up the story line. The word of the Lord came to Abram in a vision: "Do not be afraid, Abram. I am your shield, your very great reward." The negative imperative appears here and on other occasions, as with Isaac (26:24) and Jacob (46:3). With the passing of time, it came to serve as a formula for encouragement, having been tested and not found wanting. As elaborated, the *shield* implies his protection, and *great reward* his provision.

"O Sovereign Lord," Abram inquired, "what can you give me since I remain childless and the one who will inherit my estate is Eliezer of Damascus?" Then God replied: "This man will not be your heir, but a son coming from your own body will be your heir." After this, the Lord took him outside and instructed him: "Look up at the heavens and count the stars--if indeed you can count them. So shall your offspring be." It was recorded that "Abram believed God, and it was credited to him as righteousness" (v. 6).

Ten years nonetheless passed without a natural heir. Whereupon, Abram's wife Sarai confided in him: "The Lord has kept me from having children. Go, sleep with my handservant; perhaps I can build a family through her" (16:2). Since such was an acceptable practice at the time, Abram consented. Hagar subsequently conceived and bore him a son.

Later on, God appeared to Abram and confirmed his covenant with him: "No longer will you be called Abram; your name will be Abraham, for I have made you a father of many nations" (17:5). Whereas *Abram* meant *father is exalted* (perhaps a reference to the moon deity of Ur), *Abraham* is understood as *father of a multitude* (in connection with the covenant promise). "As for Sarai your wife," God continued, " you are no longer to call her Sarai; her name will be Sarah (*princess*). I will bless her so that she will be the mother of nations." "If only Ishmael might live under your blessing!" Abraham exclaimed. "Yes," God allowed, " but your wife Sarah will bear you a son, and you will call him Isaac. I will establish my covenant with him as an everlasting covenant for his descendants after him."

Still later on, Abraham entertained three visitors (18:2). "Where is your wife Sarah?" they asked him. "There, in the tent," he answered. Then the Lord said: "I will surely return to you about this time next year, and Sarah your wife will have a son." At this, Sarah laughed to herself. Whereupon, the Lord inquired of Abraham: "Why did Sarah laugh and say, 'Will I really have a child, now that I am old?' Is anything too hard for the Lord?" "Sarah was persisting in unbelief, not merely reacting in astonishment. ...Nevertheless it drew forth one of the great sayings of Scripture, which later became the starting-point of a searching colloquy on omnipotence (Jer. 32:17ff, 27ff.) and was taken up again in Zechariah 8:6."[41] The latter reads: "'It may seem marvelous to the remnant of the people at that time, but will it seem marvelous to me?' declares the Lord Almighty."

When the visitors got up to leave, Abraham walked with them toward Sodom. Then the Lord said: "Shall I hide from Abraham what I am about to do? Abraham will surely become a great and powerful nation, and all nations on earth will be blessed through him." Having considered the matter, God announced: "The outcry against Sodom and Gomorrah is so great and their sin so grievous that I will go down and see if what they have done is as bad as the outcry that has reached me." That is to say, he will judge the matter justly.

"Will you sweep away the righteous with the wicked?" Abraham inquired. "What if there are fifty righteous people in the city?" When assured that God would spare the city if there were fifty righteous people, the patriarch persisted: "What if there are forty-five," then forty, thirty, twenty, and ten. Each time God replied that he would spare the city. As a commentary of the pervasive character of sin, the city was subsequently wasted. In this regard, we are reminded of God's longsuffering, humanity's recalcitrance, and the vital role of intercession.

"Now the Lord was gracious to Sarah as he had said, and the Lord did for Sarah what he had promised" (21:1). She became pregnant and bore a son, who was given the name *Isaac*. The name means *he laughs* or *laughed*. Sarah explained: "God has brought me laughter, and everyone who hears about this will laugh with me."

The child grew and was weaned. Given the custom of the time, he was perhaps two or three years of age. Since Abraham was a person of considerable means, this was an occasion for celebration. In contrast, Ishmael mocked the proceedings. This was probably a climax to the rivalry which had been building. In any case, Sarah seized the opportunity to have Hagar and her son banished from the encampment. They went their way, protected by the Almighty.

This brings us back to the binding of Isaac. Whereas we previously considered the episode in some detail, it will suffice to touch on it in passing. In particular, as it relates to Isaac. The close relationship between father and son is expressed by the repetition "they went on together" (22:6, 8). Only once is Isaac said to speak, and then to inquire "where is the lamb for the burnt offering?" Abraham answered: "God himself will provide the lamb for the burnt offering, my son." Then, when the ordeal was over, he called the place *The Lord Will Provide*. So it was said, and so it is true from time to eternity.

Abraham was well advanced in years, God having blessed him in every way. He called for his chief servant, and made him swear an oath not to secure a wife for Isaac from the daughters of the Canaanites but from his own relatives. "The Lord, the God of heaven...will send his angel before you so that you can get a wife for my son from there" (24:7). As in the above instance, God will provide.

In due time, the servant made his way to the village of Nahor. There he paused by a well toward evening when the women come out to draw water. Then he prayed: "May it be that when I say to a girl, 'Please let down your jar that I may have a drink,' and she says, 'Drink, and I'll water your camels too'--let her be the one you have chosen for your servant Isaac." Before he had finished praying, Rebekah came out with her jar on her shoulder. She was the daughter of Milcah, wife of Abraham's brother Nahor, very beautiful, and a virgin. She moreover responded as the servant had petitioned. At this, the man bowed down and worshiped the Lord, saying: "Praise be to the Lord, the God of my master Abraham, who has not abandoned his kindness and faithfulness to my master."

Isaac took Rebekah to the tent of his mother Sarah and married her. "So she became his wife, and he loved her; and Isaac was comforted after his mother's death." Rebekah subsequently became pregnant. When it came time for her to give birth, there were twin boys in her womb (25:24). The first to come out was red and as if covered with a hairy garment. Consequently, they called him *Esau.* After this, his brother came out, with his hand grasping Esau's heel. They called him *Jacob*, meaning *he takes by the heel*, with the derived connotations of *taking the place of, deceiving, attacking from the rear.*

The naming of Jacob alerts us to what was to transpire. As the boys matured, Esau became a skillful hunter--*a man of the open country*, while Jacob was a quiet man--*staying among the tents.* Isaac, who had a taste for wild game, favored Esau, but Rebekah loved Jacob. Once, when Jacob was cooking some stew, Esau came in from the open country, famished. "Quick," the latter exclaimed, "let me have some of that red stew! I'm famished!" (25:30). Jacob replied: "First sell me your birthright." "Look, I am about to die," Esau protested. Jacob insisted: "Swear to me first." So he swore an oath to him, selling his birthright to Jacob. Then he got in return some bread and lentil stew. So we are told that *Esau despised his birthright.*

In seeking to assess the above incident, we should bear in mind that business transactions in the Near East, "while always subject to strict legal norms, have also been looked upon to some extent as a game, one in which the contestants match wits with one another. Popular lore takes delight in such 'gamesmanship,' much as official law stresses the ethical and moral side in such dealings."[42] Even so, we gather that Jacob was quite serious in his quest, and Esau strikingly unconcerned.

The writer alternates his attention from one generation to the next and back again. This is a stylistic feature of the patriarchal narratives, an effective means of heightening interest, and a subtle way of transition. Now there was famine in the land, so that Isaac went to Abimelech, king of the Philistines, in Gerar. There God appeared to him, and urged him to remain there for the time being. When the men of the place asked about his wife, Isaac said: "She is my sister," (26:7), because he was afraid that if they knew she was his wife, they might kill him on her account--*because she was very beautiful* (as earlier observed).

When Isaac had been there some time, Abimelech looked down from a window and saw Isaac caressing his wife. So the king summoned Isaac and said: "She is really your wife! Why did you say, 'She is my sister?'"

Isaac answered him: "Because I thought I might lose my life on account of her." Then Abimelech responded: "What is this you have done to us? One of the men might well have slept with your wife, and you would have brought guilt upon us." Whereupon, he decreed that should anyone molest either Jacob or his wife he would be put to death.

The mixed standard of conduct expressed by Abimelech in his rebuke of Isaac is striking. "Apparently, someone would have 'lightly' had sexual relations with Rebekah, without marrying her, and this would have been acceptable. Such behavior, however, would have 'brought guilt' upon the people if Rebekah were already married."[43] Evidently, the marriage relationship was considered inviolable even among such *pagan* people.

This is the third episode of similar character. The first concerned Abram and Sarai in Egypt (12:10-20), and the second their sojourn in Gerar (20:1-18). There is no compelling reason to believe that these were not separate instances. In fact, the use of the multiple *three* may in this context imply a *human* resolution. Otherwise stated, Jacob chose to walk by *sight* rather than by *faith*.

When Isaac was old and he could no longer see, he called for his eldest son Esau. "I am now an old man and don't know the day of my death," he observed (27:2). "Now then, get your weapons--your quiver and bow--and go out to the open country to hunt some wild game for me. Prepare me the kind of tasty food I like and bring it to me to eat, so that I may give you my blessing before I die." Now Rebekah overheard what was said, and instructed Jacob: "Go out to the flock and bring me two choice young goats, so I can prepare some tasty food for your father, just the way he likes it. Then take it to your father to eat, so that he may give you his blessing before he dies." When Jacob returned, his mother dressed him in the best clothes of Esau, and covered his hands and smooth part of his neck with goatskins to resemble the flesh of his brother. Thus were they able to deceive Isaac, and Jacob received the blessing intended for Esau.

As his life progressed, Jacob would experience little worldly happiness. "He would fear for his life at the hands of Esau. He would be deceived by his uncle Laban. Most of his children would disappoint him immensely. He would suffer the loss of his beloved wife. He would eventually die in Egypt--a stranger in a strange land."[44] In short, he would reap what he had sown. In literary terms, it was a matter of *poetic justice*.

In greater detail, Esau said to himself: "The days of mourning for my father are near; then I will kill my brother Jacob" (27:41). When Rebekah heard of this, she sent Jacob away to his uncle Laban's home--so as to secure a wife and escape his brother's wrath. On the way, he stopped for the night and had a dream concerning a stairway reaching to heaven, and the angels of God ascending and descending on it. There above it stood the Lord, who confided: "I am the Lord, the God of your father Abraham and the God of Isaac." Such qualifies as *visionary literature*. "Visionary literature pictures settings, characters, and events that differ from ordinary reality. This is not to say that the things described in visionary literature did not happen in past history or in future history."[45] Conversely, it suggests that such things can't be empirically verified.

When Jacob awoke from his sleep, he thought: "How awesome is this place! This is none other than the house of God; this is the gate of heaven." Then he made a vow that if the Lord would see him safely through his journey, he would acknowledge him as his own, and offer a tithe of all he received. Thus disposed, he arrived at his destination.

When Jacob had stayed with Laban for a month, the latter proposed that they negotiate a proper salary (29:14-15). Jacob offered to work for seven years in return for the hand of Laban's younger daughter Rachel in marriage. Rachel was quite attractive, and Jacob was in love with her. Laban agreed and so when the time was completed he brought together all the people to have a great feast. But when the evening came, he took his elder daughter Leah and gave her to Jacob, and Jacob lay with her. When morning came, "there was Leah!" What must have seemed utterly tragic to Jacob, might solicit uninhibited laughter with its telling.

"What is this you have done to me?" Jacob exclaimed. "I served you for Rachel, didn't I? Why have you deceived me?" Laban replied: "It is not our custom here to give the younger daughter in marriage before the older one. Finish this daughter's bridal week; then we will give you the younger one also, in return for another seven years of work." Since this seemed the best of a bad situation, Jacob agreed.

With the passing of time, Jacob prospered. Laban's sons complained: "Jacob has taken everything our father owned and has gained all this wealth from what belonged to our father." Jacob likewise noticed that Laban's attitude toward him had taken a decided turn for the worse. Then the Lord said to Jacob: "Go back to the land of your fathers and to your relatives, and I will be with you" (31:3). Jacob assembled his wives and their children, their flocks, and their possessions, and started his return journey.

On the third day, Laban was told of Jacob's departure. Taking his relatives with him, he pursued Jacob for seven days, until he had overtaken him. "What have you done?" Laban protested. "You've deceived me, and you've carried off my daughters like captives in war. ...Why didn't you tell me, so that I could send you away with joy and singing to the music of tambourines and harps." Suggesting he could harm Jacob, perhaps with a wave of his hand to those who were with him, he nonetheless observed that the *God of your father* had cautioned him the night before not to do so.

"Now you have gone off because you longed to return to your father's house," Laban added. "But why did you steal my gods?" Since Jacob was not aware that Rachel had taken the family idols, he urged that a thorough search be made. When the objects could not be found, Jacob's pent-up indignation broke loose. "What is my crime?" he demanded. "What sin have I committed that you hunt me down? ...Put it here in front of your relatives and mine, and let them judge between the two of us." (As for the significance of the family idols, they were associated with the rights of inheritance.)

At length, Laban proposed a covenant between them. An altar was erected as a monument between the two suspicious kinsmen, and a sacrifice offered. After they had eaten, they spent the night there. Early the next morning Laban kissed his grandchildren and his daughters and blessed them. Then he left for home, and Jacob continued his journey.

Jacob subsequently sent messengers ahead of him to his brother Esau in the land of Seir, announcing his arrival along with that of his family and extensive possessions. When the messengers returned, they brought word that Esau was coming to meet him, along with four hundred men. In great fear and distress, Jacob made preparations to lessen his losses. With this, he commended his way to God.

The next day he sent gifts on ahead of him, and tarried still another night (32:22). So Jacob was left alone, and a man wrestled with him till daybreak. Jacob insisted: "I will not let you go unless you bless me." "What is your name?" the man inquired. "Jacob," he answered. "Your name will no longer be Jacob, but Israel (*God strives*)," the other responded, "because you have struggled with God and with men and have overcome."

The identity of Jacob's assailant emerges only gradually, "and Jacob is quick to seize every clue to it. Behind the human limitations there is an awesome reserve of power, and behind the reluctance to be overtaken by the day there could be the elusiveness of some night phantom or else the holiness of God, whose face must not be seen."[46] When at last Jacob insists on God's blessing, the reader may be assured that the patriarch has had a genuine encounter with the Almighty. So it would seem that those who fear God, have nothing else to fear. Jacob's reunion with his brother was amicable, and life took on a new lease.

Thus assured, we turn to a later point in the patriarchal narratives. Joseph was Israel's favorite son, having been born to him in his old age (37:3). When his brothers saw this, they hated him and would not say so much as a kind word to him. Eventually, they sold him to Midianite merchants traveling to Egypt, and reported that he had been killed by a wild beast.

The merchants, in turn, sold Joseph to Potiphar, the captain of Pharaoh's guard. The Lord was with Joseph, so that he came into favor with Potiphar, who put him in charge of his household. Now Joseph was well-built and handsome, and after a while the master's wife took notice and invited him to cohabit with her. When he refused, she reported to her husband that Joseph had attempted to rape her. Whereupon, Joseph's master placed him in prison.

The Lord was with Joseph in prison, and showing him kindness and granting him favor in the eyes of the prison warden. So the warden put him in charge of the prison, and made him responsible for its operation. He had confidence in Joseph since the Lord gave him success in whatever he did.

Some time later, the Pharaoh's cupbearer and baker were put in the custody of the captain of the guard, in the same prison where Joseph was confined. When Joseph came to them on a certain morning, he found them dejected. "Why are your faces so sad today?" he inquired. "We both had dreams," they answered, "but there is no one to interpret them." Then Joseph said to them: "Do not interpretations belong to God? Tell me your dreams." It was as Joseph said that it would be.

Still later on, the Pharaoh had a troubling dream, which none could interpret. At this, the cupbearer recalled Joseph, who was summoned. As on the former occasion, God gave him the interpretation of the dream. Then Pharaoh said to Joseph: "Since God has made all this known to you, there is no one so discerning and wise as you. You shall be in charge of my palace, and all my people are to submit to your orders."

Now there was a severe famine in Canaan. Jacob consequently sent Joseph's brothers, with the exception of Benjamin, to buy grain in Egypt (42:1-2). They appeared before Joseph, who was in charge of distributing grain. As soon as Joseph saw his brothers, he recognized them. "If you are honest men," Joseph reasoned, "let one of your brothers stay here in prison, while the rest of you go and take grain back for your starving households. But you must bring your youngest brother to me, so that your words may be verified and that you may not die."

But when they stopped for the night, they discovered that the silver they had taken to buy grain was returned to their sacks. Their hearts sank and they turned to each other trembling and said: "What is this that God has done to us?" As they had surmised earlier, they supposed this might be because they had maltreated Joseph.

Since the famine was still severe, they were forced to return to Egypt. When Joseph saw Benjamin, he ordered his steward: "Take these men to my house, slaughter an animal and prepare dinner; they are to eat with me at noon." His brothers were frightened because they supposed it might have to do with the silver in their sacks, and that they would be reduced to slaves. Instead, they feasted heartily.

Now Joseph gave instructions that the silver would once again be returned to his brothers' sacks, and his silver cup in the mouth of Benjamin's sack. They had not gone far until Joseph's steward caught up with them. "Why have you repaid good with evil?" the steward inquired as Joseph had instructed him. "Isn't this the cup my master drinks from and also uses for divination? This is a wicked thing you have done." When the cup was discovered, the brothers were dismayed.

Upon their return to Egypt, Judah interceded on behalf of Benjamin. "So now, if the boy is not with us when I go back to your servant my father and if my father, whose life is closely bound up with the boy's life, sees that the boy isn't there, he will die. ...Now then, please let your servant remain here as my lord's slave in place of the boy, and let the boy return with his brothers." At this, Joseph could contain himself no longer, but revealed his identity. "You intended harm to me," he eventually concluded, "but God intended it for good to accomplish what is now being done, the saving of many lives" (50:20).

In conclusion, I will propose a brief response to four questions asked of *heroic literature* as applied to patriarchal narrative.[47] First, what is its view of people? The people of patriarchal narrative resemble us in most regards: they don't always do what they should, and often do what they ought not to do. But for the grace of God, we all stumble over our best intentions. Second, what is its religious perspective? God is more intent on making his way known than we are in discovering it. Third, what is its view toward society? Society can either be a blessing or curse, but is in any case necessary to our well being. Fourth, what are its values? We are called upon to love God without reservation, and others as ourselves.

THE COVENANT

Exodus contains a virtual cornucopia of types of literature, "from narrative to law to architectural instructions. All are skillfully woven together to narrate the sequence of events that led a people from feeling that God had abandoned them to understanding themselves to be God's select people with his presence in their midst."[48] More expressly, we encounter what is called in Hebrew tradition *the ten words* (commandments), leading eventually to a more fully developed covenant with Deuteronomy.

Commentators differ as to whether *the ten words* were the original kernel of the larger covenant or its summary. It would seem from the exodus account that the former is the case. The narrator begins with the decalogue, so that the remainder may be properly considered an extension. As a result, the story line is preserved.

The importance of the decalogue can hardly be overstated. The rabbis emphasized its supreme importance in virtually every connection. They speculated that it was prepared on the eve of creation in anticipation of subsequent use; they asserted that as each commandment was sounded from the lofty height of Sinai it filled the world with a pleasing aroma; they concluded that all nature hushed to hear every word as it was spoken. It subsequently charts the way for the righteous to follow.

The ten words are *apodictic* in character, as opposed to *casuistic*. That is, they are broad general principles rather than case instances. As an example of the former, "You shall not murder" (20:13). As an example of the latter, "If men who are fighting hit a pregnant woman and she gives birth prematurely, but there is no serious injury, the offender must be fined whatever the woman's husband demands and the court allows. But if there is serious injury, you are to take life, eye for eye, tooth for tooth, hand for hand, foot for foot, burn for burn, wound for wound, bruise for bruise" (21:22-25).

There is a consensus that there were ten (witness the common title), "although tradition is not agreed as to how to divide the material so as to make this ten. There seems to be no special sacredness about the number ten, although the Hebrews, like most of mankind, counted on the base of ten, probably because the possession of ten fingers made this an easy task."[49]   That is to say, what would seem curious to us may appear commonplace to others.

"God spoke all these words," the narrator assures us. "I am the Lord your God, who brought you out of Egypt, out of the land of slavery. You shall have no other gods before me" (20:2). *Before* is employed not in the sense of *priority* but *in the presence of another*. "Thus the first 'word' takes aim at atheism (we must have a God), idolatry (we must have Yahweh as our God), polytheism (we must have the Lord God alone), and formalism (we must live, fear, and serve the Lord with all our heart, soul, and strength, and mind). The ground of all morality begins here."[50]

"You shall not make for yourself an idol in the form of anything in heaven above or on the earth beneath or in the waters below. You shall not bow down to them or worship them; for I, the Lord your God, am a jealous God, punishing the children for the sin of the fathers to the third and fourth generation of those who hate me, but showing love to a thousand generations of those who love me and keep my commandments." Neither shall you *make* graven images, nor shall you *worship* them. This prohibition would include images of Yahweh, for at least three reasons. First, they would be inadequate expressions of the divine reality. Second, they would impose human misunderstandings. Third, they might give the impression that God could be localized in some manner or other.

The accompanying rationale recognizes the social implications of our actions. That is, whatever we do or fail to do impacts on others. Even so, God promises to restrain evil influence while cultivating the good we do. Evil is therefore dissipated in three or four generations, while good lingers for a thousand generations for those who love God and keep his commandments.

"You shall not misuse the name of the Lord your God, for the Lord will not hold anyone guiltless who misuses his name." Negatively considered, you shall not take the name of God casually, hypocritically, or for magical purposes. Positively considered, you are to treat it reverently, lovingly, and earnestly. All of which brings to mind the adage: "Say what you mean, and mean what you say."

"Remember the Sabbath day by keeping it holy. Six days you shall labor and do all your work, but the seventh day is a Sabbath to the Lord your God. On it you shall not do any work, neither you, nor your son or daughter, nor your manservant or maidservant, nor your animals, nor the alien within your gates." Why? Because God rested from his labors. Why? Because God gave you rest from your bondage in Egypt. Why? Because you should treat others as God treated you. Rest from your labors, celebrate life before God, and be refreshed in body and spirit.

"Honor your father and your mother, so that you may live long in the land the Lord your God is giving you." This is said to be "the first commandment with promise" (Eph. 6:2). "Those who build a society in which old age has an honored place may with confidence expect to enjoy that place themselves one day. This is not a popular doctrine in our modern world, where youth is worshiped, and old age dreaded or despised."[51] In this regard, *the modern world* seems out of step with traditional wisdom.

Honor of parents involves respect, obedience, and love. It includes taking care of their physical, social, and spiritual needs. The rabbis further reasoned that parental honor should extend beyond life as a treasured memory expressed in attitude and deed. The bond was further emphasized by the practice of being *gathered to one's fathers*, whereby the bones of the deceased shared a family crypt.

"You shall not murder." The point is that since we are all joined together in a human bond, we are charged with the safety of others. Otherwise stated, life (our own and that of others) is a sacred trust. The prohibition was understood to exclude the taking of life except as capital punishment legally imposed or to defend individual or corporate life.

"You shall not commit adultery." While insisting on marital fidelity, the prohibition extended to a variety of unacceptable sexual behavior. As an example, "No one is to approach any close relative to have sexual relations" (Lev. 18:6). As another, "Do not lie with a man as one lies with a woman" (18:22). As still another, "Do not have sexual relations with an animal and defile yourself with it" (18:23). In conclusion, "Keep my requirements and do not follow any of the detestable customs that were practiced before you came and do not defile yourselves with them. I am the Lord your God" (18:30).

"You shall not steal." According to rabbinic tradition, one is guilty whether he or she brazenly robs in public or in secret; whether in taking possessions from another or kidnaping the person; whether involving much or little; whether outright or with usury; whether concerning property or reputation. In a peasant society, where the margin for survival is minimal, any theft might result in hardship--if not death. In a covenant community, theft no matter how serious otherwise was an affront to God and a denial of life together.

"You shall not give false testimony against your neighbor." The seriousness of this offence can be seen in that false witness could result in the death of the person charged. In general, truth (like life) is a sacred trust. In religious terms, we honor God by speaking the truth. In social terms, truth serves as the catalyst for a civilized society. Those who treat truth lightly consequently invite disaster, not only on themselves but those associated with them.

"You shall not covet your neighbor's house. You shall not covet your neighbor's wife, or his manservant or maidservant, his ox or his donkey, or anything that belongs to your neighbor." "*House* means 'household', in the early sense of the word, and the thought of 'wife' is primary. ...*Ox* and *ass* are the typical wealth of the bronze age peasant or semi-nomad, for whom the perplexities of developed society have not yet arisen. 'Slaves' are the only other form of movable property."[52] This final interdict makes explicit what has been implicit up to this point: that our predatory desires are the root to our perverse practices. In this connection, we are reminded that man is his own worst enemy.

"When the people saw the thunder and lightning and heard the trumpet and saw the mountain in smoke, they trembled with fear. They stayed at a distance and said to Moses, 'Speak to us yourself and we will listen. But do not have God speak to us or we will die.'" Moses replied: "Do not be afraid. God has come to test you, so that the fear of God will be with you to keep you from sinning."

At this juncture, the narrator turns from general principles to case concerns (21:1). For instance, "Anyone who strikes a man and kills him shall surely be put to death. However, if he does not do it intentionally, but God lets it happen, he is to flee to a place I will designate. But if a man schemes and kills another man deliberately, take him away from my altar and put him to death" (21:12-14). Then, with the passing of time, the covenant was ratified (24:1-18).

Since Leviticus is basically a manual of priestly regulations and procedures, it is only natural that the purely historical elements should be subordinated to ritual and legal concerns. "Nevertheless, historical narratives are interwoven with sections of law and instructions concerning sacrificial procedures in such a way as to make it clear that Leviticus is closely connected historically with Exodus and Numbers."[53] The refrain *the Lord said to Moses* (or *Moses and Aaron*) appears time and again, and the text summarily concludes with "These are the commands the Lord gave Moses on Mount Sinai for the Israelites" (27:34).

Israel was if anything a people at worship, with sacrifice playing a prominent role. As for the former, worship extols the worthiness of God. Otherwise stated, it allows God to be God. As for the latter, sacrifice provided access to the Almighty. As such, it wasn't a substitute for devotion but an evidence of it. It was, in a manner of speaking, a visible expression of an inward commitment. The scapegoat provides us with our most vivid portrait of vicarious sacrifice. In this connection, Aaron was instructed to take two goats: one for a sin offering, and the other "for making atonement by sending it into the desert as a scapegoat" (16:10). Along this line, the psalmist enthused: "As far as the east is from the west, so far has he removed our transgressions from us" (103:12).

The sacrifices and offerings resemble parables concerning God's holiness, justice, and love; man's sinfulness and means whereby his access to God could be achieved; and the conditions under which a chosen people might fulfill their high calling. These cult parables complemented moral instruction, and dramatized the divine-human encounter. They also cultivated a spirit of thanksgiving and praise, coupled with pious resolve.

The dietary regulations have been variously explained. Some seem to reflect hygienic concerns; others so as to disassociate the people from pagan practice; still others to accent traditional ethnicity or general cultural norms. Suffice to say, the dietary code results from some combination of such concerns, more or less understood by us today.

The annual religious festivals accented the sacred character of life. They were closely related to the agricultural year: Passover was observed at the time of barley harvest and Pentecost during the wheat harvest. The celebration of Trumpets, the Day of Atonement, and Tabernacles coincided respectively with the fruit harvest of grapes, figs, and olives. Through such festivals the people were encouraged to express thankfulness to God for his rich provision.

Certain of the Hebrew festivals also came to commemorate the intercession of God on behalf of his chosen people. Passover consequently recalled their deliverance from bondage; Pentecost the giving of the Torah; Tabernacles God's providential protection through the wilderness wandering. Hebrew worship thus incorporated not only the conviction that God was sovereign over nature but history as well.

"The book of Numbers contains instructions for travel and setting up the camp, as well as records of the events that took place during the nearly forty years the Israelites spent in the wilderness. It also includes a number of ritual and legal passages."[54] As such, it commences with a census primarily for military purposes. It continues with an account of events from Sinai to Kadesh, the forty year sojourn in the wilderness, Kadesh to the plains of Moab, and what transpired thereafter.

One instance will serve to illustrative the narrative character of the text. Now Barak was king of Moab at the time the Hebrew people pressed into the area. His people were terrified and complained: "This horde is going to lick up everything around us, as an ox licks up the grass of the field" (22:4). So Barak sent word to Balaam the seer: "A people has come out of Egypt; they cover the face of the land and have settled next to me. Now come and put a curse on these people, because they are too powerful for me." But God said to Balaam: "You must not put a curse on those people, because they are blessed."

Barak again sent word to Balaam: "Do not let anything keep you from coming to me, because I will reward you handsomely and do whatever you say. Come and put a curse on these people for me." That night God said to Balaam: "Since these men have come to summon you, go with them, but do only what I tell you."

The next morning Balaam arose, saddled his donkey, and went on his way. God was nonetheless displeased with his behavior, and the angel of the Lord stood in his way. When the donkey saw the angel of the Lord with sword drawn, she turned off into the field. At which, Balaam beat her to get her to return to the road. Then the angel of the Lord moved ahead to a narrow place with walls on both sides. When the donkey saw this, she pressed close to the wall, crushing Balaam's foot against it. So he beat her again. Then the angel of the Lord moved along further to a place where there was no room to pass, either to the right or the left. When the donkey saw the angel, she lay down in the road. So Balaam beat her with his staff. Then to our astonishment, the donkey speaks: "What have I done to you to make you beat me these three times?"

To our further amazement, Balaam answers: "You have made a fool of me! If I had a sword in my hand, I would kill you right now." Then the donkey replied: "Am I not your own donkey, which you have always ridden, to this day? Have I been in the habit of doing this to you?" "No," her master admitted. Then the Lord opened Balaam's eyes, and he saw the angel of the Lord standing in the road with his sword drawn, and he bowed in submission.

As illustrated in this passage, there is more satire in the Bible than we often recognize. *Satire*, we recall, is the exposure through ridicule or rebuke of human vice or folly. It moreover involves four main elements: the object of attack, vehicle, tone, and norm.[55] As for the object, Balaam the notable seer turns out to be less sensitive to God's ways than his lowly donkey. As for the vehicle, God chooses humble means. As for the tone, it is of the more scornful variety than its more playful counterpart. As for the norm, we ought to accept what God says without hedging on it.

After forty years of wandering in the wilderness, the covenant was renewed on the plains of Moab--as recorded in Deuteronomy. In structure, it resembles a vassal treaty of the time. As such, it consists of five segments: preamble, historical prologue, stipulations, sanctions, and provision for renewal. The *preamble* was succinctly expressed: "Moses proclaimed to the Israelites all that the Lord had commanded him concerning them" (1:3). Consequently, it identifies Yahweh as the heavenly sovereign, on whose behalf Moses extends the treaty for ratification. It was a solemn moment that solicited reverence from all those assembled. They were being called upon to give their unqualified allegiance to the Great King from this point on.

In contrast, the purpose of the *historical prologue* was to justify God's reign over his people. "Benefits allegedly conferred by the lord upon the vassal were cited with a view to grounding the vassal's allegiance in a sense of gratitude complementary to the sense of fear which the preamble's grandiose identification of the suzerain had been calculated to inspire."[56] Illustrations were not difficult to come by. Yahweh had delivered his people from bondage in Egypt, graciously met with them at Sinai, sustained them in the wilderness, and given them recent victories in the Trans-Jordan. This he had done in spite of their persisting waywardness.

The *stipulations* made up the central and major portion of the vassal treaty. Having structured life with regard to a wide variety of situations, it concludes as follows: "The Lord your God commands you this day to follow these decrees and laws; carefully observe them with all your heart and with all your soul. You have declared this day that the Lord is your God and that you will walk in his ways.... And the Lord has declared this day that you are his people, his treasured possessions as he promised, and that you are to keep all his commands" (26:16-18).

The *sanctions* contrast the fortunes of those who trust their way to Yahweh, and those who pursue life on their own. If obedient, the people could anticipate blessing *in the city and in the country, of the fruit of your womb, the crops of your land, and the young of your flocks*, with *your basket and your kneading trough*, and *when you come in and go out*. If disobedient, they would be cursed in all of the above.

The final section dealt with *covenant renewal*. Such would allow the people to respond to changing times in continuity with covenant precedents. In particular, they took upon themselves the yoke of the covenant in anticipation of possessing the promised land. This time there would be no turning back.

THE CONQUEST

"The land west of the Jordan River provides the setting for most of the biblical events. This region provides the geographical background for the conquest, the period of the judges, the monarchy, the restoration after the exile, the life of Christ, and the early church."[57] Readers who ignore the setting in Biblical stories, miss much of the meaning. "Sometimes, it is true, setting functions as little more than a lead-in to a story. ...But whenever a storyteller begins to elaborate the setting, we can rest assured that it is there for a purpose, either to make the story come alive in our imagination or as a contribution to the meaning of the story."[58] Such is eminently the situation as we approach the Hebrew conquest of the promised land.

The expression "from Dan to Beersheba" (Judg. 20:1) was used to refer to the land occupied by the Hebrews from its northern to southern borders. It was approximately one hundred and fifty miles as the crow flies. The region between the Mediterranean Sea and Jordan River narrowed to thirty-five miles in northern Galilee and extended to eighty-five miles at the southern end of the Dead Sea.

It was a *land between* two great meteorological systems: the dry scorching heat from the desert and the moist breeze from the sea. These struggled to gain and maintain control as if two relentless combatants. This provided the theological imagery for the two ways, concerning the wicked and the righteous. As for the former, it resembles the grass parched by the desert heat. As for the latter, it recalls the green pastures refreshed by spring water and dew.

It was also a *land between* two great population centers of the ancient world: Egypt and Mesopotamia. As such, it lay along the fertile crescent, providing the means for commerce and military operations. Its inhabitants consequently were largely subservient to foreign powers. They could achieve some degree of autonomy only when the great kingdoms were internally weak or neutralized one another. Otherwise, they had to take the greatest care in choosing which to side with, since a wrong decision could be disastrous.

It was finally a *land between* two extended cultures which comprised the landed region and the sea peoples. With the passing of time, "Israelites under Joshua occupied the central highlands and fanned out toward the coast regions. The Sea Peoples, particularly the Philistines, occupied the southern coastal regions of the Mediterranean littoral, and challenged Israel's hold on the interior of the country."[59]   While depreciated by the Hebrews, the Philistines had a more developed culture in some respects. As a case in point, we read: "Not a blacksmith could be found in the whole land of Israel... .   So all Israel went down to the Philistines to have their plowshares, mattocks, axes, and sickles sharpened" (1 Sam. 13:19-20).

While a troubled region from antiquity, the promised land was not without its redeeming features. So it was that Sinuhe, the ancient Egyptian traveler, reported: "Figs were in it, and grapes. It had more wine than water. Plentiful was its honey, abundant its olives. Every kind of fruit was on its trees. Barley was there, and emer. There was no limit to any kind of cattle." In retrospect, "This land was fashioned by God for a particular service to Him, that its very landscape should help to mold the character and spirit of His beloved people."[60]

Rabbinic comments may be noted in passing: "Even the conversation of those who live in the Land of Israel is Torah"; "Then measures of wisdom came into the world. The Land of Israel took nine, and the rest of the world took one"; "Jerusalem is the light of the world, as it is stated 'Nations shall walk by your light' (Isa. 60:3). Who is the light of Jerusalem? The Holy One, praise be He, as it is written: 'The Lord will be your everlasting light' (Isa. 60:19)."[61]

So it was that after the death of Moses--*the servant of the Lord*, the Lord said to Joshua--the son of Nun and *Moses aide*: "Moses my servant is dead. Now then, you and all these people, get ready to cross the Jordan River into the land I am about to give to them" (Josh. 1:2). The *Jordan River* snakes its way from the Huleh Lake (seven feet above sea level) to the Dead Sea (1274 feet below sea level), negotiating a twenty mile distance in a circuitous route of two hundred miles. Behind the Israelites were the Trans-Jordan highlands, and before them the Great Rift and Central Hill Country. "No one will be able to stand up against you all the days of your life," the Lord added. As I was with Moses, so I will be with you; I will never leave you nor forsake you."

"Be strong and courageous, because you will lead these people to inherit the land I swore to their forefathers to give them. Be strong and very courageous. Be careful to obey all the law my servant Moses gave you; do not turn from it to the right or the left, that you may be successful wherever you go." The conditions as we find them in the Joshua story are as follows: (1) they must cross the Jordan River, (2) enter the promised land, (3) engage in a long, determined struggle, (4) do away with internal corruption, (5) agree to a fair distribution of the land, and (6) organize the society according to their covenant obligations.[62]   "Have I not commanded you? Be strong and courageous. Do not be terrified; do not be discouraged, for the Lord your God will be with you wherever you go."

As for the people, they promised Joshua: "Whatever you have commanded us we will do, and wherever you send us we will go. Just as we fully obeyed Moses, so we will obey you. Only may the Lord be with you as he was with Moses." It was a new generation and unlike the previous generation, one prepared to obey those God would appoint as their leaders.

Then Joshua sent out two spies. "Go, look over the land," he said, "especially Jericho" (2:1). So they went and entered into the house of Rahab and stayed there. "Rahab had, probably out of economic necessity, earned a living as a prostitute. ...In ancient cities, certain occupational groups were tolerated but, because of the nature of the work, entirely without a recognized place. Among these groups were prostitutes and slaves."[63] Since *marginalized* persons saw society at its worse, they might be more open to some new alternative.

Information concerning the spies came to the attention of the king of Jericho, who ordered that they be brought to him. "Yes, the men came to me, but I did not know where they had come from," Rahab responded to the inquiry. "At dusk, when it was time to close the city gate, the men left. I don't know which way they went." Instead, she had hidden them, and asked that she be well received once the city fell to the Israelites. Matthew subsequently mentions her in the genealogy of Jesus (Matt. 1:5). Upon returning to Joshua, the spies confidently reported: "The Lord has surely given the whole land into our hands; all the people are melting in fear because of us."

Early the next morning Joshua and all the people set out from their encampment and came to the Jordan River. "Consecrate yourselves," Joshua urged them, "for tomorrow the Lord will do amazing things among you." Joshua moreover said to the Israelites: "This is how you will know that the living God is among you... . And as soon as the priests who carry the ark of the Lord--the Lord of all the earth--set foot in the Jordan, the waters flowing downstream will be cut off and stand up in a heap." So it came to pass, and the people took heart. "That day the Lord exalted Joshua in the sight of all Israel; and they revered him all the days of his life, just as they had revered Moses."

The battle of Jericho is a well-known and often repeated story which not only entertains, but questions and challenges the attentive reader. "One NT writer found in it two examples of faith (Heb. 11:30-31). A chronicler of the Maccabean wars reported that the Jericho story inspired Judas to attack an impregnable fortress with inferior forces and slaughter the inhabitants (2 Macc. 12:15-16)."[64] We are told that the city was *tightly shut up* for fear of the Israelites (6:1). Whereupon, God commanded Joshua to march around the city with all the armed men for six days. On the seventh day, the priests were to blow their trumpets, and in turn, all the people give a loud shout. "Then the wall of the city will collapse and the people will go up, every man straight in." So God promised, and so it came to pass.

They moreover devoted the city to the Lord and destroyed every living thing in it. Walter Kaiser observes that they were cut off to prevent Israel and the rest of the world from being corrupted (Deut. 20:16-18). He subsequently elaborates: "When people start to burn their children in honor of their gods (Lev. 18:21), practice sodomy, bestiality, and all sorts of loathsome vices (Lev. 18:23, 24; 20:3), the land itself begins to 'vomit' them out as the body heaves under the load of internal poisons (Lev. 18:25)."[65] This destruction was no different in principle than that of Noah's contemporaries, except that it was more surgically selective.

Now Achan kept for himself some of the things devoted to God. Thus when the people went up against Ai, they were sorely defeated. Achan's subsequent confession contains three verbs: *I saw*, *I coveted*, and *I took* (7:21). The same three verbs are found in Genesis 3:6 concerning Eve's eating of the fruit of the tree of the knowledge of good and evil. "Then all Israel stoned him... . Then the Lord turned from his fierce anger." After this, Joshua burned Ai and made it a desolate place *to this day*. The people subsequently renewed their covenant at Mount Ebal in the Hill Country.

"Now when all the kings west of the Jordan heard about these things--those in hill country, in the western foothills, and along the entire coast of the Great Sea...they came together to make war against Joshua and Israel" (9:1). That is to say, they came from various regions so as to join together in opposition to the invaders. However, when the people of Gibeon heard what Joshua had done to Jericho and Ai, they resorted to a ruse. They went as a delegation whose donkeys were loaded with worn-out wineskins, cracked and mended. The men put on worn and patched sandals on their feet and wore old clothes. All their bread was dry and moldy. They came to Joshua and said to him and the men of Israel: "We have come from a distant country; make a treaty with us."

The men of Israel sampled their provision, but didn't *inquire of the Lord.* Then Joshua made a treaty with them, only to discover three days later that they lived near by. At this, the people grumbled against their leaders. The latter, in turn, did not want to go back on their promise, and so the people of Gibeon became woodcutters and water carriers for the community in general and ritual purposes in particular.

Whereas the prior story seems rather *ordinary*, what follows is decidedly *unique.* Now when Adoni-Zedek, king of Jerusalem, heard that Joshua had destroyed Ai as he had previously done to Jericho, and that he had made a treaty with the people of Gibeon, he "and his people were very much alarmed at this" (10:2). Since Gibeon (el-Jib) is only six miles north of Jerusalem, we can appreciate the cause of his concern. Whereupon, he organized five kings of the Amorites so as to make a pre-emptive strike against Gibeon. This, in order, forced Joshua to defend those with whom he had mistakenly become allied. Leading his troops on an all night march from Gilgal to Gibeon, he took the allied forces by surprise. The latter subsequently fled west down the ascent of Beth-horon with the Israelites hot in pursuit.

On the day that the Lord delivered the Amorites over to Israel, Joshua said to the Lord in the presence of Israel: "O sun, stand still over Gibeon, O moon, over the Valley of Aijalon. So the sun stood still and the moon stopped, till the nation avenged itself on its enemies, as it is written in the Book of Jashar." The narrator subsequently assures us: "The sun stopped in the middle of the sky and delayed going down about a full day. There has never been a day like it before or since, a day when the Lord listened to a man. Surely the Lord was fighting for Israel."

Some have made this passage a test of belief in the literal sense of the Scriptures. "Others have tried to reconcile it with natural phenomena, such as an eclipse of the sun, or planetary disturbances causing a *lost day* in terrestrial chronology. Still others say that it is impossible to understand it as anything other than the creation of a pious writer's imagination."[66] Several factors would appear relevant. First, the narrator seems to be describing an exceptional event however we may choose to account for it. Second, an alternative translation to *stand still* is *to cease from doing something.* Third, the natural way for God to keep the sun and moon from shining would be to lay out a heavy cloud layer for an extended period. Fourth, this would preempt any effort of the enemy to recoup and go on the offensive. This is but one plausible reconstruction, and there are others.

In any case, the story suggests how God may choose to wage war on the forces of evil. For one thing, we observe his intervention in the form of natural phenomena: a storm with heavy cloud cover and deadly hailstones. This occurs at a providential time to help the Israelites gain a decisive victory. For another, he employs Joshua and the people to accomplish his righteous purposes. For still another, God and Israel work together as covenant partners--in which God promises to provide on condition of their obedience.

Fresh from victory, Joshua pressed his advantage--destroying one city after another. "So Joshua subdued the whole region, including the hill country, the Negev, the western foothills and the mountain slopes, together with all their kings." "Then Joshua returned with all Israel to the camp in Gilgal."

The news of Joshua's overwhelming victory in southern Canaan soon reached the ears of Jabin, "king of Hazor, a strategic fortress city north of the Sea of Galilee. Fearing attack he organized a coalition of cities to protect the northern territory. The gathering point for Jabin's confederacy was the waters of Merom, a copious spring about seven miles northwest of Hazor (11:1-5)."[67] "They came out with all their troops and a large number of horses and chariots--a huge army, as numerous as the sand on the seashore."

The Lord encouraged Joshua: "Do not be afraid of them, because by this time tomorrow I will hand all of them over to Israel, slain." So Joshua and his whole army came against them suddenly at the Waters of Merom, "and the Lord gave them into the hand of Israel." "So Joshua took this entire land: the hill country, all the Negev, the whole region of Goshen, the western foothills, the Arabah and the mountains of Israel with their foothills." "Except for the Hivites living in Gibeon, not one city made a treaty of peace with the Israelites, who took them all in battle." "Then the land had rest from war."

While the conquest was not as yet complete, it came time to distribute the land among the several tribes. As a result, the society would differ radically from what preceded it. As for the former, "Sociological studies indicate that the aristocracy, temple, and government had control of over 50 percent of the land as patrimonial holdings. These holdings were worked by slaves or sharecropping peasants who paid over half of their produce to the landlords."[68] The rest of the land was tilled by villagers who paid heavy taxes to support the urban elite. In contrast, "God grants the whole land not to a king but to all the people, tribe by tribe, family by family. There is no privileged class."

Then the Lord said to Joshua: "Tell the Israelites to designate the cities of refuge...so that anyone who kills a person accidentally and unintentionally may flee there and find protection from the avenger of blood" (20:2-3). The institution was designed to preserve society from the escalation of violence. Six designated locations were conveniently located throughout the land, with easy access maintained at all times. Care was taken to assure that only those qualified were allowed protection. In each city, a community of priests would administer the program: welcoming the refugee, providing him shelter, and protecting him from the avengers.

So also Joshua was to set aside towns for the Levites (21:1-2). These would serve as centers for the study of the Torah. Here the teaching would be considered, interpreted, applied, and instilled. These would replace the idolatrous high places, altars, pagan priests, and cult practices which had preceded them. "The towns of the Levites in the territory held by the Israelites were forty-eight in all (twelve multiplied by four, signifying universality), together with their pasture-lands." So it was implied that the Torah should pervade all of society.

After a long time had passed and the Lord had given Israel rest from all their enemies around them, Joshua was well advanced in years. He consequently summoned all Israel--their elders, leaders, judges and officials--to say to them: "You yourselves have seen everything the Lord your God has done to all these nations for your sake; it was the Lord your God who fought for you. I have allotted as an inheritance for your tribes all the land of the nations that remain...between the Jordan and the Great Sea to the west. He will push them out before you, and you will take possession of their land, as the Lord promised you" (23:3-4).

"One of you routs a thousand," Joshua continued, "because the Lord your God fights for you, just as he promised. So be very careful to love the Lord your God." "But if you turn away and ally yourselves with the survivors of these nations that remain among you...they will become snares and traps for you, whips on your backs and thorns in your eyes, until you perish from this good land, which the Lord your God has given you."

"Now I am about to go the way of all the earth. You know with all your heart and soul that not one of all the good promises the Lord your God gave you has failed. ...But just as every good promise of the Lord

your God has come true, so the Lord will bring on you all the evil he has
threatened, until he has destroyed you from this good land he has given
you." Then, on a later occasion, the people reaffirmed their commitment:
"We will serve the Lord our God and obey him" (24:24). "See!" Joshua
said in response. "This stone will be a witness against us. It has heard all
the words the Lord has said to us. It will be a witness against you if you
are untrue to your God." So the narrator concludes in graphic terms his
audience would not readily forget.

TIME OF THE JUDGES

The seemingly inconsequential words "Now...it came to pass" at the beginning of the book of Judges (Judg. 1:1 KJV) convey an important truth. "They tell us that the ultimate context for the study of the book of Judges is the entire panorama which begins with creation, and extends on to Abraham, Moses, Joshua, the Judges, Samuel, David, the kings of Israel, and Jesus Christ."[69] It this manner, it validates the thesis of the Scripture *as* story.

More in particular, we are encouraged to view Judges as a sequel to Joshua, as Joshua was a sequel to Deuteronomy. Ruth, in turn, picks up with the time of the judges, and anticipates the monarchy. As for the past, "The people served the Lord throughout the lifetime of Joshua and of the elders who outlived him and who had seen all the great things the Lord had done for Israel" (Judg. 2:7). Then, after "that whole generation had been gathered to their fathers, another generation grew up, who knew neither the Lord nor what he had done for Israel. ...They forsook the Lord, the God of their fathers, who brought them out of Egypt. They followed and worshiped various gods of the people around them."

The book of Judges derives its name from the activities of its leading characters. These were endowed with qualities of leadership with God's Spirit coming upon them. The more spectacular evidence of this possession, and the most likely to be remembered by posterity, "was the shattering of the yoke of an oppressor. Other qualities assumed prominence when the national emergencies receded, and those who manifested these gifts were respected and sought out by those in need of advice or arbitration."[70] There are twelve judges listed in all: seven major judges and five minor judges. We will limit our attention to the seven major judges and Ruth as a supplement.

A common cycle occurs throughout the narrative. First, the Israelites do evil in the sight of the Lord. Then, seeing that they would not restrain sin within, they could not contain evil without. They were consequently oppressed by others. Thereupon, they cried out to the Lord in their distress. When they did so, he raised up for them a deliverer. After this, they enjoyed peace for a time, until again falling back into their evil ways.

Othniel sets the course for others to follow. "The Israelites did evil in the eyes of the Lord; they forgot the Lord their God and served the Baals and the Asherahs. The anger of the Lord burned against Israel so that he sold them into the hands of Cushan-Rishathaim king of Aram Naharaim, to which the Israelites were subject for eight years" (3:7-8). But when they cried out to the Lord, he raised up Othniel, *who saved them.* "So the land had peace for forty years, until Othniel son of Kenaz died."

"Once again the Israelites did evil in the eyes of the Lord, and because they did this evil the Lord gave Eglon king of Moab power over Israel" (3:12). "Again the Israelites cried out to the Lord, and he gave them a deliverer--Ehud, a left-handed man, the son of Gera the Benjamite." A *left-handed* person was thought to be at some disadvantage. As we shall see, it turns out otherwise in the story.

Ehud was sent to pay tribute. Now he "had made a double-edged sword about a foot and a half long, which he strapped to his right thigh under his clothing. He presented the tribute to Eglon king of Moab, who was a very fat man." The implication of his being *fat* is that he lived in luxury at the expense of others.

After Ehud had delivered the tribute and sent away his associates, he turned back. "I have a secret message for you," he said to Eglon. "Quiet!" the king replied, sending his attendants from the room. Ehud then approached him while he was sitting alone in the upper room of his summer palace and said: "I have a message from God for you." As the king arose from his seat, Ehud "reached with his left hand, drew the sword from his right thigh and plunged it into the king's belly." Then he went out to the porch, shut the doors of the upper room behind him and locked them. Thus he made his escape and rallied his fellow Israelites to put the Moabites to flight. "That day Moab was made subject to Israel, and the land had peace for eighty years."

We have only the briefest of record concerning Shamgar, the third of the major judges. It seems that he struck down six hundred Philistines with an oxgoad. As a result, he "too saved Israel" (3:31). Since Ehud rather than Shamgar is mentioned in the following verse, it would seem that the latter appears as one who helped to preserve the peace ushered in by Ehud's victory. His use of an impromptu weapon parallels Samson's later use of the jawbone of an ass (15:16).

"After Ehud died, the Israelites once again did evil in the eyes of the Lord. So the Lord sold them into the hands of Jabin, a king of Canaan, who reigned in Hazor" (4:1-2). Deborah, a prophetess, "was leading Israel at that time." She subsequently sent for Barak, and said to him, "The Lord, the God of Israel, commands you: 'Go, take with you ten thousand men of Naphtali and Zebulun and lead the way to Mount Tabor.' I will lure Sisera, the commander of Jabin's army with his chariots and his troops to the Kishon River and give him into your hands."

"If you go with me, I will go," Barak responded, "but if you don't go with me, I won't go." "Very well," Deborah replied, "I will go with you. But because of the way you are going about this, the honor will not be yours, for the Lord will hand Sisera over to a woman." So it was that when Sisera fled from the field of battle, he came to the tent of Jael, the wife of Heber the Kenite. "Come my lord," she welcomed him, "come right in. Don't be afraid." "I'm thirsty," he said. "Please give me some water." She opened a skin of milk, gave him drink, and covered him. "Stand in the doorway of the tent," he instructed her. "If someone comes by and asks you, 'Is anyone here?' say 'No.'" Instead, she picked up a tent peg and hammer while he lay fast asleep--thoroughly exhausted, and drove the peg through his temple. Thus when Barak arrived he found his adversary dead.

On that day God subdued Jabin, and "the hand of the Israelites grew stronger and stronger against Jabin, the Canaanite king, until they destroyed him. *On that day* Deborah and Barak sang a song extolling God for his intercession, describing the severity of the oppression, and allowing for the means of deliverance. One final clue about oppression may be seen in the thoughts attributed to Sisera's mother, "that her son might be dividing captive Israelite girls among the soldiers (5:30). With Israelite poverty created by economic exploitation, and brute force in the hands of soldiers on raids, sexual violation of women would be common."[71] Such is perhaps the context of Jael's reprisal, and Deborah and Barak's commendation of her (5:24-27).

"Again the Israelites did evil in the eyes of the Lord, and for seven years he gave them into the hands of the Midianites" (6:1). When they cried to the Lord, he sent them a prophet to remind them of their covenant obligations and their failure to keep them. After this, the angel of the Lord appeared to Gideon and said to him: "The Lord is with you, mighty warrior." "But sir," the latter protested, "if the Lord is with us, why has all this happened to us?" "Go in the strength you have and save Israel out of Midian's hand," the other insisted. "But Lord," Gideon inquired, "how can I save Israel? My clan is the weakest in Manasseh, and I am the least in my family." "I will be with you," the angel of the Lord assured him."

Now all the Midainites, Amalekites and other eastern peoples gathered together to wage war against Gideon. Whereupon, Gideon said to God: "If you will save Israel by my hand as you have promised--look, I will place a wool fleece on the threshing floor. If there is dew only on the fleece and all the ground is dry, then I will know that you will save Israel by my hand, as you said." But when this happened, he requested that the reverse might occur. "That night God did so. Only the fleece was dry; all the ground was covered with dew."

Early in the morning, Gideon and his forces encamped at the spring of Harod. "You have too many men for me to deliver Midian into their hands," the Lord observed. "In order that Israel may not boast against me that her own strength has saved her, announce now to the people, 'Anyone who trembles with fear may turn back.'" So twenty-two thousand men left, while ten thousand remained. But the Lord said to Gideon: "There are still too many men. ...Separate those who lap the water with their tongues like a dog from those who kneel down to drink. Three hundred men lapped with their hands to their mouths." Thus they demonstrated their alertness, and being few in number, assured that God would be honored for their victory. "Thus Midian was subdued before the Israelites and did not raise its head again. During Gideon's lifetime, the land enjoyed peace forty years."

"Again the Israelites did evil in the sight of the Lord" (10:6). They served the gods of the people around them, and thereby invoked God's wrath. He consequently "sold them into the hands of the Philistines and the Ammonites." Then the Israelites cried out to the Lord: "We have sinned against you, forsaking our God and serving the Baals." God was not impressed. "Go and cry out to the gods you have chosen," he replied. "Let them save you when you are in trouble!" The people persisted: "Do with us whatever you think best, but please rescue us now." *Then*, rather than *before*, they got rid of the foreign gods among them and served the Lord.

The Spirit of Lord subsequently came upon Jephthah, and he made a pledge: "If you give the Ammonites into my hands, whatever comes out of the door of my house to meet me when I return in triumph from the Ammonites will be the Lord's and I will sacrifice it as a burnt offering." So when he returned in triumph, "who should come out to meet him but his daughter, dancing to the sound of tambourines!" "Oh! My daughter!" Jephthah exclaimed. "You have made me miserable and wretched, because I have made a vow to the Lord that I cannot break." "My father," she replied, "you have given your word to the Lord. Do to me just as you promised... . But grant me this one request. Give me two months to roam the hills and weep with my friends, because I will never marry." Her request was granted, the vow kept, and the event annually commemorated.

"Again the Israelites did evil in the eyes of the Lord, so the Lord delivered them into the hands of the Philistines for forty years" (13:1). Now the angel of the Lord appeared to the wife of Zorah to announce that she would give birth to a son--Samson. Samson was decidedly unique among the judges. Endowed with the Spirit of the Lord and dedicated to a lifelong Nazirite vow, "his life seems to have revolved around illicit relationships... . It is a sad tale of a lack of discipline and true dedication, and the reader is left wondering what Samson might have achieved had his enormous potential been matched and tempered by these mental and spiritual qualities."[72]

Sampson went down to Timnah, and there saw a young Philistine woman. When he returned, he said to his father and mother: "I have seen a Philistine woman in Timnah; now get her for me as my wife." His parents responded: "Isn't there an acceptable woman among your relatives or among all our people? Must you go to the uncircumcised Philistines to get a wife?" But Samson insisted: "Get her for me. She's the right one for me." The narrator observes: "His parents did not know that this was from the Lord, who was seeking an occasion to confront the Philistines."

Samson subsequently returned to Timnah. Along the way, he was attacked by a young lion which he killed. Still later on, when he again returned to marry the woman, he came across the carcass of the lion. In it was a swarm of bees and honey. After this, he made a feast as was customary for bridegrooms. "Let me tell you a riddle," he said to his companions. "If you can give me the answer within the seven days of the feast, I will give you thirty linen garments and thirty sets of clothes. If you can't tell me the answer, you must give me thirty linen garments and thirty sets of clothes." "Tell us your riddle," they urged him. He replied: "Out of the eater, something to eat; and of the strong, something sweet."

"A riddle is a concise saying which is intentionally formulated to tax the ingenuity of the hearer or reader when he tries to explain it. ...What began in fun and festivity ended in tragedy."[73] The thirty friends of Sampson threatened to burn the girl and her father's house if she did not find out for them the answer to Sampson's riddle. So it was that before sunset on the seventh day, the men of the town said to him: "What is sweeter than honey? What is stronger than a lion?" Samuel was furious, and said in reply: "If you had not plowed with my heifer, you would not have solved my riddle." Whereupon, he went down to Ashkelon, struck down thirty of their men, stripped them of their belongings and gave their clothes to those who had explained the riddle.

The conflict between Sampson and the Philistines continued to escalate. Refused by his wife, and rejecting her younger sister as a substitute, Sampson announced: "This time I have a right to get even with them." So he burned their "shocks and standing grain, together with the vineyards and olive groves." In response, the Philistines killed his wife and burned her house. Samson responded: "Since you've acted like this, I won't stop until I get my revenge on you." True to his word, he viciously attacked them and killed many.

Some time later Samson fell in love with a woman by the name of Delilah (16:4). The Philistine officials plotted with her to discover the source of his strength. So Delilah pled with Sampson: "Tell me the secret of your great strength and how you can be tied up and subdued." He replied: "If anyone ties me with seven fresh thongs that have not been dried, I'll become as weak as any man." With men hidden in the room, she called out: "Sampson, the Philistines are upon you!" But he snapped the thongs as easily as a piece of string snaps when it comes close to a flame. Twice more Delilah attempted to ply the information from Samson. Twice more he misled her. At last she complained: "How can you say, 'I love you' when you won't confide in me?" So he confessed: "If my head were shaved, my strength would leave me, and I would become as weak as any other man."

After this, the Philistines seized him, gouged out his eyes, and set him to grinding in the prison. "But the hair on his head began to grow again after it had been shaved," the narrator observes. The story builds to a climax. So it was that when the Philistines were celebrating in the temple of Dagon, they called for Samson so that they might taunt him. "Put me where I can feel the pillars that support the temple," he requested of the servant who brought him, "so that I may lean against them." Now the temple was filled to capacity. Then when Sampson asked God to strengthen him one more time, he pushed on the pillars with all his might, and down came the temple on the rulers and all the people.

Both the accounts of Jephthah and Samson might qualify as *tragedy*. "At the level of plot or action tragedy is the story of exceptional calamity. It portrays a movement from prosperity to catastrophe. Because it depicts a change of fortune, tragedy must be differentiated from pathos, which depicts unmitigated suffering from the very start."[74]

Conditions reach their lowest point with the final episode. Everyone who witnessed it, said: "Such a thing has never been seen or done, not since the day the Israelites came up out of Egypt" (19:30). It concerned a Levite who with his concubine accepted hospitality in Gibeah. While they were enjoying themselves, some wicked men surrounded the house and demanded that the Levite come forth so that they could gang rape him. When his host refused, he offered his daughter and the man's concubine as an alternative. They settled for the concubine, and when morning came, she lay at the door--dead. At this, the Levite cut up her body and sent portions *to all parts of Israel*. This eventuated in bloody conflict, and the summary observation: "In those days Israel had no king; everyone did as he saw fit."

The editor thereby reveals his own background to be one of stability and security, conditions characteristic of the major part of David's reign and in the earlier part of Solomon's reign. "However, the historical perspective of the editor was not to be the final assessment, for the monarchy itself was to deteriorate and proved to be no lasting remedy for the evils of the land. ...But the reader must take up this story in another book."[75]

The book of *Ruth* concerns friendships. "The devotion that Ruth shows to Naomi and the care that Naomi exercises towards Ruth runs through the book. ...But it is worth noticing that all three of the principal characters of the book are depicted as being mindful of their obligations to the family."[76] Consequently, it might be more plausible to argue that it deals primarily with family obligations. Not to be overlooked, it acts as a corrective against exclusive ethnic tendencies.

One example will suffice. In the days when the judges ruled, there was a famine in the land, and Elimelech of Bethlehem, and his wife Naomi and their two sons went to live for the time being in the region of Moab. Now when Elimelech died, Naomi determined to return to her people. Meanwhile, her sons had married Moabite women, but they too had died. Naomi said to her two daughters-in-law: "Go back, each of you, to your mother's home. May the Lord grant that each of you will find rest in the home of another husband" (1:8-9). Then Orpah kissed her mother-in-law goodby, but Ruth clung to her. "Look," said Naomi, "your sister-in-law is going back to her people and her gods. Go back with her." But Ruth replied: "Don't urge me to leave you or turn back from you. Where you go I will go, and where you stay I will stay. Your people will be my people and your God my God." So it was that Ruth lived a full life, and appears in the genealogy of David and that of Jesus the Messiah.

As such, the book exemplifies from literary perspective a *comedy*. When speaking of comedy as a type of story, literary critics do not mean a humorous story but rather one with a certain shape of plot. " Comedy is the story of the happy ending. It is usually a U-shaped story that beings in prosperity, descends into tragedy, and rises again to end happily. The first phase...is often omitted, but the upward movement from misery to happiness is essential."[77]

RISE OF THE MONARCHY

There was a certain man from the hill country of Ephraim, north of Jerusalem, named *Elkanah*. He had two wives: one called *Peninnah* and the other *Hannah*. The former had children, but the latter was barren (a catastrophe by ancient standards). "And because the Lord had closed her womb, her rival kept provoking her in order to irritate her. This went on year after year. Whenever Hannah went up to the house of the Lord, her rival provoked her till she wept and would not eat" (1 Sam. 1:6-7).

Now Eli the priest was sitting on a chair by the doorpost of the Lord's temple when Hannah prayed silently: "O Lord Almighty, if you will only look upon your servant's misery and remember me, and not forget your servant but give her a son, then I will give him to the Lord for all the days of his life, and no razor will ever be used on his head." Since her mouth was moving but no words coming forth, Eli supposed that she was drunk and rebuked her.

"Not so, my lord," Hannah replied. "I am a woman who is deeply troubled. I have not been drinking wine or beer; I was pouring out my soul to the Lord." "Go in peace," Eli answered, "and may the God of Israel grant you what you have asked of him." So in the course of time Hannah conceived and gave birth to a son. She called him *Samuel* as a testimony to her prayer-answering God. Then when the child was weaned, she presented him at the sanctuary for service to the Almighty.

Eli's sons were wicked men, who had no regard for the Lord. Now when Eli was advanced in years, he heard about all the things his sons were doing. So he inquired of them: "If a man sins against another man, God may mediate for him; but if a man sins against the Lord, who will intercede for him?" Then, subsequently, Eli was visited by a man of God who confirmed his worse fears: "Those who honor me will I (God) honor, but those who despise me will be disdained."

"In those days the word of the Lord was rare; there were not many visions" (3:1). "These vision forms or experiences were occasionally in the night. However, most of them occurred during the day when God brought to the mind of the prophet the content which the prophet was later to proclaim."[78] For instance, the text of Amos begins: "The words of Amos, one of the shepherds of Tekoa--what he saw concerning Israel two years before the earthquake when Uzziah was king of Judah and Jeroboam...was king of Israel" (1:1).

One night the Lord called Samuel. "Here I am," the lad replied, running in response to what he supposed was Eli's summons. "Here I am; you called me." But Eli said: "I did not call; go back and lie down." Again the Lord called: "Samuel!" So again Samuel went to Eli and said: "Here I am; you called me." "My son," Eli replied, "I did not call; go back and lie down." The Lord called Samuel a third time, and Samuel went to Eli once again and said: "Here I am; you called me." Then Eli realized that the Lord was calling the boy. Whereupon, he instructed Samuel: "Go and lie down, and if he calls you, say 'Speak, Lord, for your servant is listening.'" So it was that Samuel learned of God's intent to remove the house of Eli from serving him.

In this account, we come across three characters: God, represented through his word, Eli the priest and Samuel. "The main character here is neither Eli nor Samuel, but the word of God. In this chapter, the Hebrew root *dbr* occurs fifteen times, both in its nominative and predicative forms."[79] In particular, God's word reveals his purpose. When we fail to heed his word, we are at cross-purposes. The narrator concludes: "The Lord continued to appear at Shiloh, and there he revealed himself to Samuel through his word. And Samuel's word came to all Israel."

Now the Israelites went out to fight against the Philistines and were defeated. When this occurred, the elders inquired: "Why did the Lord bring defeat upon us today before the Philistines? Let us bring the ark of the Lord's covenant from Shiloh, so that it may go with us and save us from the hand of our enemies" (4:3). The ark symbolized the presence of Yahweh in the midst of his people, Israel. "But the Israelites wrongly identified the symbol with the reality itself and thus mistook the material presence of the ark for the real presence of Yahweh. They believed that the ark would activate the power of Yahweh in a magical way against the enemy, the Philistines."[80] They were mistaken. The Israelites were defeated, the ark captured, and Eli's sons killed. Then when word of the ark's capture came to Eli, he fell backward from his chair and likewise died.

After the Philistines had captured the ark of God, they bore it to Ashdod, and there placed it in the temple of Dagon. When the inhabitants of Ashdod rose early the next day, "there was Dagon, fallen on his face on the ground before the ark of the Lord!" (5:3). They took Dagon and put him back in his place, but the next morning "there was Dagon, fallen on his face on the ground before the ark of the Lord! His head and hands had been broken off and were laying on the threshold; only his body remained." As with the Israelites before them, they had mistaken the symbol for reality.

The Philistines subsequently went to elaborate precautions to assure that the ark would be safely returned to Israel. These involved a guilt offering, such as in compensation for infringing on someone's rights; a new cart to bare the ark, since it would be set apart for that sole purpose; two cows that were calved but never yoked, so as to be assured that they were drawn by the spirit of Yahweh rather than their natural instincts. "Now the people of Beth Shemesh were harvesting their wheat in the valley, and when they looked up and saw the ark, they rejoiced at the sight." God nonetheless struck down seventy of them because they looked into the ark, which was then sent on to Kiriath Jearim.

"It was a long time, twenty years in all, that the ark remained at Kiriath Jearim, and all the people mourned and sought after the Lord" (7:2). Then Samuel said: "Assemble all Israel at Mizpah, and I will intercede for you." When the Philistines heard that Israel had gathered together at Mizpah, they came up to attack them. "But that day the Lord thundered with loud thunder against the Philistines and threw them into such a panic that they were routed before the Israelites." "Intimidated by the thunderstorm that broke up their battle lines, the Philistines fled downhill towards their own territory, while the Israelites had the double advantage of height from which to hurl their missiles on the enemy below, and growing confidence in their likely victory."[81] So Samuel set up a stone between Mizpah and Shen, and named it *Ebenezer* (stone of help), saying: "Thus far has the Lord helped us."

Throughout Samuel's lifetime, the hand of the Lord was against the Philistines. He continued as judge over Israel all the days of his life. From year to year, he made a circuit from Bethel to Gilgal to Mizpah, judging Israel in all those places. But he always returned to Ramah, which was his home, and he judged Israel there as well.

When Samuel grew old, he appointed his sons as judges for Israel. However, they did not walk in his ways. "They turned aside after dishonest gain and accepted bribes and perverted justice" (8:3). So all the elders of Israel came before Samuel, and said to him: "You are old, and your sons do not walk in your ways; now appoint a king to lead us, such as all the other nations have." Since this displeased him, Samuel took the matter before the Lord. At which, the Lord replied: "Listen to all that the people are saying to you; it is not you they have rejected, but they have rejected me as their king." While Yahweh had an ideal for his people, he acquiesced sufficiently in this less than ideal world for them to have a king, and incorporated the monarchy motif into his revelation concerning himself.

"Now listen to them," God continued, "but warn them solemnly and let them know what the king who will reign over them will do." Up to this time, each family was responsible for its own affairs, but under a king military and agricultural conscription would restrict Israel's liberty. "Nor would the women of the family escape, for as *perfumers and cooks and bakers* they would serve the royal house. Taxation, which had been unknown, would become increasingly oppressive, until the people were virtually slaves, and cried out for liberation."[82]

Saul appeared a likely candidate. He came from the small tribe of Benjamin, and as such would not fuel competition among the major clans. He was also "an impressive young man without equal among the Israelites--a head taller than any of the others" (9:2), and appealingly humble (9:21; 10:22). Now the day before, the Lord had revealed to Samuel that "About this time tomorrow I will send you a man from the land of Benjamin. Anoint him leader over my people Israel." When Samuel caught sight of Saul, the Lord said to him: "This is the man I spoke to you about; he will govern my people."

So with the passing of time, Samuel summoned the people before him. From the various tribes, Benjamin was chosen. Clan by clan, Matri's clan was chosen. Finally, Saul son of Kish was chosen. (The casting of lots was a common practice in antiquity, and provision was made for God to guide Israel in such a manner.) But when they looked for Saul, he was no where to be found. So they inquired of the Lord to confirm his designation. The Lord replied: "Yes, he has hidden himself among the baggage." They ran and brought him out, and he towered above all the others. Then the people shouted in unison: "Long live the king!"

Unintentionally, the Ammonites provided Saul with the opportunity for proving his leadership. They besieged Jabesh Gilead, and agreed to a treaty only on condition that the inhabitants submit to having their right eyes gouged out as an affront to all of Israel. The elders of Jabesh replied: "Give us seven days so we can send messengers throughout Israel; if no one comes to rescue us, we will surrender to you" (11:3). Saul threatened the people with reprisal if they failed to respond to the challenge, and gained a striking victory over the enemy.

Subsequently, Samuel bid farewell to the people. "Now you have a king for your leader," he observed (12:2). "Here I stand," he continued. "Testify against me in the presence of the Lord and his anointed. "Whose ox have I taken? Whose donkey have I taken? Whom have I cheated? From whose hand have I accepted a bribe to make me shut my eyes? If I have done any of these, I will make it right." None bore an accusation against him. He, in turn, admonished them to walk in the ways of Yahweh.

Power tends to corrupt and Saul proved to be no exception. Things turned from bad to worse: Saul offered sacrifice when Samuel was delayed, took plunder and rationalized it for the purpose of making sacrifice to God, attempted to slay youthful David, killed the priests of Nob, and violated the prohibition against contacting mediums. It is in the last connection that we read how the Philistines gathered their forces to fight against Israel (28:1). When Saul saw their formidable army, he was afraid. When he inquired of the Lord, the Lord did not answer him-- whether by dreams, Urim, or prophets. The heavens had turned to brass in judgment against him.

Saul then said to his attendants: "Find me a woman who is a medium, so I may go and inquire of her." "There is one in Endor," they said. So he disguised himself with other apparel, and along with two companions came by night to the woman. If at *night*, he would be more difficult to recognize; then too the narrator may mean to imply that Saul was moving away from God into the surrounding darkness. "Consult a spirit for me," he petitioned, "and bring up for me the one I name." "Surely you know what Saul has done," she replied. "He has cut off the mediums and spiritists from the land. Why have you set a trap for my life to bring about my death?" Thus would he violate the code he had insisted that others observe. "As surely as the Lord lives," he assured her, "you will not be punished for this."

"Who shall I bring up for you?" she inquired. "Bring up Samuel," Saul responded. When the woman saw Samuel, she cried out at the top of her voice and said to Saul: "Why have you deceived me? You are Saul!" Necromancy was part of popular religion in those days. The narrator doesn't question its possibility but acceptability. The king encouraged the woman: "Don't be afraid. What do you see?" "I see a spirit coming up out of the ground," she reported. "What does he look like?" Saul persisted. "An old man wearing a robe is coming up," she responded. Then Saul knew it was Samuel. Samuel said: "Why do you consult me, now that the Lord has turned away from you and become your enemy?" Hearing this, Saul despaired of life and would not be comforted.

In contrast to Saul's dismal failure, David's reign seemed even more spectacular. He became the paradigm by which subsequent kings would be judged. For instance, it was said of Solomon that "his heart was not fully devoted to the Lord his God, as the heart of David his father had been" (1 Kings 11:4). For another, God remonstrated with Jeroboam: "I tore the kingdom away from the house of David and gave it to you, but you have not been like my servant David, who kept my commands and followed me with all his heart, doing only what was right in my eyes" (1 Kings 14:6).

David nonetheless sinned grievously. He coveted the wife of another and planned the murder of her husband to satisfy his lust. He subsequently admitted under the withering indictment of Nathan the prophet: "I have sinned against the Lord" (2 Sam. 12:13). We sense in David both the depths to which a godly person can sink, and the heights reclaimed by God's grace. David was remembered primarily for the latter.

We are assured of David's virtuous qualities early on. "How long will you mourn for Saul," God inquired of Samuel, "since I have rejected him as king over Israel. Fill your horn with oil and be on your way; I am sending you to Jesse of Bethlehem. I have chosen one of his sons to be king" (1 Sam. 16:1). Then, when Samuel saw Eliab, he thought: "Surely the Lord's anointed stands here before the Lord." But Yahweh said to Samuel: "Do not consider his appearance or his height, for I have rejected him. The Lord does not look at the things man looks at. Man looks at the outward appearance, but the Lord looks at the heart."

Then Jesse called Abinadab and had him pass in front of Samuel, but Samuel announced: "The Lord has not chosen this one either." Then Jesse had Shammah passed by, and Samuel responded: "Nor has the Lord chosen this one." Jesse had seven sons pass before Samuel, but each time Samuel indicated that this was not the one. "Regardless of what else we might say about stories, the basic characteristic that determines whether they succeed or fail is the element of suspense, that is, the ability to arouse the reader's curiosity. ...To engage our continuing interest, storytellers must make us want to know how a given situation will turn out."[83] Such is the situation before us.

"Are these all the sons you have?" Samuel inquired. "There is still the youngest," Jesse replied, "but he is tending the sheep." "Send for him," Samuel mandated; "we will sit down until he arrives. So they sent for David. He was ruddy, with a fine appearance and handsome features.

"Rise and anoint him" the Lord said; "for he is the one." Thus assured, our suspense is satisfied.

We next encounter David as an accomplished musician. Profoundly disturbed by his loss of Samuel's support, "Saul needed help. At this stage he suffered from intermittent bouts of mental disturbance, for which the recognized *treatment* was evidently music. Interestingly, music is still a recognized form of therapy, often prescribed to restore troubled states of mind."[84] When David would play, then "relief would come to Saul" so that "he would feel better" (16:23).

We then recognize David as a man of valor. Now the Philistines gathered their forces for war and pitched their camp between Socoh and Azekah in the Shephelah (Judean foothills). Whereupon, their champion named *Goliath* presents himself (17:4). He was over nine feet tall, had a bronze helmet on his head and wore a coat of scale armor of bronze weighing five thousand shekels, on his legs he wore bronze greaves, and a bronze javelin was slung on his back. His spear shaft was like a weaver's rod, and its iron point weighed six hundred shekels. His shield bearer went ahead of him. In this manner, the storyteller cultivates our *imagination*, so that we may be thoroughly impressed with the imposing figure confronting the Israelites. So also we may be reminded when we confront some imposing obstacle to faith.

Goliath stood and shouted to the ranks of Israel: "Why do you come out and line up for battle. Am I not a Philistine, and are you not the servants of Saul? Choose a man and have him come down to me. If he is able to fight and kill me, we will become your subjects; but if I overcome him and kill him, you will become our subjects and serve us." For forty days the Philistine came forward every morning and evening and took his stand.

Now David had brought provisions to his older brothers. Whereupon, David said to Saul: "Let no one lose heart on account of this Philistine; your servant will go and fight him." Saul replied: "You are not able to go out against this Philistine and fight him; you are only boy, and he has been a fighting man from his youth." But David insisted: "Your servant has killed both the lion and the bear; this uncircumcised Philistine will be like one of them, because he has defied the armies of the living God. The Lord who delivered me from the paw of the lion and the paw of the bear will deliver me from the hand of the Philistine." Saul responded: "Go, and the Lord be with you."

Saul dressed David in his own armor. "I cannot go in these," David concluded, "because I am not used to them." So he laid them aside. Then he took his staff in his hand, chose five smooth stones from the stream, put them in the pouch of his shepherd's bag, and with sling in hand approached the Philistine. "Am I a dog, that you come at me with sticks?" the Philistine contemptuously inquired--cursing David by his gods. "Come here and I'll give your flesh to the birds of the air and the beasts of the field." David courageously replied: "You come against me with sword and spear and javelin, but I come against you in the name of the Lord Almighty, the God of the armies of Israel, whom you have defied." With this, David prevailed and the Philistines fled in disarray.

DIVISION OF THE KINGDOM

Previously a shepherd, musician, and warrior, David is eventually introduced in connection with his royal office. All the tribes of Israel came to David at Hebron and said: "We are your own flesh and blood. In the past, while Saul was king over us, you were the one who led Israel on their military campaigns. And the Lord said to you, 'You will shepherd my people Israel, and you will become their ruler'" (2 Sam. 5:1-2). The symbol of a *shepherd* to represent the duties of a sovereign was common in the ancient Near East. The Old Testament word *shepherd* "describes the Lord's care of his people in the early poetry of Genesis 49:24, as well as in the Psalms. The consciousness that the Lord was the shepherd of Israel meant that Israel's human shepherds had before them the highest possible model of faithfulness, justice, and loving kindness."[85]

A symbol, whether this or any other, exhibits three characteristics. First, it is a literal object. It may be a rainbow, a boiling pot, or a collection of good and bad figs. Second, it is employed to convey some lesson or truth. The collection of good and bad figs in Jeremiah represents two groups of people: one righteous and the other unrighteous. Third, it lends credibility to what the person means to convey by its use.[86] It is based on a sense of similarity between or among objects of interest.

God subsequently instructed Nathan the prophet to inform David: "I took you from the pasture and from following the flock to be ruler over my people Israel. ...Your house and your kingdom will endure forever before me; your throne will be established forever" (7:8, 16). "Who am I, O Sovereign Lord, and what is my family, that you have brought me this far?" David incredulously inquired. "And as if this were not enough in your sight, O Sovereign Lord, you have also spoken about the future of the house of your servant." "The answer he expected was 'Nothing!' He obviously felt that the blessing of God was incomparably greater than anything he deserved."[87] He was not unique in this regard, since this could be said of all. David in this sense is representative of human kind.

One evening David got up from his bed and walked around on the roof of the palace (11:1). From there he saw a woman bathing. She was very beautiful. He sent for her, she came in response, and they slept together. But Bathsheba was the wife of Uriah the Hittite. The woman conceived and sent word to David: "I am pregnant."

Now Uriah was away on a military campaign. So David sent for him, under the pretense of inquiring how the conflict was progressing, and encouraged him to "Go down to your house and wash your feet." Uriah zealously responded: "The ark and Israel and Judah are staying in tents, and my master Joab and my lord's men are camped in the open fields. How could I go to my house to eat and drink and lie with my wife? As surely as you live, I will not do such a thing!" After which, David sent word to Joab that he should put Uriah where the fighting was most fierce, and then withdraw so that he would be killed. Joab did as directed, and after Bathsheba had observed the customary time for mourning, she married David.

The Lord sent Nathan to David. The former observed: "There were two men in a certain town, one rich and the other poor. The rich man had a very large number of sheep and cattle, but the poor man had nothing except one little ewe lamb he had bought" (12:2-3). "Now a traveler came to the rich man, but the rich man refrained from taking one of his own sheep or cattle to prepare a meal for the traveler... . Instead, he took the ewe lamb that belonged to the poor man and prepared it for the one who had come to him." David burned with anger, and said to Nathan: "As surely as the Lord lives, the man who did this deserves to die! He must pay for the lamb four times over, because he did such a thing and had no pity." Nathan replied: "You are the man!" David contritely responded: "I have sinned against the Lord."

Nathan's story, like a parable, makes use of *indirection*. This serves several purposes. For one, it is less threatening. For another, it allows the person an opportunity to weigh matters. For still another, it clarifies what is involved in the situation. Finally, it invites a positive response that might otherwise be lacking.

David's *last words* were in the form of an *oracle*: a revelation of God through some representative (23:1). In this connection, he affirmed: "When one rules over men in righteousness, when he rules in the fear of God, he is like the light of morning at sunrise or a cloudless morning, like the brightness after rain that brings the grass from the earth." He spoke from experience, both good and bad.

Solomon got off to a good start. At Gibeon the Lord appeared to him during the night in a dream, and said: "Ask for whatever you want me to give to you" (1 Kings 3:5). Solomon answered: "Now, O lord my God, you have made your servant king in place of my father David. But I am only a little child and do not know how to carry out my duties. ...So give your servant a discerning heart to govern your people and to distinguish between right and wrong." This pleased God, so he responded: "I will give you a wise and discerning heart, so that there will never have been anyone like you, nor will there ever be. Moreover, I will give you what you have not asked for--both riches and honor--so that in your lifetime you will have no equal among kings."

As if to illustrate, the narrator cites a case in point. It seems that two prostitutes came before the king to settle a dispute. One of them said: "My lord, this woman and I live in the same house. I had a baby while she was there with me. The third day after my child was born, this woman also had a baby." The woman continued: "During the night this woman's son died because she lay on him. So she got up in the middle of the night and took my son from my side while your servant was asleep. She put him by her breast and put her dead son by my breast. ...But when I looked at him closely in the morning light, I saw that it wasn't my son." The other woman protested: "No! The living one is my son; the dead one is yours." But the first one insisted: "No! The dead one is yours; the living one is mine." Such use of contrast is a prominent feature of parables and stories with parabolic intent.

Then Solomon said: "Bring me a sword." So they brought a sword to the king. "Cut the living child in two and give half to one and half to the other," he commanded. The woman whose son was alive pled: "Please, my lord, give her the living baby! Don't kill him!" But the other said: "Neither I nor you shall have him. Cut him in two!" Then Solomon ruled: "Give the living baby to the first woman. Do not kill him; she is his mother." When the people heard, they held the king in awe, "because they saw that he had wisdom from God to administer justice."

As for related matters, the queen of Sheba heard about the fame of Solomon, and came to see for herself (10:1). When she "saw all the wisdom of Solomon and the palace he had built, the food on his table, the seating of his officials, the attending servants in their robes, his cupbearers, and the burnt offerings he made at the temple of the Lord, she was overwhelmed." Whereupon, she said to the king: "Indeed, not even half was told me; in wisdom and wealth you have far exceeded the report I heard."

Solomon nonetheless multiplied his alliances as indicated by a large and diverse harem. His wives, in turn, turned his heart to the contemptible worship of Ashtoreth and Molech. So Yahweh said to Solomon: "Since this is your attitude and you have not kept my covenant and my decrees..., I will most certainly tear the kingdom away from you and give it to one of your subordinates" (11:11). Nevertheless, for the sake of David, this would not occur during his lifetime, and then not altogether. All three of Israel's kings began well, but all three ended tragically. "The nation was not without a prophetic voiced to call for repentance and trust in Israel's God, but Israel's political success had within it the germs of failure. With the death of Solomon the kingdom was shattered, never to be united again."[88]

Although Solomon was said to have a thousand wives and concubines, we read of only one child--Rehoboam, who succeeded his father to the throne. However, the monarchy was not so firmly established that an orderly transition could be assumed. For one thing, it had been in existence for only three generations. For another, it had struggled at the outset and during the interim. For still another, it had taken an exceptionally wise leader to hold the kingdom together to that point. "South and north also had differing geographical and commercial orientations. The south was more isolated, hence more conservative." In contrast, "Merchant caravans and military expeditions passing through the Valley of Esdraelon en route from Damascus and the East to Egypt introduced the North to a wider world and tended to make that region more cosmopolitan."[89]

Finally, the kingdom was maintained by an intricate system of checks and balances. With the rise of the monarchy, the "king became the dominant unifying figure both religiously and politically; the people looked upon him as the mediator of divine blessing, and the royal ideology later gave rise to the Messianic hope."[90] The regent was one *of* the people, and not simply one *over* them. As such, he like they were obligated to abide by the covenant obligations.

Even so, the king could to a remarkable degree set the course for the nation as a whole. Should he fail to pay tribute, the land might be torched. If he cast his lot with the victor, the people might anticipate peace. He was expected to adjudicate among the people, and punish those at fault. He was also meant to guide by personal example. Like sovereign, like people.

Then, there were the prophets. Moses was said to be the spring from which the prophets drew their inspiration. Micah consequently recalled: "The Lord used a prophet to bring Israel up from Egypt" (12:13). Moses also served as a paradigm for subsequent prophets and a type for the

Messiah (Deut. 18:15; cf. Acts 3:23).

Prophetic activity came to full bloom with the monarchy. "Beginning with the monarchial establishment this group of dedicated individuals influenced Israel significantly at practically every successive juncture in her history."[91] God selected them to fine-tune the monarchy to the covenant ideal. Johannes Lindblom comments: "To us a single act of injustice-- cheating in business, exploitation of the poor--is slight; to the prophets, a disaster. To us injustice is injurious to the welfare of the people; to the prophets it is a death blow to their existence; to us, an episode; to them, a catastrophe, a threat to the world."[92]

The priests and their ritual practices were another important ingredient in the monarchy. Cultic roots were associated with the patriarchs: their encounters with God, the memorials set up to commemorate them, and the stories passed down from father to son concerning God's faithfulness. They vividly recalled Israel to worship "the God of Abraham, the God of Isaac, and the God of Jacob."

The narrative stresses the importance of the central shrine to the welfare of the monarchy. The people were instructed to bring their offerings to Jerusalem and not raise altars more convenient for their purposes. Jeroboam consequently reasoned: "If these people go to offer sacrifices at the temple of the Lord in Jerusalem, they will again give their allegiance to their lord, Rehoboam king of Judah" (1 Kings 12:27). When Josiah renewed the covenant with the people, he razed a plethora of altars including that which Jeroboam had built at Bethel (2 Kings 23:12-15). He thereupon received unique praise for his zeal: "Neither before nor after Josiah was there a king like him who turned to the Lord as he did--with all his heart and with all his soul and with all his strength, in accordance with the Law of Moses."

Likewise prominent in the dynastic mix were the sages. In this connection, Solomon's wisdom was favorably compared to that of *Ethan the Ezrahite* (1 Kings 4:31). Likewise, Hezekiah was urged not to rely on those giving him counsel (Isa. 36:4-7). Such would seem to suggest a royal advisory counsel similar to what we encounter in connection with other ancient Near Eastern peoples. If so, it may have been charged with compiling the proverbs of Solomon (cf. Prov. 25:1).

The deference shown to *elders* suggests the pervasive sense in which wisdom served in monarchial times. These were thought to gain insight in the process of living a full life. As such, they were viewed as a religious and social legacy. Their counsel was to be cherished and their example emulated.

Finally, there were the people. The *will of the people* was much more than a literary metaphor in monarchial times. It implied the consent to be governed, the willingness to cooperate, and the possibility of reconsideration. It could shift abruptly to take account for worsening economic conditions, a political threat, or royal arrogance.

Sennacherib's field commander recognized the importance of the people when he insisted on speaking in their language so that they could understand. "Was it only to your master and you that my master sent me to say these things, and not to the men sitting on the wall--who, like you, will have to eat their own filth and drink their own urine?" (2 Kings 18:27). After this, he appealed to the them not to heed Hezekiah's counsel, but make peace and enjoy the fruits of their land.

Such were the complex factors that the narrator describes for his readers. Rehoboam had a formidable task in acting as a royal catalyst to bring together diverse ingredients, mediate between differing cultural attitudes, and appeal to a common tradition. So it was that the people came before him with an observation and related request: "Your father put a heavy yoke on us, but now lighten the harsh labor and the heavy yoke he put on us, and we will serve you" (1 Kings 12:4). Rehoboam answered: "Go away for three days and then come back to me." This allowed him the opportunity to seek counsel from others.

He turned initially to the elders who had served his father during his lifetime. "How would you advise me to answer these people?" he inquired. They replied: "If today you will be a servant to the people and serve them and give them a favorable answer, they will always be your servants." But Rehoboam rejected their advice, and consulted with the young men who had grown up with him and were serving him. He asked them: "What is your advice?" They responded: "Tell these people...'My little finger is thicker than my father's waist. My father laid on you a heavy yoke; I will make it even heavier. My father scourged you with whips; I will scourge you with scorpions." So the king answered the people harshly.

Rehoboam certainly failed to recognize the seriousness, let alone the justice, of the people's complaint. "He had been accepted without question by the southern tribes, and he evidently felt that his journey to Shechem was but a formality, after which his acceptance in the north would be promptly followed. The northern tribes were in no mood to accept the king's arrogance."[93] When the people saw that he refused to listen to them, they responded: "What share do we have in David, what part in Jesse's son? To your tents, O Israel! Look after your own house,

O David!" Thus was the kingdom rent in two.

Jeroboam eventually fortified Shechem in the hill country of Ephraim and lived there. He moreover erected golden calves at Bethel and Dan. "It is too much for you to go up to Jerusalem" he observed. "Here are your gods, O Israel, who brought you up out of Egypt" (12:28). He likewise "built shrines on high places and appointed priests from all sorts of people, even though they were not Levites. He instituted a festival on the fifteenth day of the eighth month, like the festival held in Judah (Feast of Tabernacles), and offered sacrifices on the altar." If Jeroboam and his priests thought of the God of Israel as enthroned above the bull, their spiritual insight was likely lost on the average Israelite. "Worshipers could see the bulls, and the animals themselves became objects of popular worship. While theoretically the people were still worshiping Yahweh..., actually they were moving in the direction of Canaanite religion in which El and Baal were frequently likened to a bull."[94]

Now a man of God came from Judah to Bethel as Jeroboam was standing by the altar to make an offering. He cried out: "O altar, altar! This is what the Lord says: A son named Josiah will be born to the house of David. On you he will sacrifice the priests of the high places who now make offerings there, and human bones will be burned on you" (13:2). When Jeroboam heard what the man of God cried out against the altar, he commanded: "Seize him!" But the hand he stretched out toward the man shriveled up, so that he could not pull it back. "Intercede with the Lord your God and pray for me that my hand may be restored," the king pled. So the man of God interceded with the Lord, and the hand was restored.

Then the king invited the man of God to enjoy hospitality at his home. The latter refused, since he had been instructed not to do so. "Even after this, Jeroboam did not change his evil ways, but once more appointed priests for the high places from all sorts of people. Anyone who wanted to become a priest he consecrated for the high places." Concerning which, the narrator summarily comments: "This was the sin of the house of Jeroboam that led to its downfall and to its destruction from the face of the earth."

Meanwhile, the word of God came to Shemaiah the man of God: "Say to Rehoboam son of Solomon king of Judah, to the whole house of Judah and Benjamin, and to the rest of the people...'Do not go up to fight against your brothers, the Israelites. Go home, every one of you, for this is my doing'" (12:23-24). "So they obeyed the word of the Lord and went home again, as the Lord had ordered." In this regard, the narrator would remind us that God knows when a situation is beyond repair.

The course was set early on. The Northern Kingdom would go into a tight spiral from which there was no recovery. The Southern Kingdom would vacillate in its covenant observance: falling away only to return, until at last to succumb. But this is another story.

TALE OF TWO KINGDOMS

We have come to a phase in the story line that especially illustrates the dilemma inevitably facing the narrator. On the one hand, nothing can be more discouraging and disheartening than to listen to a simple recounting of some event or another. "What is needed in preaching on such narrative portions is some method of pointing out the abiding meanings and continuing significance for all believers of all times."[95] On the other, any effort to dilute or amend the story can prove counterproductive. As Marshall McLuhan would insist, *the medium is the message.* One is left to steer a course between two undesirable alternatives.

At that time, Jeroboam's son became ill. So Jeroboam said to his wife: "Go, disguise yourself, so you won't be recognized... . Then, go to Shiloh. Ahijah the prophet is there--the one who told me I would be king over this people. ...He will tell you what will happen to the boy." Now Ahijah was blind as a result of advanced age, but the Lord told him to expect the arrival of Jeroboam's wife. So when Ahijah heard the sound of her footsteps at the door, he cried out: "Come in, wife of Jeroboam. Why this pretense?" Were this not enough to unnerve the poor woman, the prophet announced that the family of Jeroboam would be cut off, and replaced by another dynasty.

"On the positive side, Rehoboam had the advantage of the Jerusalem shrine within his borders, and the loyalty of those who had attached themselves to the religious practices sanctioned in the Solomonic Temple."[96] Priests and Levites, scandalized by the cult practices at Bethel and Dan made their way southward to Jerusalem (2 Chron. 11:13-17), and pledged their loyalty to Rehoboam. On the negative side, he added numerous wives and concubines, with similar adverse results as his father Solomon. Idolatrous high places and heathen cult objects began to increase throughout Judah. Given such practices, the invasion of Shishak was interpreted as an evidence of God's displeasure. The narrator concludes concerning Rehoboam's son Abijah: "He committed all the sins his father had done before him; his heart was not fully devoted to the Lord his God" (1 Kings 15:3).

Asa, son of Abijah, was the first of Judah's reforming sovereigns. He "did what was right in the eyes of the Lord, as his father David had done. He expelled the male shrine prostitutes from the land and got rid of all the idols his fathers had made. He even deposed his grandmother Maacah from her position as queen mother, because she had made a repulsive Asherah pole" (15:11-13). Although he did not remove the high places, "Asa's heart was fully committed to the Lord all his life."

Nadab followed Jeroboam to the throne, Baasha followed Nadab, and Elah followed Baasha. Each invited God's wrath because of their idolatrous practices and insensitivity to the covenant. The situation in the North turned from bad to worse. Zimri reigned for merely seven days before being replaced by Omri.

The narrator has little to say about the reign of Omri himself (16:21-28). He appears to have brought a measure of stability to the Northern Kingdom. With his death, Ahab reigned in his stead. As for Ahab, the narrator observes that he "did more evil in the eyes of the Lord than any of those before him. He not only considered it trivial to commit the sins of Jeroboam..., but he married Jezebel daughter of Ethbaal king of the Sidonians, and began to serve Baal and worship him" (16:30-31).

It is in the context of Ahab's reign that we are introduced to one of the most colorful of the Biblical characters--Elijah. His name means *my God is the Lord*, an apt designation for so stalwart an opponent of Baalism. He began his recorded ministry with the announcement of a drought, a graphic way of expressing God's displeasure (17:1). He then hid himself in a ravine on the east bank of the Jordan River, near the brook Cherith, where God provided his needs. When the brook dried up, a widow shared with him her scanty resources, and was rewarded with a miraculous provision that was not depleted until the drought was ended.

Ahab had tried without success to find Elijah. Now God told Elijah to disclose himself to the king with the announcement that the drought would soon cease. When the latter saw the prophet, he said to him: "Is that you, you troubler of Israel?" "I have not made trouble for Israel," Elijah responded. "But you and your family have. You have abandoned the Lord's commands and have followed the Baals. Now summon the people from all over Israel to meet me on Mount Carmel. And bring the four hundred and fifty prophets of Baal and the four hundred prophets of Asherah, who eat at Jezebel's table."

So it was that Elijah inquired of the people: "How long will you waver between two opinions? If the Lord is God, follow him; but if Baal is God, follow him." But the people said nothing. Then Elijah said to them: "Get two bulls for us. Let them choose one for themselves, and let them cut it into pieces and put it on the wood but not set a fire to it. I will prepare the other bull and put it on the wood but not set fire to it. Then you call on the name of your god, and I will call on the name of the Lord. The god who answers by fire--he is God."

So the prophets prepared their sacrifice, and called on the name of Baal from morning till noon. "O, Baal, answer us!" they shouted. At noon Elijah began to taunt them. "Shout louder!" he urged them. "Perhaps he is deep in thought, or busy, or traveling. Maybe he is sleeping and must be awakened." So they shouted louder and slashed themselves with swords and spears, as was their custom. Midday passed and they continued their frantic prophesying until the time for the evening sacrifice. At which, the narrator pointedly observes: "But there was no response, no one answered, no one paid attention."

Then Elijah called on the people to gather around him. He rebuilt the altar to Yahweh, which was in ruins. He arranged the wood, cut the bull into pieces, and laid it on the wood. Then he said to those standing by: "Fill four large jars with water and pour it on the offering and on the wood." "Do it again," he said. "Do it a third time," he ordered. The water ran down around the altar and even filled the trench. Suspense was building: for those present and for those listening to the story.

At the time of the evening sacrifice, Elijah stepped forward and prayed: "O Lord, God of Abraham, Isaac and Israel, let it be known today that you are God in Israel and that I am your servant and have done all these things at your command." Then the fire of the Lord fell and burned up the sacrifice, the wood, the stones and the soil, and also licked up the water in the trench. When the people saw this, they prostrated themselves and cried out: "The Lord--he is God! The Lord--he is God!" In this and other ways, Elijah struggled to bring the Northern Kingdom back from the brink of disaster.

Meanwhile, things were going better with the Southern Kingdom. Jehoshaphat, son of Asa, became king of Judah in the fourth year of Ahab's reign in Israel. "In everything he walked in the ways of his father Asa and did not stray from them... . The high places, however, were not removed, and the people continued to offer sacrifices and burn incense there" (22:43).

Ahaziah, son of Ahab, became king of Israel in the seventeenth year of Jehoshaphat's reign in Judah. "He did evil in the eyes of the Lord, because he walked in the ways of his father and mother and in the ways of Jeroboam...who caused Israel to sin. He served and worshiped Baal and provoked the Lord, the God of Israel, to anger, just as his father had done" (22:52-53). Because Ahaziah had no son, Joram succeeded him.

Elijah had anointed Elisha as his successor. Now when the Lord was about to take Elijah up to heaven in a whirlwind, he inquired of Elisha: "What can I do for you before I am taken from you?" (2 Kings 2:9). "Let me inherit a double portion of your spirit," the other replied. "You have asked a difficult thing," Elijah responded, "yet if you see me when I am taken from you, it will be yours--otherwise not." As they were walking along, suddenly a chariot of fire and horses of fire appeared and separated the two of them, and Elijah went up to heaven in a whirlwind. When Elisha saw this he cried out: "My father! My father! The chariots and horsemen of Israel!" So it was that the prophetic mantle passed from one to the other.

Naaman was commander of the army of the king of Aram. He was a valiant soldier, but had leprosy. Now a young Israelite girl had been taken captive, and served Naaman's wife. She said to her mistress: "If only my master would see the prophet who is in Samaria! He would cure him of his leprosy" (5:3). So Naaman went with his horses and chariots and stopped at the door of Elisha's house. Elisha sent a messenger to say to him: "Go, wash yourself seven times in the Jordan, and your flesh will be restored and you will be cleansed." But Naaman went away angry, supposing he surely would "come out to me and stand and call on the name of the Lord his God, wave his hand over the spot and cure me of my leprosy. Are not the Abana and Pharpur, the rivers of Damascus, better than any of the waters of Israel?"

Naaman's servants went to him and said: "My father, if the prophet had told you to do some great thing, would you not have done it? How much more, then, when he tells you, 'Wash and be cleansed'!" So he went down and dipped himself in the Jordan not once, twice, three, four, five, or six, but seven times--*as the man of God had told him*, and he was healed. Then Naaman and all his attendants went back to the man of God. He stood before him and said: "Now I know that there is no God in all the world except in Israel." In this and other ways, Elisha carried on the work undertaken by Elijah.

Jehoram followed Jehoshaphat to the throne of Judah, and Ahaziah followed Jehoram. It was said of both that they "walked in the ways of the kings of Israel" (8:18; cf. 8:27). As for the former, he married a daughter of Ahab. As for the latter, he allied himself with Joram to war against Hazael king of Aram. They alike wasted a godly heritage.

Jehu took the throne of Israel with the blessing of the prophet Elisha. The army quickly pledged its allegiance to him. He subsequently set about to purge Israel of Baal worship. Although Jehu's accession to the throne had been blessed by Elisha, "it is obvious that Jehu and his descendants had overplayed their hand: (1) their zeal for bloodshed exceeded all bounds; (2) the ambition of Jehu outstripped any sense of divine commission; (3) his rule, though retarding the Baal worship, ...did little to bring a return to the worship of God."[97] In short, he got mixed reviews: "Because you have done well in accomplishing what is right in my eyes...your descendants will sit on the throne of Israel to the fourth generation. Yet Jehu was not careful to keep the law of the Lord, the God of Israel, with all his heart" (10:30-31).

The ninth century ended on a downbeat. Baalism, after permeating Israel and Judah, left both kingdoms in a very weakened condition. "Revolutions in the North in 841 B.C. and in the South in 835 B.C. provided the opportune time for Syrian expansion. During the rest of the ninth century, Syria under its powerful king, Hazael, extended its domination into Judah as well as Israel."[98]

"A flurry of prophetic activity was divinely inaugurated in the eighth century B.C. mainly to warn the northern kingdom of an impending destruction if she did not repent and reverse her way of life."[99] With little exception, Israel would remain impervious to the pleas of the prophets. It plunged headlong into destruction, eventuating in the fall of Samaria in 722 B.C. to the Assyrians. Jehu's dynasty ran its course with Jehoahaz, Jehoash, and Jeroboam II. All three were said to have done evil in the eyes of the Lord (13:2; 13:11; 14:24). The remainder (Shallum, Menahem, Pekahiah, Pekah, and Hoshea) proved no better. With the exception of Shallum, who reigned for only one month, all were said to have done evil in the eyes of the Lord.

Meanwhile, the situation in Judah continued the struggle between Yahweh and Baal. When Athaliah, mother of Ahaziah saw that her son was dead, she proceeded to destroy the entire royal family. However, Jehosheba the daughter of Jehoram and sister of Ahaziah, took Joash the son Ahaziah, and hid him so that we was not killed with the others. With the passing of time, Joash became king. It was said of him that he did right in the eyes of the Lord all the years he was instructed by the priest Jehoida. On one occasion, he inquired of Jehoida. "Why aren't you repairing the damage done to the temple?" (12:7). Whereupon, the priests made provision for the temple's restoration.

With Joash's death, his son Amaziah reigned in his stead. "He did what was right in the eyes of the Lord, but not as his father David had done. In everything he followed the example of his father Joash" (14:3). Otherwise stated, he was a copy of a copy. They conspired against him in Jerusalem, and when he fled to Lachish, they killed him there. His sixteen year old son Azariah (*Uzziah* in Chronicles, perhaps in connection with his enthronement) was made king in his place. He too did what was right in the eyes of the Lord, as his father had done.

Taking his cue, Isaiah strides on stage. Thus we read: "The vision concerning Judah and Jerusalem that Isaiah son of Amoz saw during the reigns of Uzziah, Jotham, Ahaz and Hezekiah, kings of Judah" (Isa. 1:1). "In the death year of Uzziah (Azariah), a young man named Isaiah began a prophetic ministry that was to last about forty years. Isaiah had witnessed the rapid development of Judah into a strong commercial and military state."[100] Under Uzziah, Judah attained a degree of strength and prosperity not enjoyed since the days of Solomon.

Isaiah took no confidence in these evidences of material prosperity. Instead, he denounced idolatry and hypocrisy, and warned of impending judgment. Isaiah would live to see the fall of Samaria. While he did not live to witness the destruction of Jerusalem, he could see disaster on the horizon.

As a case in point, "In the year that King Uzziah died, I saw the Lord seated on a throne, high and exalted, and the train of his robe filled the temple" (6:1). Above him were two seraphs calling to one another: "Holy, holy, holy is the Lord Almighty; the whole earth is full of his glory" "Woe is me!" Isaiah cried out. "I am ruined! For I am a man of unclean lips, and I live among a people of unclean lips, and my eyes have seen the King, the Lord Almighty."

As another case in point, "If you do not stand firm in your faith, you will not stand at all" (7:9). "But now, this is what the Lord says" (have faith): 'When you pass through the waters, I will be with you. When you walk through the fire, you will not be burned; the flames will not set you ablaze'" (43:1-2).

Jotham followed Azariah to the throne of Israel, and found favor in the eyes of the Lord, even though he failed to remove the high places. In contrast, Ahaz walked in the ways of the kings of Israel. He even went so far as to sacrifice his son in the fire, "following the detestable ways of the nations the Lord had driven out before the Israelites. He offered sacrifices and burned incense at the high places, on the hilltops and under every spreading tree" (16:3-4).

Hezekiah, in turn, "removed the high places, smashed the sacred stones and cut down the Asherah poles. He broke to pieces the bronze snake Moses had made, for up to that time the Israelites had been burning incense to it" (18:4). "Hezekiah trusted in the Lord, the God of Israel. There was no one like him among all the kings of Judah, either before him or after him."

In the fourteenth year of Hezekiah's reign, Sennacherib king of Assyria captured the fortified cities of Judah and threatened Jerusalem. "Has the god of any nation ever delivered his land from the king of Assyria?" Sennacherib's commander derisively inquired (18:33). When notified of the matter, Isaiah poured out his soul in prayer: "Now, O Lord our God deliver us from his hand, so that all kingdoms on earth may know that you alone, O Lord, are God." In response, God declared: "I will defend the city and save it, for my sake and for the sake of David my servant." That very night the formidable Assyrian army was devastated by the angel of the Lord, leaving us to speculate on the particulars. "When the people got up the next morning--there were all the dead bodies."

The seventh century marked one of the most critical periods in Israel's history, for it then tottered on the threshold of national destruction "and the long-predicted Babylonian captivity. Already, Judah's sister nation of the ten northern tribes had met disaster in the previous century after refusing to repent of her sin in spite of the battery of the prophets who were graciously sent to her and warned her of the impending danger."[101] Once again, God sent messengers to warn Judah and the surrounding nations of their precarious situation.

This included Nahum, Zephaniah, Habakkuk, and chief among them-- Jeremiah. So it was written: "The word of the Lord came to him (Jeremiah) in the thirteenth year of the reign of Josiah..., and through the reign of Jehoiakim..., down to the fifth month of the eleventh year of Zedekiah..., when the people went into exile" (Jer. 1:2-4). "When the words came, I ate them," the prophet reports; "they were a joy and my heart's delight" (15:16). They also resulted in conflict. "So the word of the Lord has brought me insult and reproach all day long " (20:8). When he would refrain from speaking the word of the Lord, it burned as if his bones were on fire. When he spoke, he could overhear the people murmuring: "Report him! Let's report him!"

Jeremiah released a relentless attack on ritual void of piety. "Are they ashamed of their loathsome conduct?" he rhetorically inquired (8:12). "No, they have no shame at all; they do not even know how to blush. So they will fall among the fallen; they will be brought down when they are punished."

The prophet's accent on *the religion of the heart* further expressed itself in the gracious promise of a *new covenant*. "'This is the covenant I will make with the house of Israel after that time,' declares the Lord, 'I will put my law in their minds and write it on their hearts. I will be their God, and they will be my people. No longer will a man teach his neighbor, or a man his brother...because they will all know me, from the least of them to the greatest'" (31:33-34). "The new covenant will be written deeply into the wills of the Israelites, who will obey it by choice rather than by compulsion. Past apostasy will be replaced by an attitude of fidelity to God, so that never again will the nation be in bondage to others."[102]

Both kings who preceded Josiah (Manasseh and Amon) did evil in the eyes of the Lord. As for the former, he "rebuilt the high places his father Hezekiah had destroyed; he also erected altars to Baal and made an Asherah pole as Ahab king of Israel had done. ...In both courts of the temple of the Lord, he built altars to all the starry hosts. He sacrificed his own son in the fire, practiced sorcery and divination, and consulted mediums and spiritists" (21:3, 5-6). As for the latter, he "walked in all the ways of his father; he worshiped the idols his father had worshiped, and bowed down to them. He forsook the Lord, the God of his fathers, and did not walk in the way of the Lord (21: 21-22).

During the eighteenth year of Josiah's reign, Hilkiah the priest discovered the Torah scroll in the temple precincts. Then, the king together with all the people went up to the temple, and he read in their hearing all the words of the Book of the Covenant. After this, they renewed the covenant in the presence of the Lord (23:3). "After renewing the covenant, Josiah sought to remove every trace of idolatry from his kingdom. High places were broken down, and idolatrous priests deposed. The altar which Jeroboam I had built at Bethel was pulled down, along with later altars at Samaria."[103] After his efforts to purify the land, he mandated that the Passover be observed. He died honorably, defending his country against Pharaoh Necho at Megiddo.

It was downhill from that point on. As for Jehoahaz, he did evil in the eyes of the Lord (23:32). So likewise with Jehoiakim (23:37), Jehoiachin (24:9), and Zedekiah (24:19). Now Zedekiah rebelled against Babylon. So in the ninth year of Zedekiah's reign, Nebuchadnezzar king of Babylon marched against Jerusalem. His forces encamped about the city and built siege works all around it. The city was kept under siege until the eleventh month of Zedekiah's administration. "By the ninth day of the fourth month the famine in the city had become so severe that there was no food for the people to eat. Then the city wall was broken through, and the whole army fled at night...though the Babylonians were surrounding the city" (25:3-4). The Babylonians overtook them in the plains of Jericho. Zedekiah's sons were killed before his eyes; thereafter he was blinded, shackled, and taken prisoner to Babylon.

Nebuchadnezzar moreover "set fire to the temple of the Lord, the royal palace and all the houses of Jerusalem. Every important building he burned down." Then, the wall defending Jerusalem was razed. Nebuzaradan, commander of the imperial guard, subsequently carried away those who remained in the city, as well as those who had gone over to the Babylonians, but left some of the poorest people to work the vineyards and fields.

Lamentations was composed as a funeral dirge upon the destruction of Jerusalem. It describes the cruelty of the plundering invaders, the ravages that attend plague and famine, the helplessness of the inhabitants, and the utter ruin of the city. It likewise illustrates how religious idealism flounders with the hard realities of life.

Implicit was the realization that they had been faithfully warned of impending doom, and had no one to blame but themselves. They therefore concluded: "We have sinned and rebelled and you have not forgiven." (3:42). Even so, a breath of hope springs up like the stirring of breeze felt in Jerusalem at the close of a scorching day. "The Lord is good to those whose hope is in him, to the one who seeks him; it is good to wait quietly for the salvation of the Lord" (3:25-26).

IN A STRANGE LAND

The caravan had made its way up the slopes of the Trans-Jordan Plateau. From there it would travel along the Kings' Highway toward Damascus and eventually Babylon. The column paused long enough to look back toward Jerusalem. The torched city was bellowing smoke into the air. Daniel, among the other deportees, wondered what the future held with the temple in ruins and Jerusalem devastated. Where does it say that? Nowhere. Such is the way our imagination attempts to reconstruct the events that transpired. It is our way of reliving the past so as to nourish our understanding of human pathos and resiliency.

This was not the first crises for the Hebrew people. Their persecution in Egypt had welded them into a unified people. Their desert wandering had firmed up their resolve to possess the promised land. The Philistine threat brought about their demand for a king and solidarity so as to contend with their common enemy. The disruption of the kingdom, followed by grievous times, left intact the David Dynasty and promise of the future. The exile, however, presented a unique challenge. In short, "Almost all the old symbol systems had been rendered useless. Almost all of the old institutions no longer functioned. What kind of future was possible for a people who had so alienated their God that categorical rejection was his necessary response?"[104] It was a question for which one hesitated to volunteer an answer.

What Jeremiah warned as imminent, Daniel declares has come to pass. "The Lord delivered Jehoiakim king of Judah into his hand, along with some of the articles from the temple of God. These he carried off to the temple of his god in Babylonia and put in the treasure house of his god" (Dan. 1:2). So described, the prophet preserves God's justice in bringing judgment on his people for their many offences. Conversely, he doesn't allow that the gods of Babylon have vanquished Yahweh.

Then the king ordered Ashpenaz, chief of his court officials, to bring some of the Israelites from the royal family and nobility: "young men without any physical defect, handsome, showing aptitude for every kind of learning, well informed, quick to understand, and qualified to serve in the king's palace." He was to teach them the language and literature of the Babylonians. Among these were Daniel, Hananiah, Mishael, and Azariah. The chief official gave them new names: to Daniel, the name Belteshazzar; to Hananiah, Shadrach; to Mishael, Meshach; and to Azariah, Abednego. In so skillful a manner, the narrator introduces the featured characters in his story.

While Daniel accepted Babylonian education and name, he petitioned for abstaining from *the royal food and wine.* "Why should he see you looking worse than the other young men your age?" the official in charge inquired. "The king would then have my head because of you." "Please test your servants for ten days," Daniel pled. "Then compare our appearance with that of the young men who eat the royal food, and treat your servants in accordance with what you see." At the end of ten days, they looked healthier than those who ate from the king's table. Once again we are reminded that those who honor God, God honors in return (cf. 1 Sam. 2:30).

When their training was completed, the Hebrews were brought before Nebuchadnezzar. After questioning them thoroughly, he concluded that in every matter of wisdom and understanding they were ten times better than all the magicians and enchanters of his whole kingdom. *Ten times* appears as idiomatic (cf. Gen. 31:41; Num. 14:22). In this instance, the Hebrews were *greatly superior* to their pagan counterparts.

In the second year of his reign, Nebuchadnezzar had disturbing dreams but could not remember their content. So he summoned his wise men. Whereupon, the astrologers said: "O king, live forever! Tell your servants the dream, and we will interpret it." "This is what I have firmly decided," the king replied, "if you do not tell me what my dream was and interpret it, I will have you cut into pieces and your houses turned into piles of rubble. But if you tell me the dream and explain it, you will receive from me gifts and reward and great honor" (2:5-6). Once again they asserted: "Let the king tell his servants the dream, and we will interpret it." Then the king answered: "I am certain that you are trying to gain time, because you realize that this is what I have firmly decided."

The astrologers protested: "There is not a man on earth who can do what the king asks! No king, however great and mighty, has ever asked such a thing of any magician or enchanter or astrologer ...No one can reveal it to the king except the gods, and they do not live among men." This made Nebuchadnezzar so angry that he decreed that all the wise men be executed. At this, Daniel requested time to inquire of God as to the dream and its interpretation.

Now Daniel reported what was revealed to him. The king had seen an enormous statue, awesome in appearance. The head of the statue was made of pure gold, its chest and arms of silver, its belly and thighs of bronze, its legs of iron, and its feet partly of iron and partly of baked clay. While the king was watching, the statue was struck by a rock cut out *but not by human hands*, and smashed the statue--leaving not a trace. The rock, in turn, became a huge mountain and filled the whole world.

Daniel then added an interpretation. The *head of gold* symbolized Nebuchadnezzar's dominion, the remainder of the statue successive kingdoms of lesser prominence, and the rock God's everlasting rule. "Surely your God is the God of gods, and the Lord of kings and a revealer of mysteries," the king concluded. Such is the climax to the story. We subsequently learn that Daniel was promoted to rule over the province and put in charge of the wise men.

Even so, Daniel's difficulties were only beginning. Nebuchadnezzar made an image of gold, ninety feet high and nine feet wide, and set it up on the plain of Dura in the province of Babylon. "O peoples, nations and men of every language," his herald proclaimed, "as soon as you hear the sound of...music, you must fall down and worship the image of gold. ...Whoever does not fall down and worship will immediately be thrown into a blazing furnace" (3:4-6). Many *peoples, nations, and languages* were subject to him, as a result of his deportation policy. "Babylon itself and its environs had become distinctly cosmopolitan. But the multiple listing of addresses is more than that; it is part of the art of the storyteller; so, too, is the constant repetition of them. By such means, and in keeping with ancient protocol, the preeminence of the king is demonstrated."[105]

Certain of the astrologers subsequently came forward to report that Shadrack, Meshach and Abednego were not obeying Nebuchadnezzar's decree. "Is it true that you do not serve my gods or worship the image of gold I have set up?" the king inquired. The Hebrews were defiant: "If we are thrown into the blazing furnace, the God we serve is able to save us from it, and he will rescue us from your hand, O king. But even if he does not, we want you to know, O King, that we will not serve your gods or worship the image of gold you have set up." As on previous occasions, the king was *furious*, and demanded that the men be bound and burned. Still clad in their court garments, they were unceremoniously tossed into the oven.

Then the king leaped to his feet in amazement. "Weren't there three men that we tied up and threw into the fire?" he inquired. They replied:

"Certainly, O king." He said: "Look! I see four men walking around in the fire, unbound and unharmed, and the fourth looks like a son of the gods." In other words, Nebuchadnezzar saw a heavenly messenger sent to rescue the three Hebrews. Approaching the furnace, the king shouted: "Shadrach, Meschach and Abednego, servants of the Most High God, come out! Come here!" In response to his summons, they came forth-- unharmed. The focus of the story is that the man of faith, who holds fast to what God requires of him, will not be forsaken. "He is not simply abandoned to alien and destructive forces. We do the story less than justice if we fail to interpret it within its own context, or if we go beyond its main theme by erecting on the basis of its particulars a general principle that might hold for all time."[106]

After some time, Nebuchadnezzar lost his sanity. Then, when it was restored, he declared: "Now I, Nebuchadnezzar, praise and exalt and glorify the King of heaven, because everything he does is right and all his ways are just. And those who walk in pride, he is able to humble" (4:37). We are not told that the king repented first; it might be difficult for a man in his condition to do so. "We are told rather that God's handling of him was effective. As they were destined to do, dethronement and restoration have brought the earthly king to praise and confession before the Most High as the one whose kingship is never set aside."[107]

Without further comment, the narrator abruptly turns our attention to Belshazzar (Nebuchadnezzar's son) on the eve of the fall of Babylon to the Medes and Persians. Now Belshazzar gave a great banquet for a thousand of his nobles. Then, he commanded that his attendants bring the gold and silver goblets that his father had taken from the temple in Jerusalem, so that they might drink from them. As they drank, suddenly the fingers of a human had appeared and wrote on the plaster wall. The king's "face turned pale and he was so frightened that his knees knocked together and his legs gave way" (5:6). He called for his wise men to read the writing and interpret its meaning, but they were of no help. So in due time Daniel was brought before him.

This is the inscription that was written: "Mene, Mene, Tekel, Parsin." This was Daniel's interpretation: *Mene*--God has numbered the days of your reign and brought it to an end; *Tekel*--You have been weighed on the scales and found wanting; *Peres* (the singular of *Parsin*)--Your kingdom is divided and given to the Medes and Persians. That very evening Belshazzar was slain, and Darius the Mede reigned in his place.

It pleased Darius to appoint three chief administrators, of which Daniel was one. Daniel so distinguished himself that the king planned to set him over the whole kingdom. At this, the other administrators and those under them tried to find grounds whereby they could bring charges against him. However, they could find no cause, because "he was trustworthy and neither corrupt nor negligent" (6:4). So they concluded: "We will never find any basis for charges against this man Daniel unless it has something to do with the law of his God." Whereupon, they encouraged the king to issue a decree that anyone who prays to any god or man during the next thirty days except the king should be cast into the lions' den.

"Now when Daniel learned that the decree had been published, he went home to his upstairs room where the windows opened toward Jerusalem. Three times a day he got down on his knees and prayed, giving thanks to his God, just as he had done before." When this came to attention of the king, Daniel was cast into the lions' den. At the first sight of dawn, Darius got up and hurried to the lions' den. When he came near, he called out in an anguished voice: "Daniel, servant of the living God, has your God, whom you serve continually, been able to rescue you from the lions?" Daniel answered: "O king, live forever! My God sent his angel and he shut the mouths of the lions. They have not hurt me, because I was found innocent in his sight. Nor have I ever done any wrong before you, O king." Then was the king overjoyed.

The narrator now recalls that in the first year of Belshazzar Daniel had a vision concerning four beasts that represented successive kingdoms. After this, the Ancient of Days would reign. "His clothing was as white as snow; the hair of his head was white like wool. His throne was flaming with fire and its wheels were all ablaze. A river of fire was flowing, coming out from before him" (7:9-10). Thousands attended him, ten thousand times ten thousand stood before him, and the books were opened. Judgment was about to begin.

Then as Daniel continued to look on, one appeared *like a son of man*. "The phrase *like a human being* formally compares with the earlier phrases *like a lion, resembling a bear*, and *like a leopard*. Each of those phrases, however, was followed by a clause that qualified the description and explained how the creatures were *like* but not identical with these animals."[108] While the imagery is obscure, it would suggest man's unique relationship with God and exalted place in creation. In that he is said to be simply *like* a man, one would assume that it has reference to a heavenly visitor.

In the third year of Belshazzar's reign, Daniel had another vision. This concerned a ram--representing Media and Persia, and a goat--representing

Greece. In this connection, Daniel overhears two *holy ones* discussing what will come to pass, especially concerning the desecration and restoration of the sanctuary. When the vision had run its course, Daniel was exhausted and troubled by what he had seen.

In the third year of Cyrus, Daniel had still another vision. This too dealt with things yet to come, the time yet remaining, and the persons involved. The concluding verse of the book is a personal word of assurance to Daniel. "Long before the predicted events take place he will go to his *rest.* But Sheol will not hold the faithful Daniel. He is heir to the promise of resurrection... . This is a fitting reward for a man who, since the early days of the Exile, has stood firm against temptation and threat."[109]

With such in mind, we turn our attention to another witness to the exile. Ezekiel was a priest who served God in the Jerusalem sanctuary. This was his life until removed by Nebuchadnezzar to the dusty plains of Babylonia. Apart from his visionary visit to Jerusalem (8:3-11:24), the only location associated with Ezekiel is either his house or the plain, near to the river Kebar at a place called Tel Abib. "It was the name given to an irrigation canal which brought the waters of the Euphrates in a loop south-eastwards from Babylon via Nippur and back to the main river near Uruk (biblical Erech)."[110]

So it was that Ezekiel found himself among the exiles by the Kebar River, when "the heavens were opened and I saw visions of God" (Ezek. 1:1). "I looked, and I saw a windstorm coming out of the north--an immense cloud with flashing lightning and surrounded by brilliant light. The center of the fire looked like glowing metal, and in the fire was what looked like four living creatures. In appearance their form was that of a man, but each of them had four faces and four wings." Perhaps his vision began by observing a natural phenomenon which eventuated in a spiritual revelation.

"As I looked at the living creatures, I saw a wheel on the ground beside each creature with its four faces. ...When the creatures moved, they also moved; when the creatures stood still, they also stood still, and when the creatures rose from the ground, the wheels rose along with them, because the spirit of the living creatures was in the wheels." In addition, "Above the expanse over their heads was what looked like a throne of sapphire, and high above on the throne was a figure like that of a man." "Son of man," he said to Ezekiel, "I am sending you to the Israelites, to a rebellious nation... . Whether they listen or not, they will know that a prophet was among them."

Ezekiel is scarcely given an opportunity to make excuses for himself, as did Moses and Jeremiah, "for God immediately forestalls any hesitations by giving him an exhortation to take courage (2:6-8), followed by a foretaste of his message (2:9-3:3). This in turn is followed by the promise of the power to persevere in the face of opposition (3:4-9)."[111] If we can judge from the prophet's subsequent ministry, he gives the impression of being virtually fearless and unwavering in the face of opposition. It brings to mind the adage, "Fear God and you need fear no one and nothing else."

"Now, son of man, take a clay tablet, put it in front of you and draw the city of Jerusalem on it. Then lay siege to it: Erect siege works against it, build a ramp up to it, set up camps against it and put battering rams around it. Then take an iron pan, place it as an iron wall between you and the city and turn your face toward it" (4:1-3). This would serve as a sign, depicting the assault on Jerusalem.

"Then lie on your left side and put the sin of the house of Israel upon yourself. ...I have assigned you the same number of days as the years of their suffering." "After you have finished this, lie down again, this time on your right side and bear the sin of the house of Judah. I have assigned you 40 days, a day for each year." "As commentators have frequently remarked, this episode represents Ezekiel as playing in part the role of the scapegoat of Lev. 16:21-22. Symbolically God lays the guilt of Israel upon Ezekiel while he rests on his left side... . After that he bears the guilt of Judah while lying on his right side... ."[112] If so, the need for atonement would appear paramount in the telling of the story.

On another occasion, Ezekiel was sitting along with the elders of Judah in his house. Whereupon, "The Spirit lifted me up between earth and heaven and in visions of God he took me to Jerusalem, to the entrance to the north gate of the inner court, where the idol that provokes to jealousy stood" (8:3). The visitor subsequently said to him: "Son of man, do you see what they are doing--the utterly detestable things the house of Israel is doing here, things that will drive me far from my sanctuary?" After further observation, he again inquires: "Son of man, have you seen what the elders of the house of Israel are doing in the darkness, each at the shrine of his own idol?" After still further observation, he concludes: "Is it a trivial matter for the house of Judah to do the detestable things they are doing here? ...I will not look on them with pity or spare them. Although they shout in my ears, I will not listen to them."

Ezekiel's literary range is quite extensive. For example, he deftly employs parable; that is, a brief allegorical story meant to express some religious or moral truth. In this connection, "Son of man, how is the wood of a vine better than that of a branch on any of the trees in the forest? ...And after it is thrown on the fire as fuel and the fire burns both ends and chars the middle, is it then useful for anything?" (15:2, 4). This therefore is what the sovereign Lord says: "As I have given the wood of the vine among the trees of the forest as fuel for the fire, so will I treat the people living in Jerusalem. I will set my face against them."

For another example, he uses allegory; which is to say, a more extended story with multiple points of comparison. Along this line, "On the day you were born your cord was not cut, nor were you washed with water to make you clean, nor were you rubbed with salt or wrapped in cloths. No one looked on you with pity or had compassion enough to do any of these things for you" (16:4-5). None that is but the Lord, who shows compassion.

"Later I passed by, and when I looked at you and saw that you were old enough for love, I spread the corner of my garment over you... . I gave my solemn oath and entered into a covenant with you." I moreover "clothed you with an embroidered dress and put leather sandals on you. I dressed you in fine linen and covered you with costly garments. ...Your food was fine flour, honey and olive oil." "But you trusted in your beauty and used your fame to become a prostitute. You lavished your favors on anyone who passed by... ."

For a final example, Ezekiel turns to a popular proverb: "The fathers eat sour grapes, and the children's teeth are set on edge" (18:1). "As surely as I live, declares the Sovereign Lord, you will no longer quote this proverb in Israel. For every living soul belongs to me, the father as well as the son--both alike belong to me. The soul who sins is the one who will die."

Things eventually begin to take a turn for the better. Ezekiel is led by the Spirit of the Lord to the middle of a valley full of dry bones. "Son of man," God inquired of him, "can these bones live?" (37:3). He replied: "O Sovereign Lord, you alone know." Then Ezekiel was commanded: "Prophesy to these bones and say to them, 'Dry bones, hear the word of the Lord!'" When he did so, "there was a noise, a rattling sound, and the bones came together bone to bone. I looked, and tendons and flesh appeared on them and skin covered them, but there was no breath in them." After this, God instructed him: "Prophesy to the breath, and say to it: 'Come from the four winds, O breath, and breathe into these slain, that they may live.'" Then in turn, "breath entered them; they came to live and stood up on their feet--a vast army." God subsequently explained to him: "Son of man, these bones are the whole house of Israel. They say, 'Our bones are dried up and our hope is gone; we are cut off.' ...This is what the Sovereign Lord says: 'O my people, I am going to open your graves and bring you up from them. I will bring you back to the land of Israel.'"

It therefore seems appropriate that Ezekiel conclude with his vision concerning the rebuilding of the sanctuary in Jerusalem. These chapters bring the book to is conclusion: the restoration of Israel in its land. "As such they form a counterpart of chs. 8-11. In Ezek. 8-11 the prophet had a vision of the people's cultic sins and the consequent departure of God from the sanctuary. In Ezek. 40-48 the prophet foresees the return of God's glory to the temple and receives the new cultic regulations."[113] From this sanctuary flow waters of abundant blessing and fertility.

The content of these chapters combine a mixture of prophetic vision for the future and some indication of the means by which the people may obtain their goal. Otherwise stated, they combine idealism and realism. As a case in point, "You are to distribute this land among yourselves according to the tribes of Israel. You are to allot it as an inheritance for yourselves and for the aliens who have settled among you and who have children. ...In whatever tribe the alien settles, there you are to give his inheritance" (47:21, 23). So it was that glimmer of light appeared from the exit of a long, dark tunnel.

JOURNEY HOME

Babylon did not have long to gloat over its hapless Hebrew captives. Within a half century, the once mighty empire had capitulated. Its seemingly impregnable walls were of no help once its defenders surrendered without resistance. When Cyrus personally entered Babylon it was to the acclaim of its populace. He moreover set about to right perceived wrongs that had been previously done. In this connection, he issued a decree: "The Lord, the God of heaven, has given me all the kingdoms of the earth and he has appointed me to build a temple for him at Jerusalem in Judah. Anyone of his people among you--may his God be with him, and let him go up to Jerusalem in Judah and build the temple of the Lord the God of Israel, the God who is in Jerusalem" (Ezra 1:2-3). The people in the region where such people now lived were instructed to provide them "with silver and gold, with goods and livestock, and with freewill offerings for the temple of God in Jerusalem."

The restoration narrative revolves around three central characters: Zerubbabel, Ezra, and Nehemiah. When the seventh month came and the people were settled in their towns, they assembled with singular determination in Jerusalem. "Despite their fear of the peoples around them, they built the altar on its foundation and sacrificed burnt offerings on it to the Lord, both the morning and evening sacrifices."

Then in the second month of the second year after their arrival, the governor Zerubbabel and his associates began the work of rebuilding the temple. When the builders laid its foundation, the priests and Levites sang unto the Lord: "He is good; his love to Israel endures forever." Then all the people gave a great shout of praise to the Lord, because the foundation was laid. "But many of the older priests and Levites and family heads, who had seen the former temple, wept aloud when they saw the foundation of this temple being laid, while many others shouted for joy. No one could distinguish the sound of the shouts of joy from the sound of weeping, because the people made so much noise. And the sound was heard far away." This time there is no ark nor temple: no visual expression of his glory. There were only some beginnings, and small beginnings at that. "But God is enthroned on the praises of Israel, and these could be as glorious as Solomon's. Perhaps they were more so for...they were sung in conditions more conducive to humility than to pride, and called for a faith that had few earthly guarantees to bolster it."[114]

When the enemies of Judah and Benjamin heard that they were building a temple to the Lord, they approached Zerubbabel with the offer of assisting them. But Zerubbabel, Jeshua the priest, and the family elders protested: "You have no part with us in building a temple to our God. We alone will build it for the Lord, the God of Israel, as King Cyrus...commanded us" (4:3). From this time on, the opposition attempted to subvert the Hebrews' efforts in any way possible.

Now Haggai and Zechariah, prophets of God, declared God's word to the people (5:1). As for the former, God instructed him to tell Zerubbabel that "I will shake the heavens and the earth. I will overturn royal thrones and shatter the power of the foreign kingdoms. I will overthrow chariots and their drivers, horses and their riders will fall, each by the sword of his brother. ...I will take you...and make you like my signet ring, for I have chosen you" (Hag. 2:21-23). As for the latter, the Lord directed him: "Administer justice; show mercy and compassion to one another. Do not oppress the widow or the fatherless, the alien or the poor. In your hearts do not think evil of each other" (Zech. 7: 9-10). So it was "that the prophets of God were with them, helping them" in the work of the Lord.

In due time, the temple was completed. "Then the people of Israel--the priests, the Levites and the rest of the exiles--celebrated the dedication of the house of God with joy. For the dedication of this house of God they offered a hundred bulls, two hundred rams, four hundred male lambs and, as a sin offering for all Israel, twelve male goats, one for each of the tribes of Israel" (Ezra 6:16-17). They also installed the priests in their divisions and the Levites in their groups for the service of God, and celebrated the Passover.

After these things, and during the seventh year of the reign of Artaxerxes, Ezra and his associates arrived in Jerusalem. As concerns Ezra, the narrator observes that he "had devoted himself to the study and observance of the Law of the Lord, and to teaching its decrees and laws in Israel." As concerns his mandate, "in accordance with the wisdom of your God, which you possess, appoint magistrates and judges to administer justice to all the people of Trans-Euphrates--all who know the laws of your God. And you are to teach any who do not know them.

Whoever does not obey the law of your God and the law of the king must surely be punished by death, banishment, confiscation of property, or imprisonment."

In the course of his labors, it was brought to Ezra's attention that the "people of Israel, including the priests and Levites, have not kept themselves separate from the neighboring peoples with their detestable practices" (9:1). When he heard this, he tore his tunic and cloak, pulled hair from his head and beard, and sat down appalled at the situation. "Then everyone who trembled at the words of the God of Israel gathered around me because of this unfaithfulness of the exiles. And I sat there appalled (repeated for emphasis) until the evening sacrifice."

A proclamation was subsequently sent throughout Judah for all the exiles to assemble in Jerusalem. "Anyone who failed to appear within three days would forfeit all his property, in accordance with the decision of the officials and elders, and would himself be expelled from the assembly of the exiles." When the people had come together, Ezra declared to them: "You have been unfaithful; you have married foreign women, adding to Israel's guilt. Now make confession to the Lord, the God of your fathers, and do his will. Separate yourselves from the peoples around you and from your foreign wives." The whole assembly responded with a loud voice: "You are right! We must do as you say."

More than half of *Nehemiah* is a personal record, punctuated with frank comments that "make it one of the liveliest pieces of writing in the Bible. Much of Ezra's story was also told in the first person, but Ezra was a quieter personality than the formidable, practical Nehemiah; he does not leap out of the page as this man does."[115] Nehemiah recalls: "While I was in the citadel of Susa, Hanani, one of my brothers, came from Judah with some other men, and I questioned them about the Jewish remnant that survived the exile, and also about Jerusalem" (Neh. 1:1-2). They replied: "Those who survived the exile and are back in the province are in great trouble and disgrace. The wall of Jerusalem is broken down, and its gates have been burned with fire." Upon hearing of this, Nehemiah sat down and wept.

Now Nehemiah was a cupbearer to the king. The cupbearer's primary duty was serving wine to the king to avoid the danger of assassination. This brought him into close contact with those in authority and sometimes allowed him to exercise considerable influence. So it was that on a certain occasion when Nehemiah brought wine to the king, the latter inquired: "Why does your face looks so sad when you are not ill? This can be nothing but sadness of heart." "I was very much afraid,"

Nehemiah admits, "but I said to the king: 'May the king live forever! Why should my face not look sad when the city where my fathers are buried lies in ruins, and its gates have been destroyed by fire?'" Whereupon, the king said to him: "What is it you want?" Then he prayed to the God of heaven, and answered the king: "If it pleases the king and if your servant has found favor in his sight, let him send me to the city in Judah where my fathers are buried so that I can rebuild it." Since it pleased the king to send him on his mission, Nehemiah set a time for his return.

Nehemiah first set out to appraise the situation. "On the debit side it is the *disgrace*, not the insecurity of their position, which strikes him--for Jerusalem should be seen as *the city of the great King* and *the joy of all the earth*."[116] On the credit side, "he speaks first of *the hand of...God* upon him, and only then of *the words (of) the king*. This was indeed the right order, as cause and effect. It was also his genuine conviction...and as such it was infectious."

He then prescribed a course of action. The repair of each section of the wall was delegated. For instance, "the Fountain Gate was repaired by Shallum...ruler of the district of Mizpah. He rebuilt it, roofing it over and putting its doors and bolts and bars in place. He also repaired the wall of the Pool of Siloam, by the King's Garden, as far as the steps going down from the City of David" (3:15). So they built the wall, *for the people worked with all their heart.*

In the process, they experienced continuing opposition. So it was that Sanballat and Geshem urged Nehemiah: "Come, let us meet together in one of the villages on the plain of Onon" (6:2). Since Nehemiah perceived that they meant to harm him, he sent back the reply: "I am carrying on a great project and cannot go down." Four times they sent him the same message, and each time he gave the same reply. The fifth message charged Nehemiah with rebellion. "Nothing like what you are saying is happening," he responded; "you are just making it up out of your heads." Nehemiah eventually stationed half of his men as guards, and the remainder as workers. Moreover, "Those who carried materials did their work with one hand and held a weapon in the other, and each of the builders wore his sword at his side as he worked." At the sound of a trumpet, all were to leave their work and gather to repulse the enemy. In the end, the wall was completed.

Nehemiah also initiated reforms. For one thing, he took a census of the people--which would serve in civil and military matters. For another, he encouraged the resettling of Jerusalem. For still another, he along with

Ezra renewed the covenant with the people. "Remember me with favor," Nehemiah prayed to the Lord in conclusion to his labors (13:31).

The book of *Esther* draws our attention to those exiles who had chosen not to return. "Comparatively few had availed themselves of the opportunity either then or on later occasions, and sixty years later large numbers of Jews remained in the eastern half of the Persian empire, many in the great imperial cities of Persia itself."[117] Very little is known of them, except from what we may derive from the text of Esther, and the brief reference to the reign of Ahasuerus in Ezra 4:6.

All things considered, the account of Esther provides us with one of the more dramatic illustrations of Biblical narrative. "Let a search be made for beautiful young virgins for the king," Xerxes' attendants proposed (Esther 2:2). "Now the king was attracted to Esther more than to any of the other women, and she won his favor and approval... . So he set a royal crown on her head and made her queen." "But Esther had kept secret her family background and nationality just as Mordecai had told her to do, for she continued to follow Mordecai's instruction as she had done when he was bringing her up." The stage was now set from what would subsequently transpire.

It came to pass that Mordecai overheard a plot against the king, and reported it to Esther. She, in turn, brought it to Xerxes' attention. Then when it was discovered that the report was true, the perpetrators were hanged. After these events, Xerxes honored Haman, "elevating him and giving him a seat of honor higher than that of all the other nobles. All the royal officials at the king's gate knelt down and paid honor to Haman, for the king had commanded this concerning him. But Mordecai would not kneel down to pay him honor" (3:1-2). In this regard, he demonstrated an integrity apparently lacking in others. Haman was nevertheless enraged.

Then Haman observed to Xerxes: "There is a certain people dispersed and scattered among the peoples in all the provinces of your kingdom whose customs are different from those of all other people and who do not obey the king's laws; it is not in the king's best interest to tolerate them." Xerxes consequently sent couriers to all the provinces "with the order to destroy, kill and annihilate all the Jews--young and old, women and little children--on a single day."

In response to Mordecai's request that Esther intercede with her husband, her attendant explained: "All the king's officials and the people of the royal provinces know that for any man or woman who approaches the king in the inner court without being summoned the king has but one law--that he be put to death. The only exception to this is for the king to extend the gold scepter to him and spare his life." It addition, it was thirty days since the queen was summoned to appear. To do so now would be to invite the death penalty.

"Do not think that because you are in the king's house you alone of all the Jews will escape?" Mordecai inquired. "For if you remain silent at this time, relief and deliverance for the Jews will come from another place, but you and your father's family will perish. And who knows but that you have come to royal position for such a time as this?" "The answer of Mordecai presents the inmost convictions of the author and at the same time moves the reader to deep sympathy with Esther. Her dilemma is at some time the dilemma of us all: circumstances hem us in and demand that we commit ourselves to act courageously and exercise faith."[118] There are three lines of argument to Mordecai's reasoning. First, Esther can't assume that she will be spared. Second, God will in any case frustrate Haman's strategy. Third, if God's deliverance does not come through Esther then by another, and she and her family will suffer the dire consequences.

Then Esther sent this reply: "Go, gather together all the Jews who are in Susa, and fast for me. Do not eat or drink for three days, night or day. I and my maids will fast as you do. When this is done, I will go to the king even though it is against the law. And if I perish, I perish." So Mordecai went away and carried out all of Esther's instructions.

"On the third day Esther put on her royal robes and stood in the inner court of the palace, in front of the king's hall. The king was sitting on his royal throne in the hall, facing the entrance. When he saw Queen Esther standing in the court, he was pleased with her and held out to her the gold scepter that was in his hand. So Esther approached and touched the tip of the scepter" (5:1-2). In this manner, we are alerted to the interplay of personal relationships and royal protocol. Then Xerxes said: "What is it, Queen Esther? What is your request? Even up to half the kingdom, it will be given you." It was a conventional way of speaking, as indicated by the context, but one that suggested that the king meant to be exceedingly generous. "If it pleases the king," Esher responded, "let the king, together with Haman, come today to a banquet I have prepared for him."

The next day Haman was in good spirits. But when he saw Mordecai at the king's gate and he showed him no deference, his anger was re-kindled. He nonetheless restrained himself. Arriving at home, he summoned his wife and friends, and "boasted about his vast wealth, his many sons, and all the ways the king had honored him and how he had elevated him above the other nobles and officials." "And that's not all," he concluded. "I'm the only person Queen Esther invited to accompany the king to the banquet she gave. And she has invited me along with the king tomorrow. But all of this gives me no satisfaction as long as I see that Jew Mordecai sitting at the king's gate." His wife and friends said to him: "Have a gallows built, seventy-five feet high, and ask the king in the morning to have Mordecai hanged on it. Then go with the king to the dinner and be happy." The suggestion delighted Haman, and he had the gallows erected in anticipation of ridding himself of Mordecai.

That night the king could not sleep, so he had the record of his reign brought in and read to him. Here it was recorded how Mordecai had reported the plan to assassinate the king. "What honor and recognition has Mordecai received for this?" the king asked. "Nothing has been done for him," his attendants answered. The king inquired: "Who is in the court?" Now Haman had just entered the outer court of the palace to speak to the king about hanging Mordecai. "Bring him in," the king ordered. When Haman entered, Xerxes inquired of him: "What should be done for the man the king delights to honor?" Now Haman thought to himself: "Who is there that the king would rather honor than me?" So he suggested that the king bring a royal robe he has worn and a horse he has ridden, *one with a royal crest on its head.* "Then let the robe and horse be entrusted to one of the king's most noble princes. Let them robe the man the king delights to honor, and lead him on the horse through the city streets, proclaiming before him, 'This is what is done for the man the king delights to honor." "Go at once," the king commanded. "Get the robe and the horse and do just as you have suggested for Mordecai the Jew, who sits at the king's gate." So Haman did as he was commanded, and returned home to share his grief with his wife and friends. They said to him: "Since Mordecai, before whom your downfall has started, is of Jewish origin, you cannot stand against him--you will surely come to ruin!"

On the second day as they were drinking wine, the king again asked: "Queen Esther, what is your petition?" She replied: "If I have found favor with you, O king, and if it pleases your majesty, grant me my life... . And spare my people... . For I and my people have been sold for destruction and slaughter and annihilation." At this, Xerxes inquired: "Who is he? Where is the man who has dared to do such a thing?" Esther responded: "The adversary and enemy is this vile Haman." The king stood to his feet in a rage, left his wine and went out into the palace garden. Haman, realizing that the king had already decided his fate, stayed behind to beg

Esther for his life. Just as the king returned from the palace garden, Haman was falling on the couch where Esther was reclining. The king exclaimed: "Will he even molest the queen while she is with me in the house?"

As soon as the king spoke, they covered Haman's face. Though the practice of covering the heads of condemned prisoners by the Persians in ancient times is otherwise not mentioned, it was the custom among the Greeks and Romans. Then one of the attendants observed: "A gallows seventy-five feet high stands by Haman's house. He had it made for Mordecai, who spoke up to help the king." Xerxes responded: "Hang him on it!" So they hanged Haman on the gallows he had prepared for Mordecai. It was a classic instance of poetic justice.

That same day the king gave Haman's estate to Esther. Esther, in turn, put Mordecai in charge of it. Xerxes moreover granted the Jews privilege to protect themselves against any who should threaten them. This they were able to do. As a celebration of their deliverance, they instituted the festival of *Purim*. Traditionally, the Esther scroll is read in the synagogue on that occasion.

"It is quite possible that the Talmudic tradition (*Bara Bathra* 15a) is correct in assigning the authorship (of *Chronicles*) to Ezra. As the chief architect of the spiritual and moral revival of the Second Commonwealth he would have had every incentive to produce a historical survey of this sort."[119] As a Levite from the priestly line, his viewpoint would have fitted well with the emphasis of this narrative. In any case, its comprehensive character provides a proper summary to the events recorded in Holy Writ from Adam to the edict of Cyrus.

The first part of *Chronicles* (1 Chron. 1-9) is preliminary in character. It incorporates genealogical tables and periodic commentary. As an example, "The fellow Levites were assigned to all the other duties of the tabernacle, the house of God. But Aaron and his descendants were the ones who presented offerings on the altar of burnt offering and on the altar of incense in connection with all that was done in the Most Holy Place, making atonement for Israel, in accordance with all that Moses the servant of God had commanded" (6:48-49). As another example, "The people of Judah were taken captive to Babylon because of their unfaithfulness. Now the first to resettle on their own property in their own towns were some Israelites, priests, Levites and temple servants" (9:1-2).

The second part (1 Chron. 10-29) focuses on the accession and reign of David. As a case in point, the narrator describes the exploits of David's *mighty men.* "At that time David was in the stronghold, and the Philistine garrison was at Bethlehem. David longed for water and said: 'Oh, that someone would get me a drink of water from the well near the gate of Bethlehem!'" (11:17). So three of his mighty men broke through the Philistine lines, drew water from the well and carried it back to David. But he refused to drink it; instead, he poured it out before the Lord. "God forbid that I should do this!" he exclaimed. "Because they risked their lives to bring it back," the narrator observes, "David would not drink it." "These mighty men belong to the close circle of David. Historically these accounts belong to the early period of David, when David moved around as a guerilla fighter and when duels were an important part of military encounters."[120]

The third part (2 Chron.) provides an account of what transpired with David's successors. For instance, we read that "after Uzziah became powerful, his pride led to his downfall" (25:16). As evidence, he "entered the temple of the Lord to burn incense on the altar of incense." Azariah and eighty other courageous priests confronted him: "It is not right for you, Uzziah, to burn incense to the Lord. That is for the priests, the descendants of Aaron, who have been consecrated to burn incense." Uzziah, who had a censer in his hand ready to burn incense, became angry. While he was raging at the priests before the altar, leprosy broke out on his forehead. When the priests saw this, they hurried him out of the temple. "Indeed, he himself was eager to leave, because the Lord had afflicted him." He remained a leper throughout his life. In this and other ways, the chronicler accents the importance of the central sanctuary in the life of the Hebrew people.

POET'S CORNER

"Next to story, poetry is the most prevalent type of writing in the Bible. Some books of the Bible are entirely poetic in form: Psalms, Song of Solomon, Proverbs, Lamentations. Many others are mainly poetic: Job, Ecclesiastes, Isaiah, Hosea, Joel, and numerous other prophetic books."[121] There is virtually no extended portion of Scripture in which we do not encounter poetry in some form or manner.

Poetry may be defined as a type of literature distinguished from prose by meter, rhythm, rhyme, sound, figurative language or a combination of these ingredients. The American poet John Ciardi insists that "Poetry lies its way to the truth." He means to say that poetry should not be taken as true in a literal but an imaginative sense. In this connection, the writer employs *poetic license.* By way of example, the godly person doesn't literally meditate on the word of God *day and night.* He or she however does make a practice of meditating on it.

"The most noteworthy characteristic of Hebrew poetry is its parallelism. The term refers to the practice of balancing one thought or phrase by a corresponding thought or phrase containing approximately the same number of words, or at least a correspondence in ideas."[122] This may be accomplished in a variety of ways. In *synonymous parallelism,* the thought expressed in the first part is repeated in different but equivalent terms. For instance, "The earth is the Lord's, and everything in it, the world, and all who live in it" (Psa. 24:1). In *antithetic parallelism,* the thought expressed in the first part is contrasted with its opposite in the second. As an example, "For the Lord watches over the way of the righteous, but the way of the ungodly will perish" (Psa. 1:6). In *synthetic parallelism,* the idea expressed in the first part is more fully developed in what follows. As an illustration, "Do not answer a fool according to his folly, or you will be like him yourself" (Prov. 26:4). In *climactic parallelism,* the first line is not complete without the addition of the second. As a case in point, "Ascribe to the Lord, O mighty ones, ascribe to the Lord glory and strength" (Psa. 29:1). In *emblematic parallelism,* the second part provides a figurative expression of the first. For example, "Like cold water to a weary soul is good news from a distant land" (Prov. 25:25).

The *Psalter* first captures our attention. "On the one hand, the psalms were in fact written by somebody in Hebrew in circumstances and for purposes that belonged to the history of Israel. ...They come to us as tradition. They are given to us as a means of standing in identity and continuity with the faith of that community."[123] On the other hand, the psalms are notoriously difficult to date. Except when ascribed, we are left to speculate.

Psalm 3 is ascribed to David when he fled from his son Absalom. As such, it recalls a narrative event. "In the course of time, Absalom provided himself with a chariot and horses and with fifty men to run ahead of him. He would get up early and stand by the side of the road leading to the city gate" (1 Sam. 15:1-2). Then, whenever anyone would come with a complaint to be placed before the king for a decision, Absalom would call out to him: "What town are you from?" In this manner, he not only demonstrated interest but established the credentials for bringing the case to court. Whereupon, Absalom would reply: "Look, your claims are valid and proper, but there is no representative of the king to hear you." After this, he would plaintively add: "If only I were appointed judge in the land! Then everyone who has a complaint or case would come to me and I would see that he gets justice." In this and other ways, Absalom "Stole the hearts of the men of Israel."

A messenger came and told David that "the hearts of the men of Israel are with Absalom." Then David said to his officials: "Come! We must flee." Along the way, David met Ittai the Gittite. "Why should you come with us?" David inquired. "Go back, and take your countrymen. May kindness and faithfulness be with you." But Ittai insisted: "As surely as the Lord lives, and as my lord the king lives, wherever my lord the king may be, whether it means life or death, there will your servant be." Then the king instructed Zadok: "Take the ark of God back into the city. If I find favor in the Lord's eyes, he will bring me back and let me see it and his dwelling place again." Whereupon, David continued up the Mount of Olives, "weeping as he went; his head was covered and he was barefoot. All the people with him covered their heads too and were weeping as they went up."

"O Lord, how many are my foes! How many rise up against me!" (Psa. 3:1). So it must have seemed as "the conspiracy gained strength, and Absalom's followers kept on increasing" (2 Sam. 15:12).

Nonetheless, "You are my shield around me;" "He answers from his holy hill;" "I wake again, because the Lord sustains me;" "I will not fear the tens of thousands drawn up against me on every side." In retrospect, David concludes: "From the Lord comes deliverance. May your blessing be on your people."

Some psalms are less specific. Psalm 17 is simply ascribed to David. As such, it may be a distillation of his experience. "Hear, O Lord, my righteous plea," David petitions. As a matter of record, others had judged him unfairly. Saul thought him an usurper to the throne (1 Sam. 18:8); Michal despised his enthusiastic worship (2 Sam. 6:16); Absalom portrayed him as unconcerned and irresponsible (2 Sam. 15:3); Sheba charged him with being partisan (2 Sam. 20:1). No doubt the list could be greatly extended. David consequently turns to the Lord for justice: "May my vindication come from you; may your eyes see what is right."

David moreover shifts his emphasis from *justice* to *compassion*. Perhaps for good reason, because we have more to fear from his justice than his severity per se. "Show me the wonder of your great love, you who save by your right hand those who take refuge in you and from their foes." As for the latter, "they have tracked me down, they now surround me." As for the former, "rescue me from the wicked by you sword."

Still other psalms seem to be composed for the express purpose of worship. Of course, these too draw upon experience. Psalm 5 provides a case in point. *In the morning*, David lifts his voice to God in prayer (v. 3). *In the morning*, he joins with others in the sanctuary for corporate worship (v. 7). *In the morning*, he assures himself concerning the day ahead (v. 12). Along this line, a Fourth Century text reads: "Be not careless of yourselves, ...neither divide His body nor disperse His members, neither prefer the occasions of this life to the word of God; but assemble yourselves together every day, morning and evening, singing psalms and praying in the Lord's house."[124]

The psalm consists of five strophes, three soliciting God's grace (1-3, 7-8, 11-12), alternating with two denouncing those opposed to his gracious rule (4-6, 9-10). "Listen to my cry for help," David pleads. "Lead me, O Lord, in your righteousness." "Let all who take refuge in you be glad; let them ever sing for joy. Spread your protection over them, that those who love your name may rejoice in you." *Listen*, and having listened, *lead*, and during the interim, *protect*. As for the wicked, may they reap what they have sown.

On the one hand, we are struck by the *Psalter*'s distinctive literary character. Its poetic structure distinguishes it from prose. On the other hand, we are reminded that its composition draws from experience. In one way or another, it blends into a narrative context. All things considered, the text is consequently enhanced.

Job and *Proverbs* illustrate wisdom literature. James Crenshaw asserts that while initially wisdom consisted of proverbial sentence or instruction, debate, and intellectual reflection; "thematically, wisdom comprises self-evident intuitions about mastering life for human betterment, gropings after life's secrets with regard to innocent suffering, grappling with finitude, and quest for truth concealed in the created order and manifested in Dame Wisdom."[125] As I commented on another occasion: wisdom literature draws from a common treasure of understanding. It calls our attention to what we know or should know. "Just as the artisan forges his sword or weaves a rug, so the sage tells us how to live life with finesse. He corrects those of us who blunder along...saying the wrong thing, doing the wrong thing, wishing we could do better."[126]

"In the land of Uz there lived a man whose name was Job. This man was blameless and upright; he feared God and shunned evil" (Job 1:1). He moreover had seven sons and three daughters, and enjoyed great wealth. "Early in the morning he would sacrifice a burnt offering for each of them, thinking, 'Perhaps my children have sinned and cursed God in their hearts.' This was Job's regular custom."

Henceforth, life for the patriarch begins to unravel. "The book of Job tells the story of a good man overwhelmed by troubles. He is stripped of his wealth, his family, his health. He does not know why God has done this to him."[127] Only the reader knows that this comes about as a means of testing, and demonstration of God's faithfulness in times of adversity. Only the reader is privy to the spiritual struggle raging between the forces of good and evil.

One day the angels came to present themselves before the Lord, and Satan came with them. "Where have you been?" God asked of Satan. Satan responded: "From roaming through the earth and going back and forth in it." Then the Lord inquired: "Have you considered my servant Job? There is no one on earth like him; he is blameless and upright, a man who fears God and shuns evil." "Does Job fear God for nothing?" Satan impugns. "Have you not put a hedge around him and his household and everything he has? ...But stretch out your hand and strike everything he has, and he will surely curse you to your face." "Very well," the Lord responded, everything he has is in your hands, but on the man himself do not lay a finger."

So it was that on a certain day a messenger reported to Job: "The oxen were plowing and the donkey were grazing nearby, and the Sabeans attacked and carried them off. They put the servants to the sword, and I am the only one who has escaped to tell you!" *While he was still speaking*, another messenger came and said: "The fire of God fell from the sky and burned up the sheep and the servants, and I am the only one who has escaped to tell you!" *While he was still speaking*, a third messenger arrived with the word: "The Chaldeans formed three raiding parties and swept down on your camels and carried them off. They put the servants to the sword, and I am the only who has escaped to tell you!" *While he was still speaking*, a fourth messenger informed Job: "Your sons and daughters were feasting and drinking wine at the oldest brother's house, when suddenly a mighty wind swept in from the desert and struck the four corners of the house. It collapsed on them and they are dead, and I am the only one who has escaped to tell you!"

At this, Job got up and tore his robe and shaved his head. "Naked I came from my mother's womb," he allowed, "and naked I will depart. The Lord gave and the Lord has taken away, may the name of the Lord be praised." "In all this," the narrator observes, "Job did not sin by charging God with wrongdoing."

On another day the angels came to present themselves before the Lord, and Satan also came with them. Then the Lord said to Satan: "Where have you come from?" Satan replied: "From roaming through the earth and going back and forth in it." At this, the Lord inquired: "Have you considered my servant Job? There is no one on earth like him, he is blameless and upright, a man who fears God and shuns evil. And he still maintains his integrity, though you incited me against him to ruin him without any reason." "Skin for skin!" Satan retorted. "A man will give all he has for his own skin. But stretch out your hand and strike his flesh and bones, and he will surely curse you to your face." The Lord replied: "Very well, then, he is in your hands; but you must spare his life."

So Satan went out from the presence of the Lord and afflicted Job with painful sores from the soles of his feet to the top of his head. "Then Job took a piece of broken pottery and scraped himself with it as he sat among the ashes." Whereupon, his wife urged him: "Curse God and die!" He resolutely responded: "You are talking like a foolish woman. Shall we accept good from God and not trouble?" At this, the narrator again observes: "In all this, Job did not sin in what he said."

Much of what follows consists of dialogue among Job and his friends turned tormentors. One instance will suffice. Eliphaz comments: "Blessed is the man whom God corrects; so do not despise the discipline of the Almighty" (5:17). Job replies: "Teach me, and I will be quiet; show me where I have been wrong." "Eliphaz and Job drew from the same revelation but arrived at different conclusions. Eliphaz derived a precise formula to explain Job's distress; Job puzzled over the meaning of the turn of events."[128] In this regard, Job was accurate in assuming that life is plagued by ambiguity.

In the end, Job is commended. After the Lord had spoken to Job, he said to Eliphaz: "I am angry with you and your two friends, because you have not spoken to me what is right, as my servant Job has. ...My servant Job will pray for you, and I will accept his prayer and not deal with you according to your folly" (42:7-8). So it came to pass that the Lord "blessed the latter part of Job's life more than the first."

Proverbs is as mentioned earlier another example of wisdom literature. It largely consists of a collection of wise sayings, ascribed to Solomon and others. As for its cast, the *wise person* welcomes instruction; with understanding, gains insight, with insight, skill in living, with skill, the ability to plan ahead; with all, to orient life toward God and his benevolent purposes. The *fool* resists instruction; otherwise put, is obstinate; as the saying goes: *resembles an accident waiting to happen*; as such, is a menace to self and others. The *scoffer* contrasts to the wise and is coupled with the fool; not only dislikes correction but holds the truth up to ridicule. The *sluggard* is disinclined to initiate worthwhile activity; if initiated, fails to carry it through; is reluctant to face up to issues; is characterized from time to time as restless, helpless, useless, and exasperating. A *good friend* is constant in his or her love; hence also candid, accepting, reassuring, and tactful. The *simple person* may be readily influenced, whether for good or evil--but more likely the latter.

Proverbs 9 provides a classic case in point. "Wisdom has built her house; she has hewn out its seven pillars. She has prepared her meat and mixed her wine; she has also set her table." In such manner, wisdom is portrayed as an aristocratic lady preparing a sumptuous feast. "Come, eat my food and drink the wine I have mixed. Leave your simple ways and you will live."

"The woman Folly is loud; she is undisciplined and without knowledge. She sits at the door of her house...calling to those who pass by... ." Much as would a prostitute. "Let all who are simple come in here... . Stolen water is sweet; food eaten in secret is delicious." At which, the narrator observes: "But little do they know that the dead are there, that her guests are in the depths of the grave."

As for select sayings, the following are representative. "The mouth of the righteous is a fountain of life, but violence overwhelms the mouth of the wicked" (10:11). "The Lord tears down the proud man's house but he keeps the widow's boundaries intact" (15:25). "Gold there is, and rubies in abundance, but lips that speak knowledge are a rare jewel" (20:15). "Do not answer a fool according to his folly, or you will be like him yourself. Answer a fool according to his folly, or he will be wise in his own eyes" (26:4-5). "These twin sayings, which would have invited the charge of inconsistency had they not stood together, bring out the dilemma of those who would reason with the unreasonable."[129]

Ecclesiastes and *Song of Solomon* round out the so-called *Poetic Books. Ecclesiastes* is said to be the words of the *teacher*, son of David, king in Jerusalem (1:1). One would assume this a reference to Solomon. Its purpose "was to convince men of the uselessness of any world view which does not rise above the horizon of man himself. ...It is only God's work that endures, and only He can impart abiding value to the life and activity of man."[130] "Now all has been heard; here is the conclusion of the matter: fear God and keep his commandments, for this is the whole duty of man. For God will bring every deed into judgment, including every hidden thing, whether it is good or evil" (12:13-14).

Song of Solomon (Song of Songs in the Hebrew text) appears to be "an example of a universal type of poem--the love poem. The world of the Old Testament provides numerous examples of the genre. These are of widely differing styles and from widely scattered places, but they share certain common elements."[131] Such exhibit a common theme of sexual attraction, extended description of the beloved, and sexual intimacy. In this instance, it is meant to typify the relationship between God and his people. As such, it draws not only on a covenant relationship but historical precedence.

The beloved speaks: "I am a rose of Sharon, a lily of the valleys" (2:1). The lover responds: "Like a lily among thorns is my darling among the maidens." The beloved continues: "Like an apple tree among the trees of the forest is my lover among the young men." The lover again responds: "My dove in the clefts of the rock, in the hiding places on the mountainside, show me your face, let me hear your voice; for your voice is sweet, and your face is lovely." The beloved is allowed the final word: "Come away, my lover, and be like a gazelle or like a young stag on the spice-laden mountains" (8:14).

SILENT YEARS

There is cause for referring to the era between the testaments as the *silent years*. It seemed as if God had tired of speaking to those who continued to turn a deaf ear toward him. The school of the prophets had withered on the vine. While this was a relief for some, it seemed a tragedy for others. "For if you remain silent," the psalmist observed, "I will be like those who have gone down to the pit" (Psa. 28:1).

The silent years were decidedly not uneventful. Philip of Macedon took the initial step toward forming the Hellenic League as a rival to Persia. Murdered in 336 B.C., he was succeeded by his youthful son Alexander. Alexander had the distinction of being educated by Aristotle, carried the *Illiad* and *Odyssey* with him on his campaigns, and became a zealous embassador of Hellenic culture.

The Persians were slow to take Alexander seriously. He won a close contest at the river Granicus, and proceeded to *liberate* the Greek cities in Asia Minor--sometimes against their will. One victory followed on the heels of another. Alexander subsequently extended his empire from the Balkans south to Egypt and east to India. Eleven years after his invasion of Asia Minor, he lay dead at the age of thirty-three. Hellenism would survive its militant apostle.

Alexander's generals were quick to tear apart his empire, each seeking to extend his territory at the expense of others. Two impacted directly on the Jewish people: Ptolemy seized control of Egypt and Seleucus I consolidated the region from Syria in the west to Iran in the east. Both coveted the Jewish buffer-zone.

Ptolemy was first to realize his political ambition concerning Canaan. Josephus comments as follows: The Jews "have a custom of abstaining from work every seventh day; on those occasions they neither bear arms nor take any agricultural operations in hand.... . Consequently, because the inhabitants, instead of protecting their city, persevered in their folly, Ptolemy was allowed to enter with his army... ."[132] The territory thus fell prey to a cruel master. Ptolemy carried away many captives to Egypt, and armed others as mercenaries.

The Ptolemies administered the region for approximately a century. The Jews were forced to pay tribute. "The high priest, who apparently had personal responsibility for yielding tribute to the crown, was both spiritual head of the community and, increasingly, a secular prince. Records of the next century document clearly the development of a priestly aristocracy."[133] It was not the best, but neither was it the worst of times.

Meanwhile, the Seleucid fortunes took a turn for the better under Antiochus III. When successful in annexing Canaan in 130 B.C., he assumed a conciliatory posture: ordering the return of Jewish refugees and prisoners, tax concessions to allow for rebuilding from the devastation caused by warfare, the right to live according to the dictates of conscience, and revenue to support ritual activity. It was an auspicious beginning that failed to anticipate the difficult times ahead.

Hellenism was making substantial inroads into the Jewish community. Such influence was not necessarily calculated. " It was simply that Greek thought was in the air and inevitably made its impact on the minds of Jewish thinkers as they grappled with the new problems that their age had raised. Merely to breathe in the Hellenistic period involved absorption of Greek culture!"[134] There were also economic and social incentives for accommodation.

Hellenism played to mixed reviews. Some saw it as a serious threat to prized religious traditions, their identity as Jews being at stake. Others welcomed Hellenism as a liberating force from ethnic constraints, so much so that their tradition proved an embarrassment. Antiochus IV brought matters to a head. In a dramatic encounter outside Alexandria, a Roman envoy demanded that Antiochus promise to cut short his invasion of Egypt. With dreams of grandeur shattered and prestige diminished, Antiochus bitterly retreated. Along the way, he decided to take out his frustration on Jerusalem and solidify his southern flank. Swine were sacrificed on the altar. "The drunken orgy associated with the worship of Bacchus was made compulsory. Conversely, Jews were forbidden, under penalty of death, to practice circumcision, Sabbath observance, or the observance of the feasts of the Jewish year. Copies of the Hebrew Scriptures were ordered destroyed."[135] The mandate promulgating Hellenism and prohibiting Judaism was enforced with utmost severity.

"In those days Mattathias the son of John, son of Simeon, a priest of the sons of Joarib, moved from Jerusalem and settled in Modein" (1 Macc. 2:1). When he saw what was being done, he complained: "And behold, our holy place, our beauty, and our glory have been laid waste; the Gentiles have profaned it." Mattathias and his sons rent their clothes, put on sackcloth, and mourned greatly.

The king's officers who were enforcing the edict came to Modein to make its inhabitants offer sacrifice. Singling our Mattathias, they said to him: "You are a leader, honored and great in this city, and supported by sons and brothers. Now be the first to come and do what the king commands, as all the Gentiles and the men of Judah and those that are left in Jerusalem have done. Then you and your sons will be numbered among the friends of the king, and you and your sons will be honored with silver and gold and many gifts." But Mattathias answered in a loud voice so that all could hear: "Even if all the nations that live under the rule of the king obey him, and have chosen to do his commandments, departing each from the religion of his fathers, yet I and my sons and my brothers will live by the covenant of our fathers. ...We will not obey the king's words by turning aside from our religion to the right hand or to the left."

When he had finished speaking, a Jew came forward in the sight of all to offer sacrifice on the altar, according to the king's command, and no doubt supposing that he would benefit as a result. "When Mattathias saw it, he burned with zeal and his heart was stirred. He gave vent to righteous anger; he ran and killed him upon the altar. At the same time he killed the king's officer who was forcing them to sacrifice, and he tore down the altar." Then Mattathias cried out in a loud voice: "Let every one who is zealous for the law and supports the covenant come out with me!" So it was that he and his followers fled into the hills, and carried on gorilla warfare against their oppressors.

Judas the Maccabee (hammer) replaced his father as head of the revolutionary forces. Subsequently, "At daybreak Judas appeared in the plain with three thousand men, but they did not have armor and swords such as they desired. And they saw the camp of the Gentiles, strong and fortified, with cavalry round about it; and these men were trained in war" (1 Macc. 4:7). Then Judas said to the men with him: "Do not fear their numbers or be afraid when they charge. Remember how our fathers were saved at the Red Sea, when Pharaoh with his forces pursued them. And now let us cry to Heaven, to see whether he will favor us and remember his covenant with our fathers and crush the army before us today. Then all the Gentiles will know that there is one who redeems and saves Israel." As unequal as the contest may have appeared, they supposed that with God they were in the majority. So it came to pass that the "Gentiles were

crushed and fled into the plain, and all those in the rear fell by the sword."
On their return, Judas and his associates "sang hymns and praises to
Heaven, for he is good, for his mercy endures for ever." At this, the
narrator succinctly observes: "Thus Israel had a great deliverance that
day."

Increasing numbers of Jews joined the struggle as time wore on. Judas
was eventually able to recover Jerusalem. The altar dedicated to Jupiter
was removed and one erected in its place to the worship of Yahweh. The
Seleucids lay siege to Jerusalem, but had to retire to deal with an
insurrection at home. They eventually promised to refrain from
interfering with the internal affairs of Judea. Laws against the practice of
Judaism were repealed. Judas and his followers were granted immunity
and a fragile peace ensued.

The Jews were eventually freed from taxation under the administration
of Simon, an act considered tantamount to independence. A convocation
of Jewish leaders declared Simon "should be their leader and high priest
for ever, until a trustworthy prophet should arise" (1 Macc. 14:41). He
was the last of Mattathias' sons and first in a hereditary line of
Hasmonean rulers. Judea retained its independent status on condition of
loyalty to Syria and the promise of military assistance as needed.

The religious idealism of the Maccabees began to decline. "In
Palestine the strength--both moral and physical--of the Maccabees was
fast waning. The news of the chaos in Palestine reached Rome. Pompey,
the Roman general who had been so successful in bringing Roman power
to the East, determined to intervene."[136] Judea was subsequently in the
cogent words of Josephus "made tributary to the Romans."

Herod the Great was an enterprising son of the Idumean governor
Antipater. His finesse earned for him the title *Procurator of Judea* and
the promise that he would succeed himself as king. Herod's rule spanned
the eventful years of 37 B.C. to 4 A.D. His building projects were legion.
He zealously protected his office against any usurper. His atrocities are
well documented.

In so brief a resume of the *silent years*, we have nonetheless touched
on the two prime historical sources: 1 and 2 Maccabees and the writings
of Josephus. But there were literary works of other types. Some were
represented as additions to select Old Testament books. As a case in
point, we turn to *Bel and the Dragon* as an appendage to *Daniel*. Its
author introduces his story with the reign of Cyrus, when "Daniel was a
companion of the king, and was the most honored of his friends."

"Now the Babylonians had an idol called Bel, and every day they spent on it twelve bushels of fine flour and forty sheep and fifty gallons of wine. The king revered it and went every day to worship it. But Daniel worshiped his own God." "Why do you not worship Bel?" the king inquired. Daniel responded: "Because I do not revere man-made idols, but the living God, who created heaven and earth and has dominion over all flesh." "Do you not think that Bel is a living God?" the king inquired further. "Do you not see how much he eats and drinks every day?" At this, Daniel laughed and said: "Do not be deceived, O king; for this is but clay inside and brass outside, and it never ate or drank anything."

Then the king was angry, and summoned his priests. "If you do not tell me who is eating these provisions, you shall die," he said to them. "But if you prove that Bel is eating them, Daniel shall die, because he blasphemed against Bel." Hearing this, Daniel replied: "Let it be done as you have said."

So it was that the priests proposed: "Behold, we are going outside; you yourself, O King, shall set forth the food and mix and place the wine, and shut the door and seal it with your signet. And when you return in the morning, if you do not find that Bel has eaten it all, we will die; or else Daniel will, who is telling lies about us." They were not concerned, because beneath the table they had made a hidden entrance through which they used to go in regularly and consume the provision.

When they had gone out, the king set out the food intended for Bel. Then Daniel ordered his servant to bring ashes and sift them throughout the temple in the presence of the king alone. Then they went out, sealed the door, and departed. During the night, the priests and their families came, as they were accustomed to do, and ate and drank everything. Early the next morning, it could be seen that the seals were not broken. Then when the doors were opened, the king exclaimed: "You are great, O Bel; and with you there is no deceit, none at all." At this, Daniel laughed once again and said: "Look at the floor, and notice whose footsteps these are." The king observed: "I see the footsteps of men and women and children." Now the king was enraged, put the deceivers to death, and turned Bel over to Daniel to be likewise destroyed.

Along a different line, *Tobit* and *Judith* qualify as romantic tales. A fascinating combination of *Arabian Nights* romance, kindly Jewish piety, and sound moral teaching, Tobit is one of the most popular of the books of the Apocrypha. "Besides the intrinsic interest of the tale, which is compounded in large part of themes derived from ancient folklore, the books' principal value lies in the picture it gives of Jewish culture and religious life in an age not too remote, either in time or temper, from that of the New Testament."[137]

The setting of the story is the Assyrian capital Nineveh, when Israel was made captive. There lives Tobit, who in spite of his charitable deeds, has become blind and poor. But God hears his prayer, and heals him. He commissions his son Tobias to go on a mission for him, from which the latter returns with Sarah as his wife.

We pick up the story line with Tobias' arrival at the house of his relative Raguel. Now Raguel said to his wife Edna: "How much the young man resembles my cousin Tobit!" Then Raguel asked them: "Where are you from, brethren?" They answered him: "We belong to the sons of Naphtali, who are captives in Nineveh." So he said to them: "Do you know our brother Tobit?" They replied: "Yes we do." And he asked them: "Is he in good health?" They responded in the affirmative. Then Tobias added: "He is my father." At this, Raguel sprang to his feet, and welcomed him gladly.

Now Tobias' father had instructed him to "take a wife from among the descendants of your fathers and do not marry a foreign woman, who is not of our father's tribe; for we are the sons of the prophets" (4:12). So it was that he pursued the prospect of marriage to Sarah. Raguel responds: "Eat, drink, and be merry; for it is your right to take my child. But let me explain the true situation to you. I have given my daughter to seven husbands, and when each came to her he died in the night. But for the present be merry."

As Tobias was about to go into his wife, he remembered the words of the angel Raphael, and took the live ashes of incense and put the heart and liver of the fish upon them and made a smoke. "And when the demon (who had disposed of Sarah's previous husbands) smelled the odor he fled to the remotest parts of Egypt, and the angel bound him." After this, Tobias prayed: "and now, O Lord, I am not taking this sister of mine because of lust, but with sincerity. Grant that I may find mercy and may grow old together with her." Then they said "Amen," and went to sleep for the night.

But Raguel arose and went and dug a grave, with the thought: "Perhaps he too will die." When he returned to the house, he said to his wife: "Send one of the maids to see whether he is alive; and if he is not, let us bury him without letting any one know." So the maid opened the door and went in, and found them both asleep. When she returned with word that he was alive, Raguel blessed God and said: "Blessed art thou, because thou hast had compassion on two only children. Show them mercy, O Lord; and bring their lives to fulfilment in health and mercy."

So it came to pass.

Then, too, we have examples of wisdom literature from the period. *Ecclesiasticus*, otherwise called *The Wisdom of Jesus the Son of Sirach,* is the only apocryphal book which bears the author's name. He appears to have been a Jewish scribe, who conducted an academy--most likely in Jerusalem--concerning religious and ethical matters. Sirach is an important link in the history of the development of ancient Jewish reflection. "It is the last great example of the type of wisdom literature represented in the Old Testament book of Proverbs, and the first specimen of that form of Judaism which subsequently developed into the rabbinical schools of the Pharisees and the Sadducees."[138]

Whence comes wisdom? "The Lord himself created wisdom; he saw her and apportioned her, he poured her out upon all his works. She dwells with all flesh according to his gift, and he supplied her to those who love him" (1:9-10). How ought we to regard our parents? "Whoever honors his father atones for sins, and whoever glorifies his mother is like one who lays up treasure. Whoever honors his father will be gladdened by his own children, and when he prays he will be heard" (3:3-5). What is the nature of our social obligations? "Incline your ear to the poor, and answer him peaceably and gently. Deliver him who is wronged from the hand of the wrongdoer; and do not be fainthearted in judging a case. Be like a father to orphans, and instead of a husband to their mother; you will then be like a son of the Most High" (4:8-10). What ought we to conclude? "So now sing praise with all your heart and voice, and bless the name of the Lord" (38:35). "Do your work before the appointed time, and in God's time he will give you your reward" (51:30).

We see that the Hebraic hope was only in a qualified sense satisfied by their restoration. Shalom went unrealized. Most Jews remained in the diaspora. The nations showed no inclination to assemble in Jerusalem for worship. There was no turning back the clock to the golden age with David and Solomon nor ahead to the glories depicted by Isaiah and Ezekiel. They had to struggle with an uncertain future.

So it was that they cultivated a striking concern for keeping the law. In this regard, we must distinguish it from the religion of pre-exilic Israel. "This does not mean that it was a new religion, or represented the importation of some strange new element into Israel's faith. Rather, it resulted from a heightened stress, one-sided perhaps, but inevitable, on a feature at all times of central importance."[139] More in particular, it accented the continuing relevance of the Torah at a time when no prophetic voice could be heard. The silent years had generated a solemn obligation, and as a result, the stage was set for the dawn of the Messianic Age.

PROMISE FULFILLED

A literary approach to the Gospels begins with the conviction that they are essentially stories. Once this premise is accepted, "the reader's attention focuses on a cluster of related concerns: unifying plot conflicts that move toward a final resolution; the overall structure and progression of the story; narrative and artistic patterns such as repetition, contrast, and framing; the characters who generate the action... ."[140] In addition, "the settings in which events occur; the point of view from which the story is told...; image patterns and symbolism; style...; and the characteristics of the narrative *world* that each Gospel builds in the reader's imagination."

"Nevertheless, if we come to the Gospels with the characteristic narrative expectations...we will be continuously frustrated. The Gospels are too episodic and fragmented, too self-contained in their individual parts, and too thoroughly a hybrid form...to constitute this type of unified story."[141] Among such are biographical elements, historical allusion, parables, oration, dialogue, proverb, poem, tragedy, and comedy.

In particular, we first encounter the so-called *Synoptic Gospels*: *Matthew*, *Mark*, and *Luke*. "Each contains both events and sayings purporting to be from Jesus' life; these events and sayings, however, were not recorded immediately in the Gospels but were instead transmitted through various means, the most notable of which were word of mouth and written collections."[142] With such in mind, a *narrative harmony* seems the preferred alternative for approaching the life and ministry of Jesus from synoptic perspective.

The *motif* common to these three works is the *gospel*. The term *motif* is used for a theme which permeates an author's presentation. "A motif is different from a word in that, whereas a word is restricted to one lexical unit, a motif encompasses associated words. ...If a word is sufficiently broad in meaning, a word study may accidentally result in a good motif study."[143] Since the term *gospel* means *good news*, the Synoptic Gospels might be said to resemble extended newspaper articles.

Even so, each of the Synoptic Gospels has its own *set* (sub-division).

Luke is the only one to make his *set* explicit. He writes: "Many have undertaken to draw up an account of the things that have been fulfilled among us... . Therefore, since I have carefully investigated everything from the beginning, it seemed good also to me to write an orderly account for you, most noble Theophilus, so that you may know the certainty of the things you have been taught" (1:1, 3). What he means by an *orderly account* can only be determined by examining the text. Having done so, it would appear that he follows a plausible chronological order with perhaps two or three exceptions. These exceptions seem for topical reasons.

As for Matthew and Mark, their *sets* are implicit rather than explicit. As for Matthew, Scot McKnight introduces *discipleship* as its *motif*, which corresponds to my use of *set*. As an example, he explores the tasks of the disciple as to (1) proclaim the gospel, pronounce judgment, and participate in the ministry of Jesus, (2) influence the world around, (3) experience table fellowship and communion with Jesus, (4) perform the ministry of Jesus, (5) teach the doctrines of Jesus, and (6) worship and confess Jesus.[144]

As for Mark, *tragedy* seems to provide us its peculiar *gospel set*. I wrote on an earlier occasion: "Jesus plays the tragic hero from beginning to last. ...That is, (his courage) not only contrasted to evil but transcended the good. We can characterize what this entails, but not exhaust it. The whole remains greater than its parts."[145]

Since the story line is obviously most critical to Luke's *gospel set*, we will defer to his order in the *synoptic harmony* that follows. In the time of Herod king of Judea, there was a priest named *Zechariah*. His wife Elizabeth was also descended from Aaron. "Both of them were upright in the sight of God, observing all the Lord's commandments and regulations blamelessly" (1:6). But Elizabeth was barren, and both she and her husband advanced in age.

Having introduced his characters, Luke turns to the narration. Once when Zechariah's division was serving at the temple, an angel of the Lord appeared to him and said: "Do not be afraid, Zechariah; your prayer has been heard. Your wife Elizabeth will bear you a son, and you are to give him the name John. ...And he will go on before the Lord, in the spirit and power of Elijah, to turn the hearts of the fathers to their children and the disobedient to the wisdom of the righteous--to make ready a people prepared for the Lord."

God subsequently sent the angel Gabriel to Nazareth, to a virgin pledged to be married to a man named *Joseph*--a descendant of David.

The virgin's name was *Mary*. "Greetings, you who are highly favored!" Gabriel exclaimed (1:28). "Do not be afraid," the angel continued. "You will be with child and give birth to a son, and you are to give him the name Jesus. He will be great and will be called the Son of the Most High. The Lord God will give him the throne of his father David, and he will reign over the house of Jacob forever; his kingdom will never end."

"How can this be since I am a virgin?" Mary inquired. The angel answered: "The Holy Spirit will come upon you, and the power of the Most High will overshadow you." Gabriel's message to Mary is four-fold: "she will have a son to be named Jesus; the child will be the Son of God and will occupy forever the throne of David; the birth of the child will be effected by the overshadowing descent of the Holy Spirit; and as a sign ...Gabriel informs Mary of the pregnancy of her kinswoman Elizabeth."[146] After this, he adds the cogent observation: "For nothing is impossible with God."

Elizabeth subsequently gave birth to a son. When they came to circumcise him, they supposed that he would be called *Zechariah*--after his father. Elizabeth however indicated that they would call him *John*. Now Zechariah was unable to speak since his encounter with the angel, but when asked what to call the child, he wrote "His name is John." Zechariah moreover prophesied: "And you, my child, will be called a prophet of the Most High, for you will go on before the Lord to prepare the way for him, to give his people the knowledge of salvation through the forgiveness of sins, because of the tender mercy of our God, but which the rising sun will come to us from heaven to shine on those living in darkness and in the shadow of death, to guide our feet into the path of peace." At which the narrator adds: "And the child grew and became strong in spirit; and he lived in the desert until he appeared publicly to Israel."

"This is how the birth of Jesus Christ came about," Matthew informs us. "His mother Mary was pledged to be married to Joseph, but before they came together, she was found to be with child through the Holy Spirit. Because Joseph her husband was a righteous man and did not want to expose her to public disgrace, he had in mind to divorce her quietly" (1:18-19). But after this, an angel of the Lord appeared to him in a dream and said: "Joseph son of David, do not be afraid to take Mary home as your wife, because what is conceived in her is from the Holy Spirit. She will give birth to a son, and you are to give him the name Jesus, because he will save his people from their sins." The name *Jesus* means *Yahweh saves*.

In those days, Caesar Augustus issued a decree that a census should be taken throughout the Roman Empire. So Joseph journeyed from Nazareth to Bethlehem with Mary expecting to register, since he belonged to the house of David (Luke 2:4-5). While they were there, Mary gave birth, and wrapped her son in cloths and placed him in a manager-- because there was no room for them in the inn. This was likely the residence of a relative, whose accommodation for their animals was enclosed along with that for the household.

Now there were shepherds living out in the fields nearby, keeping watch over their flocks at night. An angel of the Lord appeared to them, the glory of the Lord shone around them, and they were terrified. But the angel said to them: "Do not be afraid. I bring you good news of great joy... ." Suddenly a great company of the heavenly host appeared along with the angel, praising God and saying: "Glory to God in the highest, and on earth peace to men on whom his favor rests." *Peace* implies comprehensive well-being. It is here portrayed as resulting from God's favorable attitude. Otherwise stated, this is good news for God's people. When the angels had left them, the shepherds said to one another: "Let's go to Bethlehem and see this thing that has happened, which the Lord has told us about." Then when they had seen for themselves, the "shepherds returned, glorifying and praising God for all the things they had heard and seen, which were just as they had been told."

When the time of purification according to the Torah was completed (i.e., forty days after the child's birth), Joseph and Mary took Jesus to Jerusalem for dedication. Now there was a man in Jerusalem called *Simeon*, who was righteous and devout. He moreover was waiting for the consolation of Israel, and the Holy Spirit had revealed to him that he would live to see the Messiah. So it was that when Jesus' parents brought him into the temple courts, Simeon took the child in his arms and praised God, saying: "Sovereign Lord, as you have promised, you now dismiss your servant in peace. For my eyes have seen your salvation, which you have prepared in the sight of all people, a light for revelation to the Gentiles and for the glory to your people Israel" (Luke 2:29-32). There was also an aged prophetess by the name of *Anna*. She never left the temple, but worshiped there night and day. Coming up to them at that very moment, she gave thanks to God and spoke of the child to all those looking for the redemption of Jerusalem.

After Jesus was born and during the reign of Herod, Matthew tells us that Magi came from the east to Jerusalem and inquired: "Where is the one who has been born king of the Jews? We saw his star in the east and have come to worship him" (2:2). The *star* has been variously explained.

As a plausible example, Ethelbert Stauffer associates it with a conjunction of Jupiter and Saturn in the Sign of the Fishes during 7 B.C. He explains that Jupiter was regarded as the star of the ruler of the universe, "and the constellation of the Fishes as the sign of the last days. In the East, Saturn was considered to be the planet of Palestine. If Jupiter encountered Saturn in the sign of the Fishes, it could only mean that the ruler of the last days would appear in Palestine."[147] The *Magi* were probably astrologers.

When Herod heard of this, he was disturbed and all Jerusalem with him. After he had called together the chief priests and teachers of the Torah, he asked them where the Messiah was to be born. "In Bethlehem," they replied. Then Herod sent for the Magi, and inquired of them as to when the star had appeared. He moreover sent them on their way to search for the child, and report back to him--so that he might also go and worship him.

The star went before them until it stopped over the place where the child resided. On coming into the house, they saw Jesus with his mother, and bowed down to worship him. Then they opened their treasures and presented him with gifts of gold, incense, and myrrh. Having been warned in a dream not to go back to Herod, they returned to their country by another route.

When they had gone, an angel of the Lord appeared to Joseph in a dream. "Get up," he urged, "take the child and his mother and escape to Egypt. Stay there until I tell you, for Herod is going to search for the child to kill him." He did as directed. When Herod heard that the Magi had deceived him, he was furious and gave orders that all the boys in Bethlehem and its vicinity who were two years old and under should be put to death. So it was done, and the people mourned their loss. After Herod died, an angel of the Lord again appeared to Joseph, and encouraged him to return since "those who were trying to take the child's life are dead." "And the child grew and became strong; he was filled with wisdom, and the grace of God was upon him" (Luke 2:40).

Every year Jesus' parents went to Jerusalem for the Passover celebration. When he was twelve years of age, they went up according to their custom (Luke 2:42). In due time, Joseph and Mary started their journey home, supposing Jesus was among their relatives and friends. After a day's travel and when Jesus was no where to be found, his parents returned to Jerusalem to look for him. After three days, they found him in the temple courts, sitting among the teachers, listening to them and asking them questions. "Everyone who heard him was amazed at his understanding and his answers." *After three days* should probably be understood as the day of travel, the day of return, and on following day they found him.

When his parents saw him, they were astonished. His mother inquired of him: "Son, why have you treated us like this? Your father and I have been anxiously searching for you." "Why were you searching for me?" he asked. "Didn't you know I had to be in my Father's house?" They, in turn, did not understand what he was saying to them. He went down to Nazareth with them and was obedient to them. His mother treasured all these things in her heart, and Jesus "grew in wisdom and stature, and in favor with God and men." "As Mark states explicitly (Mark 3:31-35) and as Luke implies in the episode, family love and loyalties have their place and flourish under the higher love and loyalty to God."[148]

In the fifteenth year of the reign of Tiberius Caesar, the word of God came to John son of Zechariah in the wilderness. Whereupon, he went into all the country around the Jordan, preaching a baptism of repentance for the forgiveness of sins. As is written in Isaiah: "A voice of one calling in the desert, 'Prepare the way for the Lord, make straight paths for him. Every valley shall be filled in, every mountain and hill made low. The crooked roads shall become straight, the rough ways smooth. And all mankind will see God's salvation'" (Luke 3:4-6; cf. Isa. 40:3-5).

John said to the multitude coming out to be baptized by him: "You brood of vipers! Who warned you to flee from the coming wrath? Produce fruit in keeping with repentance." "What shall we do then?" they asked him. John answered: "The man with two tunics should share with him who has none, and the one who has food should do the same." Tax collectors also inquired of him: "What should we do?" He responded: "Don't collect any more than you are required to." Then certain soldiers likewise asked: "What shall we do?" He answered: "Don't extort money and don't accuse people falsely--be content with your pay."

The people wondered if John might be the Messiah. He answered them all: "I baptize you with water. But one more powerful than I will come, the thongs of whose sandals I am not worthy to untie. He will baptize you with the Holy Spirit and with fire." He was a prophet with an urgent message. From a personal perspective, one "heard John's challenge to unconditional confrontation, he repented to John's call, he decided in favor of the authenticity of the message, he was willing to submit to the imminent appearance of the Messiah, he chose to give concrete expression to his response through John's baptism."[149]

Then Jesus came from Galilee to the Jordan to be baptized by John. But John tried to deter him, saying: "I need to be baptized by you, and do you come to me?" (Matt. 3:13). Jesus replied: "Let it be so now; it is proper for us to do this to fulfill all righteousness." John then consented. As soon as Jesus was baptized, he went up out of the water, and he saw the Spirit of God descending like a dove and lighting on him. And a voice from heaven said: "This is my Son, whom I love; with him I am well pleased." Why would Jesus insist on being baptized? "The most likely answer to this question stressed Jesus' solidarity with sinners. The one who will save his people from their sins...must consecrate himself to his vocation by joining the sinful multitude in the waters of the Jordan. ...In so doing, however, he takes the first step on the road to Calvary."[150]

Luke introduces Jesus' genealogy at this point rather than at the outset, as with Matthew. The reason is obscure. Some suppose that he meant to follow a precedent established concerning Moses, whose call and ministry were separated by a genealogy (cf. Exod. 6:14-25). This would accent Jesus as *the prophet like Moses.* Certain differences between the two genealogies have also been explained in various ways. The reason is also obscure. Perhaps Luke records the actual genealogy of Joseph, and Matthew records the official genealogy--concerning succession to the throne. The latter would not necessarily pass from father to son.

Then Jesus was led by the Spirit into the wilderness to be tempted by the devil. After fasting forty days and nights, he was famished. The devil came to him and said: "If you are the Son of God, tell this stone to become bread" (Luke 4:3). "Give the tempter his due: the timing is perfect. Jesus has not preached a sermon, cast out a demon, or healed a sick person. He is alone and hungry in the desert, poised at the edge of his ministry."[151] Jesus was nonetheless ready for the challenge. "It is written," he answered, "'Man does not live on bread alone.'"

The devil then led him up to a high place, showed him in an instant all the kingdoms of the world, and said to him: "I will give you all their authority and splendor, for it has been given to me, and I can give it to anyone I want to. So if you worship me, it will all be yours." "It is written," Jesus replied, "'Worship the Lord your God and serve him only.'" At this, the devil led him to Jerusalem and had him stand on the highest point of the temple. "If you are the Son of God," he said, "throw yourself down from here. For it is written: 'He will command his angels concerning you to guard you carefully; they will lift you up in their hands, so that you will not strike your foot against a stone.'" "It says," Jesus responded, "'Do not put the Lord your God to the test.'" When the devil had finished all this tempting, he left him for a more convenient time. No doubt any time that the opportunity afforded itself, but especially as Jesus' impending death approached.

The first temptation is not only personal but social. "The second is political.... The third is religious.... Stones to bread--the hungry hope so; take political control--the oppressed hope so; leap from the temple-- those longing for proof of God's power among us hope so. All this is to say that a real temptation is an offer not to fall but to rise."[152] In any case, Jesus would not compromise his stand against the world, the flesh, and the devil. This moreover brings to a conclusion the formative years, in anticipation of Jesus' public ministry.

PUBLIC MINISTRY

Jesus returned to Galilee in the power of the Spirit, and news concerning him spread throughout the whole region. He taught in their synagogues, and was well received. He came to Nazareth, where he had been brought up, and on the Sabbath went to the synagogue as was his custom. He stood (out of respect) to read and the Isaiah scroll was handed to him. Unrolling it, he found the place where it was written: "The Spirit of the Lord is on me, because he has anointed me to preach good news to the poor. He has sent me to proclaim freedom for the prisoners and recovery of sight for the blind, to release the oppressed, to proclaim the year of the Lord's favor" (Luke 4:18-19; cf. Isa. 61:1-2). Then he rolled up the scroll, gave it back to the attendant, sat down (to teach), and announced: "Today this scripture is fulfilled in your hearing."

He had stopped pointedly short of "and the day of vengeance of our God." This was the time of God's visitation. Jesus came preaching good news. All spoke well of him and were amazed at the gracious words he spoke. Jesus nonetheless said to them, "Surely you will quote this proverb to me: 'Physician, heal yourself!' Do here in your hometown what we have heard that you did in Capernaum." "I tell you a truth," he continued, "no prophet is accepted in his hometown." At this, they were furious with him and would have killed him, but "he walked right through the crowd and went on his way." Luke offers no explanation.

Then Jesus went down to Capernaum. In doing so, he made his way along a branch of the *Via Maris* (*Way of the Sea*) trade route, through the Arbel pass, and along the shore of the Sea of Galilee. On the Sabbath, he began to teach the people, and they were amazed because he spoke with authority--rather than rely on religious precedent as was the rabbinic custom. In the synagogue there was a man possessed by a demon, who cried out at the top of his voice: "Ha! What do you want with us, Jesus of Nazareth? Have you come to destroy us? I know who you are--the Holy One of God!" (Luke 4:34). "Be quiet!" Jesus sternly rebuked him. "Come out of him!" The demon threw the man down, as if in disgust, before taking its leave; and the people were amazed. Jesus went on to heal others, and establish his credentials as a miracle worker.

He also began to enlist disciples. As Jesus was walking beside the Sea of Galilee, he saw two brothers, *Simon* called *Peter* and his brother *Andrew*. They were casting their nets into the lake, for they were fishermen. Jesus said to them: "Come, follow me, and I will make you fishers of men" (Matt. 4:19). At once they left their nets and followed him. Going on from there, he came to two other brothers: *James* and his brother *John*. They were in a boat with their father Zebedee, preparing their nets. Jesus called them and immediately they left the boat and their father and followed him. In this regard, Matthew emphasizes both their readiness and unconditional response.

On a certain day, Jesus went out to a moutainside to pray, and spent the night in prayer (Luke 6:12). When the morning came, he called his disciples to him and chose twelve of them whom he designated *apostles*. An *apostle* is *one who is sent*. "The twelve apostles symbolize the foundation of God's new people of faith.... Just as the twelve patriarchs fathered the twelve tribes of (old) Israel, so the twelve apostles are the spiritual fathers of the *twelve tribes* (as in James 1:1) of repentant and believing Israel."[153]

Then Jesus went down with them and stood on a level place. Many of his disciples were there, along with a multitude of people. Looking at his disciples, Jesus said: "Blessed are you who are poor, for yours is the kingdom of God. Blessed are you who hunger now, for you will be satisfied. Blessed are you who weep now, for you will laugh. Blessed are you when men hate you, when they exclude you and insult you and reject your name as evil, because of the Son of Man." "Rejoice in that day and leap for joy," Jesus continued, "because great is your reward in heaven. For that is how their fathers treated the prophets."

"Love your enemies, do good to those who hate you, bless those who curse you, pray for those who mistreat you." "Forgive, and you will be forgiven. Give, and it will be given to you. A good measure, pressed down, shaken together and running over, will be poured into you lap." In these and other ways, Jesus admonished his disciples. Whereas Luke's *Sermon on the Plain* is sketchy, Matthew's *Sermon on the Mount* appears as if a resume of Jesus' teaching during this early period of his public ministry.

He also spoke to them in parables. The *parable* was the most striking literary feature of Jesus' public ministry. "The parables of Jesus are masterpieces of storytelling. We should first of all enjoy them in the same ways that we enjoy other stories. These simple stories are didactic in their purpose."[154]

Now Jesus' mother and brothers came to see him, but they were not able to get near because of the crowd. Someone reported to him: "Your mother and brothers are standing outside, wanting to see you" (Luke 8:20). Jesus responded: "My mother and brothers are those who hear God's word and put it into practice." This incident provides us with an excellent opportunity for observing how the context influences our understanding of the text. Mark tells this story in a setting of intense controversy between Jesus and his critics. He "also locates it prior to the parable of the sower. In Luke's location immediately after the parable of the sower, the episode illustrates the truth of the parable: hearing and doing the word of God is the way into the fellowship created by Jesus."[155]

Once when Jesus had withdrawn in prayer, he asked his disciples: "Who do the crowds say I am?" (Luke 9:18). They replied: "Some say John the Baptist; others say Elijah; and still others, that one of the prophets of long ago has come back to life." But what about you?" Jesus inquired. Peter answered: "The Christ of God." At this, Jesus warned them not to tell anyone, since the "Son of Man must suffer many things and be rejected by the elders, chief priests and teachers of the law, and he must be killed and on the third day be raised to life."

The disciples are commanded not to talk about this discovery, for their understanding is deficient. "Like the blind man whom Jesus asked 'Do you see anything?' (Mark 8:23), the disciples see indistinctly. ...He must lay his hands upon them again. He does so in the remainder of this unit, throughout the discipleship section, throughout the Gospel, and beyond."[156] On the other hand, the disciples stand in contrast to the multitude, which is largely oblivious to the course of redemptive history.

About eight days later, Jesus took Peter, John, and James with him up onto a mountain to pray (Luke 9:28). As he was praying, the appearance of his face changed, and his clothes became as bright as a flash of lightning. At this, Moses and Elijah appeared in glorious splendor, talking with Jesus. They spoke concerning his departure that was about to take place. As they were about to leave, Peter proposed: "Master, it is good for us to be here. Let us put up three shelters--one for you, one for Moses and one for Elijah." This solicited from Luke the comment: "He did not know what he was saying." While he was speaking, a cloud appeared and enveloped them, and they were afraid. Then a voice came from the cloud, declaring: "This is my Son, whom I have chosen; listen to him." So are we to understand that the teachings of Jesus fulfill and expand upon those of Moses and the prophets.

The next day, after they had come down from the mountain, a large crowd met them. A man in the crowd cried out: "Teacher, I beg you to look at my son.... A spirit seizes him and he suddenly screams; it throws him into convulsions so that he foams at the mouth. ...I begged your disciples to drive it out, but they could not." "O unbelieving and perverse generations," Jesus replied, "how long shall I stay with you and put up with you? Bring your son here." Then, when he had healed the boy, the people were amazed at God's greatness.

As the time approached for Jesus to be taken up to heaven, he resolutely set out for Jerusalem (9:51). He moreover sent messengers on ahead to prepare for his arrival. But when the villagers would not extend hospitality to him, because he was headed for Jerusalem and since they worshiped at Mount Gerizim, James and John asked: "Lord, do you want us to call fire down from heaven to destroy them?" Whereupon, Jesus rebuked them, and they went on to another village.

As they were walking along the road, a man said to Jesus: "I will follow you wherever you go." Jesus replied: "Foxes have holes and birds of the air have nests, but the Son of Man has not place to lay his head." He said to another man: "Follow me," but the man responded: "Lord, first let me go and bury my father." Otherwise stated, "Let me fulfill my filial obligations." Jesus said to him: "Let the dead bury their own dead, but you go and proclaim the kingdom of God." Still another said: "I will follow you, Lord; but first let me go back and say good-by to my family." That is, "Let me tie together loose ends." Jesus answered: "No one who puts his hand to the plow and looks back is fit for service in the kingdom of God."

After this, Jesus appointed seventy-two others and sent them two by two ahead of him to every place where he would go (Luke 10:1). He told them: "The harvest is plentiful, but the workers are few. Ask the Lord of the harvest, therefore, to send out workers into his harvest field. Go! I am sending you out like lambs among wolves." He moreover encouraged them to travel light, not to be distracted, and gratefully accept what is offered. They subsequently returned rejoicing that "even the demons submit to us in your name." Jesus responded: Do "not rejoice that the spirits submit to you, but rejoice that your names are written in heaven." The idiom does not imply not this but that, but rather one more than the other.

On one occasion, an expert in the Torah decided to test Jesus. "Teacher," he asked, "what must I do to inherit eternal life?" "What is written in the Law?" Jesus asked in return. "How do you read it?" This, incidently, conforms to a Jewish practice of answering a question with a question. He replied: "'Love the Lord your God with all your heart and with all your soul and with all your strength and with all your mind', and 'Love your neighbor as yourself.'" "You have answered correctly," Jesus replied. "Do this and you will live." Some see in this support for the way of works. "If you want a way of salvation by doing, this is it (with the implication that you won't be able to do it). It is perhaps more likely that it is a repudiation of works. ...If we really love God in the way of which Jesus speaks, then we rely on him, not ourselves."[157]

With such in mind, we listen in on the expert's response. But he wanted to justify himself, so he asked Jesus: "And who is my neighbor?" Jesus thereupon told a story concerning a man who was going down from Jerusalem to Jericho, when he fell into the hands of robbers. They stripped him of his clothes, beat him, and went away, leaving him half dead. A priest came that way, and when he saw the man passed by on the other side of the road. So too a Levite, when he came to the place and saw the man, passed by on the other side. But a Samaritan, when he saw the man, took pity on him. He went to him and bandaged his wounds. Then he put the man on his own donkey, and took him to an inn and took care of him. The next day he gave two silver coins to the inn-keeper, with the instruction: "Look after him, and when I return, I will reimburse you for any extra expense you may have."

"Which of these three do you think was neighbor to the man who fell into the hands of robbers?" Jesus pointedly inquired. In this manner, he shifted the question from *who is my neighbor* to *who am I neighbor to*. The expert replied: "The one who had mercy on him." Jesus, in turn, replied: "Go and do likewise."

One day Jesus was praying at a certain place. When he had finished, one of his disciples said to him: "Lord, teach us to pray, just as John taught his disciples. Jesus replied to them, "When you pray, say: 'Father, hallowed be your name, your kingdom come. Give us each day our daily bread. Forgive us our sins, for we also forgive everyone who sins against us. And lead us not into temptation.'" Not only is Matthew's account more extended, but incorporated into his Sermon on the Mount--so as to illustrate the correct way to pray, as opposed to the ostentatious prayers of the hypocrites (Matt. 6:5) and the meaningless repetitions of the Gentiles (Matt. 6:7). Conversely, Luke "chose to place it in the Central Section (or Travel Narrative) in order to illustrate the need for faith and persistence in prayer."[158] As a matter of fact, there is ample evidence for concluding that Jesus repeated aspects of his teachings from time to time.

Jesus admonished his disciples: "Do not worry about your life, what you will eat; or about your body, what you will wear. ...Consider how the lilies grow. They do not labor or spin. Yet, I tell you, not even Solomon in all his splendor was dressed like one of these. If that is how God clothes the grass of the field, which is here today, and tomorrow is thrown into the fire, how much more will he clothe you, O you of little faith" (Luke 12:22, 27-28).

"Do not be afraid," Jesus continued, "for the Father has been pleased to give you the kingdom. Sell your possessions and give to the poor. Provide purses for yourselves that will not wear out, a treasure in heaven that will not be exhausted, where no thief comes near and no moth destroys. For where your treasure is, there will be your heart also." On the one hand, if one focuses his or her attention on the kingdom, and in particular, ministry to those in need, he or she invests in eternity. On the other, in response to the question "How much did he leave?" the pointed conclusion is *everything*.

Some time later, Jesus said to the multitude: "When you see a cloud rising in the west, immediately you say: 'It's going to rain.' and it does. And when the south wind blows, you say, 'It's going to be hot,' and it is. Hypocrites! You know how to interpret the appearance of the earth and the sky. How is it that you don't know how to interpret this present time?" (Luke 12:54-56). "They understood the winds of earth, but not the winds of God; they could discern the sky, but not the heavens. Their religious externalism prevented them from seeing the significance of the coming of Jesus."[159]

Whereupon, certain of the Pharisees came to Jesus and said to him: "Leave this place and go somewhere else. Herod wants to kill you" (Luke 13:31). He responded: "Go tell that fox, 'I will drive out demons and heal people today and tomorrow, and on the third day I will reach my goal.'" "O Jerusalem, Jerusalem," Jesus continued, "you who kill the prophets and stone those sent to you, how often I have longed to gather your children together, as a hen gathers her chicks under her wings, but you were not willing!" It is curious to find *Pharisees* warning Jesus of impending danger. Perhaps this indicates that regardless of differences, they felt themselves closer to Jesus than Herod, or they may have been acting on Herod's behalf. The *fox* was used to suggest a sly, worthless, or destructive person. In any case, Jesus means to say that God rather than Herod will determine when his mission is complete.

One Sabbath, when Jesus went to eat in the house of a prominent

Pharisee, he was being carefully watched. There in front of him was a man suffering from dropsy. Jesus asked the Pharisees and experts in the Torah: "Is it lawful to heal on the Sabbath or not?" (Luke 14:3). When they remained silent, he healed the man and sent him away. Then he inquired of them: "If one of you has a son or an ox that falls into a well on the Sabbath day, will you not immediately pull him out?" The subtle features of the dialogue may readily escape us. On the one hand, there was nothing in the Mosaic code to prohibit healing on the Sabbath. On the other, rabbinic tradition prohibited healing unless one's life was in danger. Finally, such custom seemed inconsistent with the inclination to rescue a son (or *ass*, seeing the textual evidence is divided) or ox when endangered.

When Jesus noticed how the guests picked the places of honor at the table, he told them this parable: "When someone invites you to a wedding feast, do not take the place of honor, for a person more distinguished than you may have been invited. If so, the host who invited both of you will come and say to you, 'Give this man your seat.' Then, humiliated, you will have to take the least important place." Instead, "take the lowest place, so that when your host comes, he will say to you: 'Friend, move up to a better place.' ...For everyone who exalts himself will be humbled, and he who humbles himself will be exalted." With Jesus' closing comment, we are alerted that his teaching extends in parabolic fashion beyond the case in point, to life in general.

Then Jesus said to his host: "When you give a luncheon or dinner, do not invite your friends, your brothers or relatives, or your rich neighbors; if you do so, they may invite you back and so you will be repaid. But when you give a banquet, invite the poor, the crippled, the lame, the blind, and you will be blessed. Although they cannot repay you, you will be repaid at the resurrection of the righteous."

When one of those at the table with Jesus heard this, he said to him: "Blessed is the man who will eat at the feast in the kingdom of God." Jesus replied: "A certain man was preparing a great banquet and invited many guests. ...But they all alike began to make excuses. The first said, 'I have just bought a field, and I must go and see it. Please excuse me.' Another said, 'I have just bought five yoke of oxen, and I'm on my way to try them out. Please excuse me.' Still another said, 'I just got married, so I can't come.'" When the servant reported back, his master was angry and ordered him: "Go quickly into the streets and alleys of the town and bring in the poor, the crippled, the blind, and the lame." Consequently, his servant went to the roads and country lanes to recruit still more persons so that his house would be full. If the parable proper terminates at this point, rather than at verse 21 or 24, one would think of God's offer first to the religiously and socially deprived in Israel (on the streets of the city) and then to the Gentiles (strangers on the outskirts of the city).

Now tax collectors and sinners were gathering around Jesus to hear him, but the Pharisees and teachers of the Torah complained: "This man welcomes sinners and eats with them" (Luke 15:2). The term *sinner*, used in this comprehensive sense, was one who due to vocation or disposition failed to live by the exacting religious code of the time. In response to the complaint, Jesus told three parables: concerning the lost sheep, coin, and son. The first will suffice to preserve the story line. "Suppose one of you has a hundred sheep and loses one of them," Jesus began. "Does he not leave the ninety-nine in the open country and go after the lost sheep until he finds it? ...Then he calls his friends and neighbors together and says: 'Rejoice with me; I have found my lost sheep.'" In the same way, "there will be more rejoicing in heaven over one sinner who repents than over ninety-nine righteous persons who do not need to repent."

To some who were confident in their own righteousness and looked down on everyone else, Jesus told another parable. "Two men went up to the temple to pray, one a Pharisee and the other a tax collector. The Pharisee stood up and prayed about himself: 'God I thank you that I am not like other men--robbers, evildoers, adulterers--or even like this tax collector. I fast twice a week and give a tenth of all I get.'" In contrast, "the tax collector stood at a distance. He could not even look up at heaven, but beat his breasts and said, 'God, have mercy on me, a sinner.'" Jesus concluded: "I tell you that this man, rather than the other, went home justified before God. For everyone who exalts himself will be humbled, and he who humbles himself will be exalted." In this connection, Jesus re-affirms the principle he introduced earlier.

As Jesus approached Jericho, a blind man was sitting by the roadside begging. When he heard the crowd going by, he asked what was happening. They told him: "Jesus of Nazareth is passing by" (Luke 18:35). At this, he cried out: "Jesus, Son of David, have mercy on me!" When rebuked, he shouted all the more: "Son of David, have mercy on me!" Jesus stopped, ordered the man brought to him, and asked him what he wanted. "Lord, I want to see," he replied. Jesus said to him: "Receive your sight; your faith has healed you." Immediately he received his sight, and he followed Jesus.

Jesus entered Jericho and was passing through. A wealthy tax collector named *Zacchaeus* wanted to see Jesus but could not because he has short of stature. So he ran ahead and climbed up into a sycamore tree. When Jesus reached the spot, he looked up and said to him: "Zacchaeus, come down immediately. I must stay at your house today." So he came down, and welcomed Jesus gladly. All the people saw this and began to mutter: "He has gone to be the guest of a sinner." But Zacchaeus stood up and said: "Lord, Lord! Here and now I give half of my possessions to the poor, and if I have cheated anybody out of anything, I will pay back four times the amount." Jesus responded: "Today salvation has come to this house, because this man, too, is a son of Abraham. For the Son of Man came to seek and to save what was lost." So we observe that what comes as *good news* for one solicits complaints from others.

The road from Jericho to Jerusalem winds its way some seventeen miles through desolate country in an assent of over 3000 feet. Jesus was near to his destination. His public ministry was coming to a close. His passion was at hand. What he said would take place was about to take place, but with narrative detail none would have anticipated.

PASSION ACCOUNT

The term *passion* is derived from the Latin meaning *suffering*. "After his *suffering*," Luke observes, "he showed himself to these men and gave many convincing proofs that he was alive" (Acts 1:3). The *passion narratives* are characterized by Jesus' resolve to do God's will in the face of adversity and suffering. We will pick up the story line with his triumphant entry.

As Jesus was approaching Bethpage and Bethany at the Mount of Olives, he instructed two of his disciples: "Go to the village ahead of you, and as you enter it, you will find a colt tied there, which no one has ever ridden. Untie it and bring it here. If anyone asks you, 'Why are you untying it?' Tell him, 'The Lord needs it.'" (Luke 19:30-31). Since it had not been ridden, it was suitable for a sacred purpose. *The Lord needs it* was likely a pre-arranged password.

They brought it to Jesus, threw their cloaks on the colt, and put Jesus on it. As they went along, people spread their cloaks on the road, while others cut branches from the trees and spread them on the road. When they came near the place where the road goes down the Mount of Olives, the whole crowd of disciples began joyfully to praise God in loud voices for all the miracles they had seen: "Blessed is the king who comes in the name of the Lord! Peace in heaven and glory in the highest!" Some of the Pharisees in the crowd urged Jesus: "Lord, rebuke your disciples!" "I tell you," he replied, "if they keep quiet, the stones will cry out." While *the stones will cry out* is no doubt a figure of speech, it reminds us that creation is involved in events that "we tend to think affect humans alone. ...Matthew says a special star appeared to announce Jesus' birth, and that the earth shuddered, cracking rocks, when he died; and all the Synoptists agree that when Jesus was put on the cross, for three hours there was an eclipse of the sun."[160]

As they approached Jerusalem, Jesus wept, saying: "If you, even you, had only known on this day what would bring you peace--but now it is hidden from your eyes. The days will come upon you when your enemies will build an embankment against you and encircle you and hem you in on every side. ...They will not leave one stone on another, because you did not recognize the time of God's coming to you."

Then Jesus entered the temple area and began driving out those who were selling. "It is written," he said to them, "'My house will be a house of prayer'; but you have made it a den of robbers" (Luke 19:46). "If the Temple system was to carry on, it was necessary that such facilities be provided. However, "it was not necessary that they should be in the Temple precincts, and it was to this that Jesus took exception. ...Luke does not mention those who bought nor the money-changers, but Matthew and Mark tell us that he dealt with them as well."[161]

Such could be calculated to especially offend the Sadducees, who considered the temple precincts their privileged domain. So it was that though they tolerated Jesus teaching daily in the temple area, they conspired with others to put him to death. "Yet they could not find any way to do it, because all the people hung on their words." On this and other occasions, Luke takes care to distinguish between the prevailing attitude of the Jewish hierarchy and the general populace.

One day when Jesus was teaching in the temple courts and *preaching the gospel*, certain of the religious leaders demanded: "Tell us by what authority you are doing these things?" (Luke 20:2). He replied: "Tell me, John's baptism--was it from heaven, or from men?" They discussed it among themselves. "If we say, 'From heaven,' he will ask, 'Why didn't you believe him?' But if we say, 'from men,' all the people will stone us, because they are persuaded that John was a prophet.'" So they answered: "We don't know where it was from." Jesus replied: "Neither will I tell you by what authority I am doing these things." Since dialogue with such biased and hostile people served no purpose, Jesus put an end to the discussion.

Matthew introduces a parable at this point. It seems that a man had two sons. He went to the first and said: "Son, go and work today in the vineyard" (Matt. 21:28). "I will not," he answered, but later he changed his mind and went. Then the father went to the other son, and said the same thing. "I will, sir," he said, but didn't keep his promise. "Which of the two did what his father wanted?" Jesus inquired. "The first," they replied. Jesus said to them: "I tell you the truth, the tax collectors and the prostitutes are entering the kingdom of God ahead of you."

Jesus also told a parable concerning certain tenants. A man planted a vineyard, rented it to some farmers and went away for an extended period. At harvest time, he sent a servant to the tenants so that they would give him some of the fruit of the vineyard. But the tenants beat him and sent him away empty-handed. He sent a second servant, and a third, but they treated them in like manner. At this, the owner decided to send his son, supposing they would respect him. But when the tenants saw him, they reasoned: "Let's kill him, and the inheritance will be ours." So this is what they did. "What then will the owner of the vineyard do to them?" Jesus raised a rhetorical question. "He will come and kill those tenants and give the vineyard to others." When the people heard this, they said: "May this never be!" Jesus looked directly at them and asked, "Then what is the meaning of that which is written: 'The stone the builders rejected has become the capstone'?" (Luke 20:17; cf. Psa. 18:22). The religious establishment looked for a way to arrest him, because they knew he had spoken this parable against them. But they were afraid of the people.

They hoped to catch Jesus in something he said. So it was that they sent persons to pose the question: "Is it right for us to pay taxes to Caesar or not?" Seeing through their duplicity, Jesus responded: "Show me a denarius. Whose portrait and inscription are on it?" "Caesar's," they replied. He said to them: "Then give to Caesar what is Caesar's and to God what is God's." They were unable to trap him in what he said, and were astonished at his answer.

Then some of the Sadducees, who say there is no resurrection, came to Jesus with a question: "Teacher, Moses wrote for us that if a man's brother dies and leaves a wife but no children, the man must marry the widow and have children for his brother. Now there were seven brothers. The first one married a woman and died childless." So it was with the remainder. "Finally, the woman died too. Now then, at the resurrection whose wife will she be, since the seven were married to her? Jesus replied: "You are in error because you do not know the Scriptures or the power of God. At the resurrection people will neither marry nor be given in marriage.... He is not God of the dead but of the living" (Matt. 22:29-30, 32).

After this, Jesus said to them: "How is that they say the Christ is the Son of David? ...David calls him *Lord.* How then can he be his son?" (Luke 20:41, 44). At which, Matthew observes: "No one could say a word in reply, and from that day on no one dared to ask him any more questions" (22:46). "Matthew rounds out this major section of his narrative by making the point that Jesus' opponents had to give up trying to outsmart Jesus or trap him in his words. The wisdom of Jesus the teacher has been vindicated. His opponents cannot so much as answer a *word*, and none dared to engage him in such debates again."[162]

As he looked up, Jesus observed the rich putting their gifts into the temple treasury. He also saw a poor widow put in two very small copper coins. "I tell you a truth," he said, "the poor widow has put in more than all the others. All these people gave their gifts out of their wealth, but she out of her poverty put in all she had to live on" (Luke 21:3-4). As sometimes said, the size of one's gift is not the amount given but in consideration of what is left.

Jesus left the temple and was walking away when his disciples called his attention to its construction. "I tell you the truth," he responded, "not one stone here will be left on another; every one will be thrown down" (Matt. 24:2). Then as he was sitting on the Mount of Olives, they asked him: "When will this happen, and what will be the sign of your coming and of the end of the age?" In Jesus' reply, he distinguished between *these things* (concerning the destruction of the temple), and *that day* (concerning the consummation). As for the former, when you witness such things as sacrilege in the temple (Matthew) or Jerusalem being surrounded by armies (Luke), you know that the desolation is near. "Then let those who are in Judea flee to the mountains. Let no one on the roof of his house go down to take anything out of the house. Let no one in the field go back to get his cloak."

As for the latter, "No one knows about that day or hour, not even the angels in heaven, nor the Son, but only the Father. As it was in the days of Noah, so it will be at the coming of the Son of Man. For in the days before the flood, people were eating and drinking, marrying and giving in marriage, up to the day Noah entered the ark" (Matt. 24:36-38). *But of that day and hour* marks a deliberate change of subject from *these things*. The analogy with *the days of Noah* suggests that persons will carry on their routine way of living without regard for what will most assuredly befall them. All things considered, one does not prepare for the consummation by calculating the time of its arrival, but by a life of constant devotion and vibrant expectation.

Now the Feast of Unleavened Bread was at hand, and the religious hierarchy continued to look for some way of disposing of Jesus (Luke 22:1-2). An opportunity presented itself when Judas approached them with the prospect of betraying him. They were delighted and agreed to reward him. It remained to find a convenient time.

Jesus subsequently directed Peter and John to make preparations for the Passover meal. "Where do you want us to prepare for it?" they asked. Jesus replied that once they entered the city, they would meet a man carrying a jar of water. They were to follow him to the house he would enter, and request from its owner the use of his upper room. *A man carrying a jar of water* would be unusual, since this was customarily a woman's task. Some have speculated that he was a celibate member of an Essene group quartered in Jerusalem. The disciples did as they were instructed, found things as Jesus told them, and prepared for the Passover meal.

When the hour was come, Jesus and his disciples reclined at the table. Then he said to them: "I have eagerly desired to eat this Passover with you before I suffer" (Luke 22:15). He subsequently took bread, gave thanks, broke it, and gave to his disciples. "This is my body given for you," he explained; "do this in remembrance of me." In the same way, after the supper he took the cup, saying: "This cup is the new covenant in my blood, which is poured out for you." Whatever chronology of the Last Supper one adopts, "it seems clear that Jesus instituted the Lord's Supper by associating it with the third cup of wine, which came after the Passover meal was eaten. It was known as the *cup of redemption*... . ...He refused, however, to drink the fourth cup (Mark 14:25), referred to as the *cup of consummation*. [163]

Jesus solemnly continued: "But the hand of him who is going to betray me is with mine on the table." The disciples began to question among themselves as to who this might be. There also arose a dispute among them as to which of them should be considered greatest. Whereupon, Jesus said to them: "The kings of the Gentiles lord it over them, and those who exercise authority over them call themselves Benefactors. But you are not to be like that. Instead, the greatest among you should be like the youngest, and the one who rules like the one who serves."

Turning his attention to Peter, Jesus observed: "Simon, Simon, Satan has asked to sift you as wheat. But I have prayed for you, Simon, that your faith may not fail. And when you have turned back, strengthen your brothers." Peter confidently replied: "Lord, I am ready to go with you to prison and to death." Jesus answered: "I tell you, Peter, before the rooster crows today, you will deny three times that you know me."

Jesus went out as usual to the Mount of Olives and his disciples followed him. On reaching his destination, he admonished them: "Pray that you will not fall into temptation." He then withdrew about a stone's throw beyond them and prayed: "Father, if you are willing, take this cup from me; yet not my will, but yours be done." At this, an angel appeared to strengthen him. Being in anguish, he prayed more earnestly, and his sweat was like drops of blood falling to the ground. When he returned to his disciples, he found them asleep--worn out from their grief. "Why are you sleeping?" he inquired. "Get up and pray so that you will not fall into temptation."

While Jesus was still speaking, a crowd appeared led by Judas. When he approached Jesus to kiss him, Jesus asked him: "Judas, are you betraying the Son of Man with a kiss?" When Jesus' followers saw this, they inquired: "Lord, should we strike with our swords?" Then one of them (identified by John as Peter) struck the servant of the high priest, cutting off his right ear. "No more of this," Jesus commanded, and healed the man. Then he said to them: "Am I leading a rebellion, that you have come with swords and clubs? Every day I was with you in the temple courts, and you did not lay a hand on me. But this is your hour--when darkness reigns." "The darkness of night symbolizes the moral and spiritual darkness of the moment. When Jesus taught in the temple during the daylight hours the religious authorities were afraid to act, but no, under the cover of darkness, and away from the purified temple, they act."[164]

Then seizing him, they led Jesus away to the house of the high priest. Peter followed at a distance. But when they had kindled a fire in the middle of the courtyard and sat down together, Peter sat down with them. A servant girl saw him seated there in the firelight, and observed: "This man was with him." "Woman, I don't know him," Peter responded. A little later, someone else saw him and said: "You also are one of them" "Man, I am not!" Peter exclaimed. About an hour later, another asserted: "Certainly this fellow was with him, for he is a Galilean." Peter replied: "Man, I don't know what you're talking about!" Just as he was speaking the rooster crowed. At this, the Lord turned and looked straight at Peter. Then Peter remembered what Jesus had said to him, and he went out and wept bitterly.

Following Jesus' arrest, he was mocked and suffered just as he predicted. Since he was acknowledged as a prophet by the people, "he was blindfolded and asked to prophesy who beat him. ...Throughout the scene, however, we sense that he who predicted that all these things would take place was in charge and was allowing this to take place in order to fulfill the divine plan."[165] At daybreak the Sanhedrin met to interrogate Jesus. "If you are the Christ," they said, "tell us." Jesus answered: "If I tell you, you will not believe me, and if I asked you, you would not answer. But from now on, the Son of Man will be seated at the right hand of the mighty God." "Are you then the Son of God?" they inquired. Jesus replied: "You are right in saying I am." At this, they concluded: "Why do we need any more testimony? We have heard it from his own lips." Jesus' words appeared to them as blasphemous.

Then the whole assembly rose and led him off to Pilate. Upon their arrival, they began to accuse Jesus, saying: "We found this man subverting our nation. He opposes payment of taxes to Caesar and claims to be Christ, a king." So Pilate asked him: "Are you the king of the Jews?" "Yes, it is as you say," Jesus answered. Then Pilate announced to the chief priests and the crowd: "I find no basis for a charge against this man. But they insisted: "He stirs up the people all over Judea by his teaching. He started in Galilee and has come all the way here." On hearing this, Pilate asked if he were a Galilean. Since he was within Herod's jurisdiction, and Herod was in Jerusalem at the time, Pilate ordered that Jesus be taken before him.

Herod was delighted to see Jesus, because he hoped that he would perform some miracle. He questioned Jesus at length, but Jesus refused to respond. The religious leaders continued to vehemently accuse him. Then Herod and his soldiers ridiculed and mocked him. Dressing him in an elegant role, they sent him back to Pilate. With a touch of irony, Luke observes that as a result Herod and Pilate became friends.

Pilate called together the religious leaders and the people, and said to them: "You brought me this man as one who was inciting the people to rebellion. I have examined him in your presence and have found no basis for your charges against him. Neither has Herod... . Therefore, I will punish him and then release him." With one voice they cried out: "Away with this man! Release Barabbas to us!" Luke observes that Barabbas was thrown into prison for insurrection and murder. Wanting to release Jesus, Pilate again appealed to them. But they kept shouting: "Crucify him! Crucify him!" For a third time he spoke to them: "Why? What crime has this man committed? I have found in him no grounds for the death penalty. Therefore I will have him punished and then release him." But *their shouts prevailed.*

As they led Jesus away to be crucified, a large number of people followed--including women who mourned and wailed for him. Jesus turned and said to them: "Daughters of Jerusalem, do not weep for me; weep for yourselves and for your children. ...For if men do these things when the tree is green, what will happen when it is dry?" (Luke 23:28, 31). No doubt a proverbial saying, it would seem to suggest that if this would happen to one who is innocent, much greater will be the suffering of those who are culpable.

Two other men, both criminals, were also led out with him to be executed. When they came to the place called the Skull, there they crucified him, along with the criminals--one on his right, the other on his left. "In this form of execution a person was fastened by ropes or nails to a cross.... . There was a horn-like projection which the crucified straddled, which took most of the weight and stopped the flesh from tearing from the nails. ...Crucifixion was a slow and painful death."[166] The synoptic writers focus our attention on other concerns. "Father, forgive them," Jesus interceded, "for they do not know what they are doing."

They divided his clothes by casting lots. The people stood watching. In contrast to their silence, *the rulers* sneered: "He saved others; let him save himself if he is the Christ of God, the Chosen One." The soldiers joined in: "If you are the king of the Jews, save yourself. One of the criminals likewise hurled insults at him: "Aren't you the Christ? Save yourself and us!" But the other rebuked him: "Don't you fear God, since you are under the same sentence? We are punished justly, for we are getting what our deeds deserve. But this man has done nothing wrong." Then he said: "Jesus, remember me when you come into your kingdom." Jesus answered: "I tell you the truth, today you will be with me in paradise."

It was about the sixth hour (noon) when darkness came over the whole land until the ninth hour, and the curtain of the temple was torn in two. Perhaps neither could be readily explained. The impact on those who had witnessed the spectacle of the crucifixion and now this eerie disturbance in nature must have been profound. "Let the normal processes of nature be unaccountably disturbed, and men's sense of insecurity will make them conscious...of their own littleness, and of the awesomeness of God... ."[167] Since *the curtain of the temple* symbolized God's remoteness, its rending would signify accessibility.

Jesus called out with a loud voice: "Father, into your hands I commit my spirit." When he had said this, he breathed his last. The centurion, seeing what had happened, praised God and said: "Surely this was a righteous man." The people, who had come to view a spectacle, beat their breasts in grief. Those who had followed Jesus stood at a distance, watching the dramatic events unfold.

They laid Jesus' body in a tomb belonging to Joseph of Arimathea, a member of the Sanhedrin and a good man. Then the women who had come with Jesus from Galilee went home and prepared spices and perfumes. But they rested on the Sabbath as enjoined in the Torah. On the first day of the week they took the spices they had prepared, and made their way to the tomb. They found the stone rolled away, and Jesus' body absent. While they were wondering about this, suddenly two glowing figures appeared to them. "Why do you look for the living among the dead" they inquired. "He is not here; he has risen!" (Luke 24:5-6). When the women returned, they told the eleven and those with them of all these things.

Now that same day two of the disciples were going to a village called Emmaus. As they discussed what had transpired, Jesus himself came up and walked along with them--but they were kept from recognizing him. He asked them: "What are you discussing together as you walk along?" One of them replied: "Are you only a visitor to Jerusalem and do not know the things that have happened there in these days?" "What things?" Jesus responded. "About Jesus of Nazareth," they answered. "He was a prophet, powerful in word and deed before God and all the people. The chief priests and our rulers handed him over to be sentenced to death, and they crucified him... . In addition, some of our women...told us that they had seen a vision of angels, who said he was alive." Still later, as Jesus was breaking bread with them, their eyes were opened and they recognized him. Then, after he disappeared, they returned to Jerusalem to share their experience with the others.

While they were still talking, Jesus stood among them and said: "Peace be with you." They were frightened, supposing they saw a ghost. He said to them: "Look at my hands and my feet. It is I myself! Touch me and see; a ghost does not have flesh and bones, as you see I have." "This is what I told you while I was still with you," Jesus continued. "Everything must be fulfilled that is written about me in the Law of Moses, the Prophets and the Psalms."

Mark's short ending concludes with the women at the tomb. Matthew adds Jesus' commission to disciple all nations. Luke will pick up the story line with Jesus' ascension to add an extended treatment with *Acts*. As such, the *Synoptic Gospels* conclude not with a period but an exclamation mark.

FOURTH GOSPEL

The *Fourth Gospel* combines a simple literary style with profound insight. Early tradition assigns it to John the apostle, in keeping with the author's claim to be an eyewitness to the events that transpired (1:4), seeming allusion to himself as *the disciple whom Jesus loved* (19:26; 20:2; 21:7, 20), and his familiarity with historical detail. While not necessarily excluding John, others associate it with his apostolic mission, thereby involving others. This, it is said, would accommodate the allusion to "we know" (21:24), differences in writing style, and supposed late first century composition. To state the obvious, these features could be accounted for otherwise.

"In the beginning was the Word, and the Word was with God, and the Word was God" (1:1). "The purpose of the Gospel writer is to place the story of Jesus in a cosmic perspective. The word that created all things, as well as the life that it created, now finds expression in a particular person and a particular life lived *among us.*"[168]

In the above connection, we recall the creation refrain: *And God said.* So it is that we read in Isaiah: "As the rain and the snow come down from heaven, and do not return to it without watering the earth and making it bud and flourish, so that it yields seed for the sower and bread for the eater, so is my word that goes out from my mouth: it will not return to me empty, but will accomplish what I desire and achieve the purpose for which I sent it" (55:10-11). Herein, the prophet emphasizes the *efficacy* of God's word, and bears witness to a rich theological tradition from which John liberally draws.

John the Baptist bore witness of him, saying: "He who comes after me has surpassed me because he was before me." John the apostle comments: "From the fullness of his grace we have all received one blessing after another. For the law was given through Moses; grace and truth came through Jesus Christ." The contrasts in this verse are not solely between law and grace, and between Moses and Jesus,"but between *was given* and *came.* Grace and truth are as much gifts of God as the law;

but, while the law can be separated from Moses the lawgiver, and is in some of its aspects of a temporary nature, grace and truth cannot be separated from Him in whom they are embodied."[169]

On a certain day, John saw Jesus coming toward him and said: "Look, the Lamb of God, who takes away the sin of the world" (1:29). The next day, John again referred to Jesus as the *Lamb of God*, and was overheard by two of his disciples. They, in turn, followed him. One of these was Andrew, Simon Peter's brother. After spending time with Jesus, the first thing that he did was to find Simon and tell him: "We have found the Messiah." Then, he brought him to Jesus. Jesus looked at the new arrival and said: "You are Simon son of John. You will be called Cephas (Peter)." All things considered, the *Lamb of God* seems to recall the *suffering servant* motif. As a case in point, "But he was pierced for our transgressions, he was crushed for our iniquities; the punishment that brought us peace was upon him, and by his wounds we are healed" (Isa. 53:5). *Cephas* means rock, a characterizing name perhaps implying *stalwart*. If so, this would seem a classic example of Jesus perceiving a person not for what he was but would become. After this, Jesus called other disciples.

Now a wedding took place at Cana in Galilee. Jesus' mother was there, and Jesus and his disciples were also invited. When the wine was gone, Mary reported the matter to her son. "Dear woman, why do you involve me?" Jesus replied. "My time is not yet come" (2:4). Mary said to the servants: "Do whatever he tells you." Nearby stood six stone water jars, each holding from twenty to thirty gallons. Jesus said to the servants: "Fill the jars with water," so they filled them to the brim. Then he told them: "Draw some out and take it to the master of the banquet." When the master had tasted of the waster turned to wine, he called the bridegroom aside and commented: "Everyone brings out the choice wine first and then the cheaper wine after the guests have had too much to drink; but you have saved the best till now." At this, John observes: "This, the first of his miraculous signs, Jesus performed in Cana of Galilee. He thus revealed his glory , and his disciples put their faith in him."

Miracle stories as a rule consist of the setting, the act itself, and an astonished response from the audience. The most distinctive feature about Jesus' miracles is that they attest to his authority. As such, they resemble an earnest of things yet to come. This would not be the last of Jesus' *miraculous signs*. In retrospect, John writes: "Jesus did many other miraculous signs in the presence of his disciples, which are not recorded in this book. But these are written that you may believe that Jesus is the Christ, the Son of God, and that by believing you may have life in his name" (20:30-31). He records such as would serve his design *that they might believe.*

Now there was a Pharisee named *Nicodemus,* a member of the Sanhedrin. He came to Jesus by night, and said: "Rabbi, we know you are a teacher who has come from God. For no one could perform the miraculous signs you are doing if God were not with him" (3:2). Jesus replied: "I tell you the truth, no one can see the kingdom of God unless he is born again." "How can a man be born when he is old?" Nicodemus asked. "Surely he cannot enter a second time into the mother's womb to be born!" Jesus answered: "I tell you the truth, no one can enter the kingdom of God unless he is born of water and the Spirit. Flesh gives birth to flesh, and the Spirit gives birth to spirit." In context, *water* appears a reference to physical birth.

After this, Jesus expanded on the notion of *belief.* "For God so loved the world that he gave his one and only Son, that whoever believes in him shall not perish but have eternal life. For God did not send his Son into the world to condemn the world, but to save the world through him. Whoever believes on him is not condemned, but whoever does not believe stands condemned already because he has not believed in the name of God's one and only Son."

On another occasion, Jesus was returning from Judea to Galilee by way of Samaria. He paused by Jacob's well, since he was tired from the journey. When a Samaritan woman came to draw water, Jesus inquired: "Will you give me a drink?" (4:7). She replied: "You are a Jew and I am a Samaritan woman. How can you ask me for a drink?" John explains: "For Jews do not associate with Samaritans." Jesus answered: "If you knew the gift of God and who it is that asks you for a drink, you would have asked him and he would have given you living water." "Sir," the woman responded, "you have nothing to draw with and the well is deep. Where can you get this living water?" Jesus answered: "Everyone who drinks this water will be thirsty again, but whoever drinks the water I give him will never thirst. Indeed, the water I give him will become in him a spring of water welling up to eternal life." The woman responded: "Sir, give me this water so that I won't get thirsty and have to keep coming here to draw water."

The Samaritan woman takes the words literally. "Jesus' promise of the Spirit and eternal life means only that she will never have to come back to this well to draw water! This sequence ends in misunderstanding, yet the woman's remark is curiously apt, for when the Spirit comes, such holy places as the well of Jacob will in fact lose their significance."[170]

Jesus' 'subsequent reply signals a turn in the narrative. "Go, call your husband and come back," he instructed her. "I have no husband," she replied. "You are right when you say you have no husband," Jesus allowed. "The fact is, you have had five husbands, and the man you now have is not your husband." "Sir," the woman responded, "I can see that you are a prophet. Our fathers worshiped on this mountain, but you Jews claim that the place where we must worship is in Jerusalem. Jesus declared: "Believe me, woman, a time is coming...and now has come when the true worshipers will worship the Father in spirt and truth, for they are the kind of worshipers the Father seeks. God is spirit, and his worshipers must worship in spirit and in truth." The woman said: "I know that Messiah is coming. When he comes, he will explain everything to us." Then Jesus revealed: "I who speak to you am he."

Then, leaving her water jar, the woman went back to the town and said to the people: "Come, see a man who told me everything I ever did. Could this be the Christ?" So when the Samaritans came to him, they urged Jesus to stay with them, and he remained for two days. After this, they said to the woman: "We no longer believe just because of what you said; now we have heard for ourselves, and we know that this man really is the Savior of the world."

Some time after this, Jesus crossed to the far shore of the Sea of Galilee, and a great crowd of people followed him. When Jesus looked up and saw the multitude coming toward him, he asked Philip: "Where shall we buy bread for these people to eat?" (6:5). Philip responded: "Eight months wages would not buy enough bread for each one to have a bite!" Andrew volunteered: "Here is a boy with five small barley loaves and two small fish, but how far will they go among so many?" Jesus replied: "Have the people sit down." He then took the loaves, gave thanks, and distributed to people--as much as they wanted. So also with the fish. When they had eaten, the disciples filled twelve baskets with the bread that remained.

After the people saw this miraculous sign, they began to say: "Surely this is the Prophet who is come into the world." Jesus, perceiving that they intended to force him to become king, withdrew again to a mountain by himself. Later on, he would respond to Pilate: "My kingdom is not of this world. If it were, my servants would fight to prevent my arrest by the Jews. But now my kingdom is from another place" (18:36-37).

Jesus subsequently asserted: "I am the bread of life. He who comes to me will never go hungry, and he who believes in me will never be thirsty" (6:35). Such should have been received with gratitude. Instead, they grumbled, much as had the Israelites concerning God's giving them manna to eat in the wilderness. "From this time many of his disciples turned back and no longer followed him."

Now it was time for the Feast of Tabernacles. Jesus arrived late and in secret. Among the pilgrim crowds there was widespread whispering about him. Some said: "He is a good man" (7:12). Others replied: "No, he deceives the people." Not until halfway through the Feast did Jesus go up to the temple courts and begin to teach. Those who heard him were amazed and asked: "How did this man get such learning without having studied?" Jesus answered: "My teaching is not my own. It comes from him who sent me. If anyone chooses to do God's will, he will find out whether my teaching comes from God or whether I speak on my own."

On the last day of the Feast, Jesus stood and declared in a loud voice: "If anyone is thirsty, let him come to me and drink. Whoever believes in me, as the Scripture has said, streams of living water will flow from within him." On hearing this, some said: "surely this man is the Prophet." Others said: "He is the Christ." Still others asked: "How can the Christ come from Galilee?" "No one ever spoke the way this man does," the temple guards reported. "You mean he has deceived you also?" the Pharisees retorted. "Has any of the rulers or of the Pharisees believed in him? No! But this mob that knows nothing of the law--there is a curse on them." Nicodemus inquired: "Does our law condemn anyone without first hearing him to find out what he is doing?" They replied: "Are you from Galilee, too? Look into it, and you will find that a prophet does not come out of Galilee."

As Jesus walked along, he saw a man born blind. "Rabbi," his disciples asked him, "who sinned, this man or his parents, that he was born blind?" (9:2). "Neither this man nor his parents," Jesus replied, "but this happened so that the work of God might be displayed in his life." Having said this, he spit on the ground, made some mud with the saliva, and put it on the man's eyes. "Go," he told him, "wash in the Pool of Siloam." So the man went and washed, and went home seeing. "This miracle is a sign that Jesus can open the eyes of the spiritually blind so that they can receive the complete sight which constitutes perfect faith. Faith means passing from darkness to light; and to bring men to faith...is the primary purpose for which Jesus has been sent into the world."[171] It moreover dismisses the idea that there is a simple correlation between sin and physical affliction, much as does *Job* at an earlier date.

Now the healing took place on the Sabbath. Therefore, the Pharisees asked the man how he had received his sight. "He put mud on my eyes," the man replied, "and I washed, and now I see." Some of the Pharisees concluded: "This man is not from God, for he does not keep the Sabbath." But others asked: "How can a sinner do such miraculous signs?" So they were divided. Finally, they turned to the man: "What have you to say about him? It was your eyes he opened." The man replied: "He is a prophet."

Having confirmed that the man was born blind, they again summoned the man. "Give glory to God," they said. "We know this man is a sinner." He responded: "Whether he is a sinner or not, I don't know. One thing I do know. I was blind but now I see!" They repeated their earlier question. He answered: "I have told you already and you did not listen. Why do you want to hear it again? Do you want to become his disciples, too?" "You are this fellow's disciple!" they impugned. "We are disciples of Moses! We know that God spoke to Moses, but as for this fellow, we don't even know where he comes from." The man responded: "Now that is remarkable! You don't know where he comes from, yet he opened my eyes. ...If this man were not from God, he could do nothing." To this they replied: "You were steeped in sin at birth; how dare you lecture us!" With that they threw him out (excommunicated him).

When Jesus heard of this, he found the man and asked: "Do you believe in the Son of Man?" "Who is he, sir?" the man inquired. "Tell me so that I may believe in him." Jesus said: "You have now seen him; in fact, he is the one speaking with you." Then the man said: "Lord, I believe." After this, Jesus told a story concerning the good shepherd. "I am the good shepherd," he declared. "The good shepherd lays down his life for the sheep." "I am the good shepherd," he repeated; "I know my sheep and my sheep know me... . I have other sheep that are not of this sheep pen. I must bring them also. They too will listen to my voice, and there shall be one flock and one shepherd."

Now a man named *Lazarus* was sick. He was from Bethany, and the brother of Mary and Martha. So the sisters sent word to Jesus: "Lord, the one you love is sick" (11:1). When he heard this, Jesus said: "This sickness will not end in death. No, it is for God's glory." After two days, Jesus proposed to his disciples: "Let us go back to Judea." "But Rabbi," they replied, "s short while ago the Jews tried to stone you, and yet you are going back there?" Jesus speaks to their concern about the danger of returning to Judea with a kind of riddle, "contrasting the safety of the daylight hours with the perils of traveling at night. The riddle is an elaborate way of saying what has been said several times before, that Jesus' hour (i.e., the hour of his death) has not yet come and that until it comes he is perfectly safe."[172]

After this, Jesus went on to tell them: "Our friend Lazarus has fallen asleep; but I am going there to wake him up." His disciples replied: "Lord, if he sleeps, he will get better." So then he said to them plainly: "Lazarus is dead, and for your sake I am glad I was not there, so that you may believe. But let us go to him." Then Thomas encouraged the rest: "Let us also go, that we may die with him." In this regard, he perhaps picked up on the *suffering servant* motif.

On his arrival, Jesus found that Lazarus had already been in the tomb for four days. "Lord," Martha greeted Jesus, "if you had been here, my brother would not have died. But I know that even now God will give you whatever you ask." Jesus said to her: "Your brother will live again." She replied: "I know he will rise again in the resurrection at the last day." He responded: "I am the resurrection and the life. He who believes in me will live, even though he dies; and whoever lives and believes in me will never die. Do you believe this?" "Yes, Lord," she confessed. "I believe that you are the Christ, the Son of God, who was to come into the world."

When Mary reached the place where Jesus was, she fell at his feet and said: "Lord, if you had been here, my brother would not have died." When Jesus saw her weeping, and those who had come with her weeping, he was deeply moved. "Where have you laid him?" he asked. "Come and see, Lord," they replied. Jesus wept. Then the Jews observed: "See how much he loved him!" But some of them questioned: "Could not he who opened the eyes of the blind man have kept this man from dying?"

Once they had reached the tomb, Jesus ordered that they remove the stone which covered its entrance. "But Lord," Martha protested, " by this time there is a bad odor, for he has been there four days." Jesus inquired: "Did I not tell you that if you believed, you would see the glory of God?" So they took away the stone. After this, Jesus looked up and said: "Father, I thank you that you have heard me. I knew that you always hear me, but I said this for the benefit of the people standing here, that they may believe that you sent me." When he had said this, he called in a loud voice: "Lazarus, come out!" So he did, his hands and feet wrapped with strips of linen, and a cloth around his face. Jesus said to them: "Take off the grave clothes and let him go."

John buttresses this *miraculous sign* in at least three ways. First, it was witnessed by those present. Second, the incident was widely published. Third, it sparked "Gentile interest. John was not unmindful of the differences in religious background between Jews and their pagan neighbors. Time had already illustrated Jesus' appeal across religious/cultural boundaries, and John affirms that it was so from the beginning."[173] Why, then, did not more believe? As a matter of record, "Even after Jesus had done all these miraculous signs in their presence, they still would not believe in him˙ (12:37). This fulfilled the prophesy of Isaiah concerning the hardness of man's heart. In addition, there were social pressures which kept some from speaking out, and others from deriving their counsel (12:42).

Then Jesus cried out: "When a man believes in me, he does not believe in me only, but in the one who sent me. When he looks at me, he sees the one who sent me. I have come into the world as a light, so that no one who believes in me should stay in darkness" (12:44-46). "As for the person who hears my words but does not keep them, I do not judge him. ...There is a judge for the one who rejects me and does not accept my words; that very word which I spoke will condemn him at the last day."

"Do not let your hearts be troubled," Jesus encouraged his disciples (14:1). "Trust in God; trust also in me. In my Father's house are many rooms; if it were not so, I would have told you. I am going there to prepare a place for you. And if I go to prepare a place for you, I will come back and take you to be with me that you may be where I am." Thomas said to him: "Lord, we don't know where you are going, so how can we know the way?" Jesus answered: "I am the way and the truth and the life. No one comes to the Father except through me." Jesus is not *a way* but *the way*. He does not simply teach truth but embodies it. He does not merely exemplify life but defines it.

"All this I have spoken while still with you," Jesus observed (14:25). "But the Counselor, the Holy Spirit, whom the Father will send in my name, will teach you all things and will remind you of everything I have said to you. Peace I leave with you... . I do not give to you as the world gives. Do not let your heart be troubled and do not be afraid." In this and other ways, Jesus prepared his disciples for the time when he would no longer be with them.

After Jesus had finished speaking, he looked toward heaven and prayed for his disciples: "Sanctify them by the truth; your word is truth. ...My prayer is not for them alone. I pray also for those who will believe in me through their message, that all of them may be one, Father, just as you are in me and I am in you. May they also be in us so that the world may believe that you have sent me" (17:17, 21). Consecrated for God's service, and joined together in their life and ministry, they would provide a convincing witness. Lacking in either regard, their credibility would flounder.

John's passion account differs less from the *Synoptic Gospels* than his text up to this point. With such in mind, several narrative additions will suffice. Near the cross of Jesus stood his mother, his mother's sister, Mary the wife of Clopas, and Mary Magdalene. When Jesus saw his mother there, and the disciple whom he loved, he said to her: "Dear woman, here is your son," and to the disciple: "Here is your mother" (19:26-27). From that time on, this disciple took her into his home. Since a primary responsibility associated in honoring one's father and mother involved providing for their needs in their declining years, Jesus entrusted this obligation to the disciple. From the perspective of a disciple, this would be an honor and privilege.

The Jews petitioned Pilate to have the legs of the crucified broken, so as to hasten their death, and their bodies could be removed before the Sabbath. The soldiers consequently broke the legs of the two criminals, but when they came to Jesus they found that he was already dead. Instead, one of the soldiers pierced Jesus' side with a spear, bringing a sudden flow of blood and water. John moreover adds: "The man who saw it has given testimony, and his testimony is true. He knows that he tells the truth, and he testifies so that you also may believe" (19:35). The physician John Cameron comments: As a Roman, the soldier would be well trained, proficient, and would know his duty. "He would know which part of the body to pierce so as to "obtain a speedily fatal result or ensure that the victim was undeniably dead. ...Blood from the greatly engorged veins, pulmonary vessel and dilated right side of the heart, together with water from the acutely dilated stomach, would flow forth in abundance."[174] His demise was not apparent but actual.

In response to the report that the tomb was empty, Peter and *the disciple Jesus loved* raced to see what had happened. The latter reached the tomb first, and when he looked in he saw the strips of linen lying there. When Peter arrived, he went into the tomb and saw both the strips of linen and burial cloth that was around Jesus' head. The cloth was folded by itself. Finally, the other disciple went inside. Whereupon, "He saw and believed" (20:8). By way of commentary, Craig Keener observes: that the face cloth separate from the linen was not merely "*folded up* (NIV) but *rolled up* (NASB, NRSV, TEV), which could be an indication of neatness, or that it was still rolled the way it had been when it was wrapped around Jesus' head--that his body had risen straight out of the wrappings and cloth."[175].

Now Thomas was not with the other disciples when Jesus appeared to them. So they said to him: "We have seen the Lord!" (20:25). He skeptically responded: "Unless I see the nail marks in his hands and put my finger where the nails are, and put my hand into his side, I will not believe it." A week later his disciples were together again, and Thomas was with them. Though the doors were locked, Jesus came and stood among them, and said: "Peace be with you!" Then he said to Thomas: "Put your finger here; see my hands. Reach out your hand and put it into my side. Stop doubting and believe." Thomas said to him: "My Lord and my God!" After this, Jesus told him: "Because you have seen me, you have believed; blessed are those who have not seen and yet have believed."

On another occasion, Jesus again appeared to his disciples. "I'm going out to fish," Peter announced (21:3). Certain of the others replied: "We'll go with you." So they went out but that night they caught nothing. Early the next morning, Jesus stood on the shore, but the disciples didn't know it was him. He called out to them: "Friends, haven't you any fish?" "No," they answered. He said: "Throw out your net on the right side of the boat and you will find some." When they did so, they were unable to haul the net in because of the large number of fish. Then the disciple whom Jesus loved said to Peter: "It is the Lord!"

When they had finished eating, Jesus said to Peter: "Simon son of John, do you truly love me more than these?" "*More than these* may mean *either* 'more than these others do', in which case Jesus would be recalling to Peter's mind the boastful assertion he had made before the passion, or 'more than you love anything else'. Perhaps both meanings are implied."[176] "Yes, Lord," Peter answered, "you know that I love you." "Feed my sheep," Jesus responded. Twice more Jesus inquires, twice more Peter responds affirmatively, and twice more Jesus enjoins him to minister. In this connection, his three affirmations correspond to his three earlier denials.

"Jesus did many other things as well," John concludes. "If every one of them were written down, I suppose that even the whole world would not have room for the books that would be written." So are we to assume that all of the gospels taken together contain no more than a fragmentary account of Jesus's earthly sojourn.

PENTECOST

"In my former book," Luke allows, "I wrote about all that Jesus began to do and to teach until the day he was taken up to heaven, after giving instructions through the Holy Spirit to the apostle he had chosen. After his suffering, he showed himself to these men and gave many convincing proofs that he was alive" (Acts 1:1-3). Thus he focuses our attention on a two-part work designated as *Luke/Acts*. In a more extended fashion, Luke begins his account with the reign of Herod the Great, whose obsession with building is still evident at Jerusalem, the Herodion, and Masada. "However, we must begin our historical review at an earlier point. All that Luke writes presupposes a grasp of the Old Testament in general and the nature of God's covenant in particular."[177]

As we earlier observed, the covenant set forth God's sovereign rule over his people. They, in turn, might anticipate his ample provision. If, however, they fail to abide by its stipulations, life would begin to unravel. So it was that Stephen complained: "You stiff-necked people, with uncircumcised hearts and ears! You always resist the Holy Spirit! Was there ever a prophet your fathers did not persecute? ...And now you have betrayed and murdered (the Righteous One)--you who have received the law that was put into effect through angels but have not obeyed it" (7:51-53).

A common theme running through *Luke/Acts* "is the atoning sacrifice of Christ. Jesus is come that men everywhere may experience God's redemption. ...The sacrifice took place, not in the privileged sanctuary of a temple, but on a hill outside the city wall, where a mixed multitude wandered aimlessly to and fro."[178] Two examples, one from *Luke* and the other from *Acts*, will suffice. They crucified Jesus between two criminals. "Jesus," one of them pled, "remember me when you come into your kingdom" (Luke 23:42). Jesus confidently assured him: "I tell you the truth, today you will be with me in paradise." While the hour was late, the occasion was opportune. In this interchange, Luke records an act of salvation in context where "the word *save* has been used in taunts and ridicule. Three times he has been mocked with *save yourself*, the lone criminal adding *and us*. Here Jesus does save someone, and that the one saved is a dying criminal is totally congenial to the types of persons blessed by Jesus through his ministry."[179]

Once the Holy Spirit had come, Peter was asked for his guidance. He responded: "Repent and be baptized, everyone of you, in the name of Jesus Christ so that your sins may be forgiven. And you will receive the gift of the Holy spirit" (Acts 2:38). Those who accepted his counsel were baptized, and about three thousand were added to the community of faith that day. "*Repentance* and *faith*, as related to the Pentecost event, resemble two sides of a coin. This can be seen from their setting, where the admonition to repent and acceptance leading to baptism appear in parallel construction. Those who repent believe, and those who believe repent."[180]

As noted above, the Holy Spirit plays a prominent role in this redemptive narrative. So it was that the angel announced to Mary: "The Holy Spirit will come upon you, and the power of the Most High will overshadow you. So the holy one to be born will be called the Son of God" (Luke 1:35). He also appears at Jesus' baptism (3:22), at the beginning of his temptation (4:1), and the announcement of his ministry (4:18). In these and other regards, he keeps a low visibility in deference to Jesus as the Christ of God.

With the transition from *Luke* to *Acts*, we encounter Christ in community. It was nonetheless in a qualified sense *a community of the Spirit*. One ignored this fact at his or her peril, as evidenced by the case of Ananias and Sapphira. They agreed to keep back a portion of the sale of property under pretense of contributing the entire amount. "Ananias," Peter addressed the man, "how is it that Satan has so filled your heart that you have lied to the Holy Spirit and have kept for yourself some of the money you received for the land? Didn't it belong to you before it was sold? And after it was sold, wasn't the money at your disposal?" (5:3-4). When Ananias heard this, he fell down and died. About three hours later, Sapphira came in. "Tell me," Peter inquired, "is this the price you and Ananias got for the land?" "Yes," she replied. Peter responded: "How could you agree to test the Spirit of the Lord? Look! The feet of the men who buried your husband are at the door, and they will carry you out also."

Luke likewise accents the *joy* that attended the coming of Jesus and subsequent indwelling of the Holy Spirit. So it was that when the shepherds returned they were "glorifying and praising God for all the things they had heard and seen" (Luke 2:20). So also "the people were delighted with all the wonderful things he was doing" (13:17). So likewise Peter quoted from the *Psalter* on the occasion of Pentecost: "You have made known to me the paths of life; and will fill me with joy in your presence" (Acts 2:28; cf. Psa. 16:11).

There are other distinctive characteristics of *Luke/Acts* that are perhaps more loosely related to the salvation theme. *Prayer* serves a prime case in point. Luke describes Jesus praying at his baptism (Luke 3:21), in private moments with growing opposition (5:16), following conflict and before choosing the Twelve (6:12), before gathering feedback from His disciples as to whom the crowd thought Him to be (9:18), at the transfiguration (9:29), and from the cross (23:46).[181] The apostles moreover devoted themselves "to prayer and the ministry of the word" (Acts 6:4), and when Peter was imprisoned, "the church was earnestly praying to God for him" (12:15).

On one occasion, while Jesus was eating with his disciples, he gave them instruction: "Do not leave Jerusalem, but wait for the gift my Father promised, which you have heard me speak about. For John baptized with water, but in a few days you will be baptized with the Holy Spirit" (1:4-5). In particular, baptism symbolized death and resurrection: death to the former life and birth of its spiritual replacement. Even so, the analogy seems strained to account for the transformation envisaged. One could little imagine how dramatic an event would transpire in the near future.

When they met together, they asked him: "Lord, are you at this time going to restore the kingdom to Israel?" He responded to them: "It is not for you to know the times or dates the Father has set by his own authority. But you will receive power when the Holy Spirit comes on you; and you will be my witnesses in Jerusalem, and in all Judea and Samaria, and to the ends of the earth" (1:7-8). As in the prior instances, he encouraged them not to speculate on future events but to take up the task at hand. In order to do so, they would soon be endowed with power from on high.

After he had said this, he was taken up before their very eyes, and a cloud hid him from their sight. They were gazing intently into the heavens when suddenly two men dressed in white stood beside them. "Men of Galilee," they said, "why do you stand here looking into the sky? This same Jesus, who has been taken from you into heaven, will come back in the same way you have seen him go into heaven." Their question was an implicit reproach of the disciples dawdling there rather than getting on with the agenda set for them. More in general, it serves as a rebuke for those who opt for a sentimental journey rather than harvesting.

Then they returned to Jerusalem from the Mount of Olives, a Sabbath day's journey (about 3/4 of a mile). They had established themselves in an upstairs room, perhaps the same as served for the Last Supper. If so, it was likely in the vicinity of the modern day *Cenacle*. Bellarmino Bagatti comments: "Disregarding the later additions and the medieval structures, whose scope throughout the centuries was to preserve the liturgical memory, we find a corner of the building, that to the southeast has, without any doubt, an ancient piece that must be taken into consideration."[182] In particular, he supposes that it is a remnant of a first century Jewish-Christian synagogue that commemorates the event and served as a place of assembly.

The apostles joined together in prayer, along with the women and Mary the mother of Jesus, and his brothers. In those days Peter stood up among the believers (a group numbering about 120), and proposed that they select one who would take Judas' place. "Therefore," he concluded, "it is necessary to choose one of the men who have been with us the whole time the Lord Jesus went in and out among us, beginning from John's baptism to the time when Jesus was taken up from us. For one of these must become a witness with us of the resurrection" (1:21-22). So they proposed two men: Joseph called Barsabbas and Matthias. After this, they prayed and cast lots, and the lot fell to Matthias. As for *casting lots*, it was a legitimate means, but we do not hear of its subsequent use-- which may suggest that with the coming of the Holy Spirit it was thought unnecessary.

When the day of Pentecost was come, they were all together in one place. Suddenly a sound like the blowing of a violent wind came from heaven and filled the whole house where they were sitting. They saw what seemed to be tongues of fire that separated and came to rest on each of them. All of them were filled with the Holy Spirit and began to speak in other tongues as the Spirit enabled them (2:1-4). *Pentecost* is the New Testament name for the Feast of Weeks, "when the wheat harvest was celebrated by a one-day festival during which special sacrifices were offered. Just as other festivals were associated with important events in Israel's history, so in Judaism the festival was associated with the renewal of the covenant made with Noah and then with Moses."[183]

Since the term for *spirit* and *wind* can be used interchangeably, it comes as no surprise that the coming of the Holy Spirit should first be associated with *a sound like the blowing of a violent wind.* In particular, *wind* suggests *life* and *power*. It was moreover *like* the sound of wind, and so differentiated. Since it *came from heaven*, we are to conclude that it was not an altogether natural event.

Along with the sound like a wind, there appeared *tongues of fire* separating and settling on each of them. "Again the description is analogical--*as* of fire. And again we are reminded of Old Testament theophanies, especially of that at Sinai, but the primary background is probably John the Baptist's association of the Spirit with fire as a means of cleansing and judgment."[184] This moreover involved a related symbolism, since the tongues of fire came to rest on *each of them.* So are we to gather that the gift was not to a select few, but to all present.

Speaking *in other tongues* would seem "to mean something different from similar references elsewhere. Here, because *tongue* is used interchangeably with a word meaning *language* or *dialect* and because what was said was apparently intelligible, we must suppose that recognized languages were spoken."[185] Seemingly in contrast, the Corinthian phenomena might pass for ecstatic utterance. In any case, the speaking in tongues appears to be a complex expression. Nils Hohm elaborates: "One may also speak of different glossolalia dialects, or forms of speaking, which recur in several individuals in the same environment. ...Sometimes, however, exotic features are borrowed from completely different languages... ."[186] In this instance, it would appear that the event should be understood as representing God's reversal to confounding language at the Tower of Babel.

This was likewise a subjective experience. As described, they were *filled with the Holy Spirit.* The term *fill* is on occasion used as if *to satisfy.* It is also associated with empowering for service. Perhaps both are implied. It results in a holy boldness. No distinction is made in this context between *baptism* and *filling,* and probably none intended.

Now there were staying in Jerusalem God-fearing Jews from every nation under heaven. When they heard this sound, a crowed came together in bewilderment, because each one heard them speaking in his own language. Utterly amazed (repeated for emphasis), they asked: "Are not all these men who are speaking Galileans? Then how is it that each of us hears them in his own native language?" Amazed and perplexed (again repeated for emphasis), they inquired of one another: "What does this mean?" Some nonetheless made fun of them and said: "They have had too much wine."

Then Peter stood up with the Eleven, raised his voice and addressed the crowd: "Fellow Jews and all of you who live in Jerusalem, let me explain this to you; listen carefully to what I say. These men are not drunken as you suppose. It's only nine in the morning!" It was not customary to take wine so early, let alone become intoxicated. "No, this is what was spoken by the prophet Joel: "In the last days, God says, I will pour out my Spirit on all people. Your sons and daughters will prophesy, your young men will see visions, your old men will dream dreams. ...And everyone who calls on the name of the Lord will be saved." Peter's primary emphasis is that God is pouring out his Spirit on all peoples. Along with this, he appeals as did Joel that the people repent of their sins and seek forgiveness in light of impending disaster.

"Men of Israel," Peter continued, "listen to this: Jesus of Nazareth was a man accredited by God to you by miracles, wonders and signs, which God did among you through him, as you yourselves know. This man was handed over to you by God's set purpose and foreknowledge, and you, with the help of wicked men, put him to death by nailing him to the cross." *This* is what you did. "But God raised him from the dead, freeing him from the agony of death, because it was impossible for death to keep its hold on him." *This* is what God did in response.

David declared: "I saw the Lord always before me. Because he is at my right hand, I will not be shaken. Therefore my heart is glad and my tongue rejoices; my body also will live in hope, because you will not abandon me to the grave, nor will you let your Holy One see decay." "Brothers," Peter continued, "I can tell you confidently that the patriarch David died and was buried, and his tomb is here to this day. But he was a prophet and knew that God had promised him on oath that he would place one of his descendants on his throne. Seeing what was ahead, he spoke of the resurrection of the Christ, that he was not abandoned to the grave, nor did his body see decay."

"God has raised Jesus to life," Peter further asserted, "and we are all witnesses of the fact. Exalted to the right hand of God, he has received from the Father the promised Holy Spirit and has poured out what you now see and hear." The *right hand of God* signifies the place of supremacy. Jesus' resurrection was followed by his ascension, and his ascension by the pouring out of the Holy Spirit. In due time, this will be followed by his return. As for now, one must contend with present realities. "Therefore let all Israel be assured of this: God has made this Jesus, whom you crucified, both Lord and Christ." Peter is not content that they recognize Jesus as *Christ* but *Lord.* He has ascended to the right hand of God, the position of power, from which he carries on his unrelenting purpose in the world. As ample evidence of this fact, he has poured out the Holy Spirit.

When the people heard this, they were cut to the heart and said to Peter and the other apostles: "Brothers, what shall we do?" Peter replied: "Repent and be baptized every one of you, in the name of Jesus Christ for the forgiveness of sins. And you shall receive the Holy Spirit. The promise is for you and your children and for all who are far off--for all whom the Lord our God will call." With many other words he warned them: "Save yourselves from this corrupt generation."

Luke intersperses in his narrative in these early chapters "with little cameos of life in the early church, intended, no doubt, as models for the church of his own day. This section (2:42-47) contains the first of these sketches. It touches on a number of matters: the teaching, the miracles, the fellowship, and the prayers."[187] So it was that they devoted themselves to *the apostles' teaching.* From the use of the definite article, one would assume that this refers to a specific body of instruction. They similarly devoted themselves to *the fellowship.* That is, to life together in Christ. They likewise shared in *the breaking of bread.* It seems best to understand this as sharing table fellowship rather than a specific reference to the Lord's Supper.

"Everyone was filled with awe, and many wonders and miraculous signs were done by the apostles," Luke reports. Of course, they were simply God's agents. They had no power in and of themselves. Perhaps if they were not so ordinary, the fact would not have been so obvious. As it was, God used common folk for uncommon purposes.

"Selling their possessions and goods, they gave to anyone as he had need. The poverty prevailing in Palestine in the first century was pronounced, "but the already desperate case of most Palestinians must have been exacerbated for the church by the fact that many of its early members had abandoned their source of livelihood in Galilee and many of its subsequent converts from elsewhere had stayed on in the city... ."[188] Then, too, those excommunicated would lose their recourse to the temple treasury.

So it was that the Lord added daily those who were being saved. As the believers were observed and spoke with those outside the faith community, they bore an individual and corporate witness. As a result, there was an on-going response from those who found their faith appealing. This, we would gather, was as Luke thought things should be.

IN JEWISH ENVIRON

It must have seemed that the followers of Christ constituted a Jewish sect. Of the then current sects, it appeared more similar to the Pharisees than Sadducees, Essenes, or Zealots. Jesus was a Jew, as were his earliest followers. They traveled primarily in Jewish circles and ministered to the Jewish populace. From this perspective, *Luke/Acts* explains how a small, inconsequential Jewish sect becomes a vigorous cosmopolitan movement.

One day Peter and John were going up to the temple at the time of prayer--at three p.m. Now a man crippled from birth was being carried to the temple gates, where he was stationed to beg from those going into the temple courts. When he saw the apostles about to enter, he asked them for alms. Peter demanded: "Look at us!" (3:4), and so the man gave them his attention. Peter continued: "Silver or gold I do not have, but what I have I give you. In the name of Jesus Christ of Nazareth, walk." Then he went with them into the temple courts, walking and jumping, and praising God. When all the people recognized the man, they were filled with wonder and amazement at what had happened to him.

Peter seized on the opportunity to proclaim the good news. "Men of Israel," he said, "why does this surprise you? Why do you stare at us as if by our own power or godliness we had made this man walk? ...By faith in the name of Jesus, this man whom you see and know was made strong. It is Jesus' name and the faith that comes through him that has given this complete healing to him, as you can all see."

"Now, brothers," Peter assumed a conciliatory attitude, "I know that you acted in ignorance, as did your leaders. But this is how God fulfilled what he had foretold through all the prophets, saying that his Christ would suffer. Repent, then, and turn to God, so that your sins may be wiped out, that times of refreshing may come from the Lord, and that he may send the Christ, who has been appointed for you--even Jesus."

The priests, captain of the temple guard, and Sadducees came up to Peter and John as they were speaking to the people. They were greatly disturbed because the apostles were proclaiming in Jesus the resurrection.

They seized the two, and because it was evening, put them in prison until the next day. But many who heard the message believed, and the number of men grew to about five thousand. "Critics have protested that this presupposes an audience of thousands for Peter's speech, and also that the total is disproportionate with the total population of Jerusalem. But the church was growing daily (2:47), and it is not necessary to ascribe the increase since 2:41 simply to this one public meeting."[189] Nor is it necessary to suppose that the number is restricted to those living in Jerusalem.

The next day the Sanhedrin met to interrogate Peter and John. They asked the apostles: "By what power or what name did you do this?" Then Peter, filled with the Holy Spirit, responded: "Rulers and elders of the people! ...It is by the name of Jesus Christ of Nazareth, whom you crucified but whom God raised from the dead, that the man stands before you healed." Having answered their question, the apostle comments: "He is 'the stone you builders rejected, which has become the capstone' (4:11; cf. Psa. 118:22). Salvation is found in no one else, for there is no other name under heaven given to men by which we must be saved." As Jesus had in a manner of speaking *saved* the man, he is God's appointed means for redeeming mankind.

When they saw the courage of these men and realized that they were unschooled, ordinary persons, they were astonished and took note that they had been with Jesus. This is not to say that they necessarily regarded Peter and John as completely ignorant and unlettered, but only that they were lacking in the formal training of the scribes. "The same complaint had been made of Jesus (John 7:15), who had also surprised his hearers with his boldness of bearing and speech. Indeed, it may have been the council's recollection of Jesus that lay behind the comment."[190]

After this, the Sanhedrin deliberated in private. "What are we going to do with these men?" the council members asked. "Everybody living in Jerusalem knows they have done an outstanding miracle, and we cannot deny it. But to stop this thing from spreading any further among the people, we must warn these men to speak no longer to anyone in this name." Then they called the apostles, and commanded them to refrain from speaking in Jesus' name. But Peter and John replied: "Judge for yourselves whether it is right in God's sight to obey you rather than God. For we cannot help speaking about what we have seen and heard." After further threatening them, the authorities let them go.

On their release, Peter and John returned to their own people, and reported all that was said to them. When they heard this, they raised their voices together in prayer to God. "Now, Lord," they petitioned, "consider their threats and enable your servants to speak your word with great boldness. Stretch out your hand to heal and perform miraculous signs and wonders through the name of your holy Servant Jesus." After they had prayed, the place where they were meeting was shaken, and they were all filled with the Holy Spirit and spoke the word of God boldly.

After this, Luke introduces a second portrait of the early church. "All the believers were one in heart and mind," he observes. "No one claimed that any of his possessions was his own, but they shared everything they had. With great power the apostles continued to testify to the resurrection of the Lord Jesus, and much grace was upon them. There were no needy persons among them." From time to time, those who owned lands or houses sold them, and distributed to those less fortunate than themselves.

As noted earlier, the death of Ananias and Sapphira alerted the church and all others who heard of God's awesome presence in the community. This, in turn, leads into still another portrait of the early church (5:12-16). In this connection, we learn that the apostles continued to perform many miraculous signs, the believers met regularly in the temple court for instruction and fellowship, and persons were reluctant to meet publically with them although they were highly regarded by the people. All things considered, many believed and were added to their number.

This intensified persecution. The apostles were arrested and put in prison. But during the night, an angel of the Lord opened the doors of the jail and brought them out. "Go," he said, "and tell the people the full message of this new life" (5:20). At daybreak they entered the temple court, as they had been told, and began to teach the people. Meanwhile, the Sanhedrin sent for the apostles. When the guards returned, they reported: "We found the jail securely locked, with the guards standing at the doors, but when we opened them, we found no one inside." Then someone came and said: "Look! The men you put in jail are standing in the temple courts teaching the people."

Once again the Sanhedrin admonished the apostles not to teach in Jesus' name. Once again the apostles appealed to a higher authority. Once more the religious authorities were furious. This time a Pharisee and renowned rabbi by the name of *Gamaliel* appealed for restraint. He argued, on the one hand, that if it were no more than a human movement, it would soon disappear. "On the other hand, if the Christian movement had its origin in God, how could they hope to withstand it? Such advice was typically Pharisaic in both temper and content. It picked up the leading point in their theology...that God rules the world by a wise providence."[191] Conversely, the Sadducees accented self-determination.

In this instance, Gamaliel's counsel prevailed. The apostles were flogged, again ordered not to teach in Jesus' name, and released. They went on their way rejoicing that they were counted worthy to suffer for the Name. Day after day, in the temple courts and from house to house, they never stopped teaching and proclaiming the good news that Jesus is the Christ.

In those days the number of Grecian Jews was increasing, and complained that they were being overlooked in the daily distribution of food (6:1). The contrast between *Grecian* and *Hebraic Jews* is as rule thought to distinguish between those whose first language was Greek or Aramaic. However, the use of one tongue or the other implies an extended difference in cultural orientation. As a matter of record, Paul identifies himself with the latter (Phil. 3:5). In any case, the apostles proposed that seven persons be selected to oversee the operation, while they give their attention to prayer and the ministry of the word.

"So the word of God spread. The number of disciples in Jerusalem increased rapidly, and a large number of priests became obedient to the faith" (6:7). Although most upper class priests were Sadducees, the poorer priests, many who came to Jerusalem only several weeks of the year, were not. "Priests did not represent any given ideology or economic status, but their conversion here shows that the Christians are making inroads even into the temple establishment, or at least the lower echelon of priests who served there."[192]

Now Stephen, variously described as *a man full of faith and of the Holy Spirit* and *a man full of God's grace and power*, performed great wonders and miraculous signs among the people. Opposition nonetheless arose from members of the *Synagogue of the Freedmen.* This was a synagogue which served diasporan Jews (those dispersed among the nations), and to which Stephen may have belonged. "These men began to argue with Stephen, but they could not stand up against his wisdom or the Spirit by whom he spoke" (6:10). Then they persuaded some to charge Stephen with blasphemy, and stir up the people. So it was that he was brought before the authorities. As those sitting in the Sanhedrin looked intently at Stephen, they saw that his face was like the face of an angel.

Then the high priest asked him: "Are these charges true?" At the conclusion of an labored account of the waywardness of his people, Stephen charged: "You are just like your fathers, you always resist the Holy Spirit!" When they heard this, they were furious and gnashed their teeth at him. "Look," Stephen said, "I see heaven open and the Son of Man standing at the right hand of God." At this they covered their ears, and shouting to drown out his words, dragged him outside the city and began to stone him. Meanwhile, the witnesses laid their clothes at the feet of a young man named *Saul*. Thus while Saul (Paul) may not have taken part in the gruesome proceedings, he approved the action. While they were stoning him, Stephen prayed: "Lord Jesus, receive my spirit." He then fell on his knees and cried out: "Lord, do not hold this sin against them." When he had said this, he *fell asleep*.

On that day a great persecution broke out against the church at Jerusalem, and all except the apostles were scattered through Judea and Samaria. It may be since the apostles remained, the persecution was directed primarily against the Grecian believers. In any case, godly men buried Stephen and mourned deeply for him. Saul conversely began to destroy the church. Going from house to house, he dragged off men and women and put them in prison. So it was that it took persecution to launch the church on its mission to disciple the nations. The familiar Jewish environ would increasingly fade into the background, as the Christian task force took on the challenge of winning converts from ethnically diverse people.

Along a related line, The New Testament epistle has a relatively fixed form, "consisting of five main parts: 1. Opening or salutation. 2. Thanksgiving (including such features as prayer for spiritual welfare, remembrance of the recipient (s), and eschatological climax). 3. Body of the letter. 4. Paraenesis (moral exhortations). 5. Closing (final greeting and benediction)."[193] "The corresponding skills that they require from the readers are the ability to determine the overall structure of an epistle, to *think paragraphs* in following the logical flow of ideas, to interpret figurative language, and to be sensitive to the effects of artistic patterning."[194] In addition, it helps to consider the correspondence in context of the story line.

A number of the New Testament epistles were directed to a Jewish constituency. *James* serves as a prime example. His *salutation* reads as follows, "James, a servant of God and of the Lord Jesus Christ, to the twelve tribes scattered among the nations: Greetings." James, brother of Jesus, seems the best candidate as author of the letter. It was this James who presided over the Jerusalem Council in Acts 15. This, in turn, would imply that he assumed leadership of the mother church, and as such was the most influential figure in the church so long as it remained primarily within the Jewish environ.

At the very least, this would date source material to the decade of the 40s. As to subsequent editing, the matter is subject to speculation. Peter Davids concludes that the church of James' day consisted of a series of house churches or Christian synagogues, "each one having no more than about sixty members.... . They met for worship, probably a modified form of the synagogue liturgy, and then celebrated the Lord's Supper immediately afterward. They also enjoyed the celebration of Jewish festivals and the temple services, as Acts shows."[195] Acts likewise suggests that it was a poverty stricken and persecuted church.

James wastes no time in coming to the issue at hand. "Consider it all joy," he admonishes his readers, "whenever you face trials of many kinds, because you know that the testing of your faith develops perseverance. Perseverance must finish its work so that you may be mature and complete, not lacking anything" (1:2-3). "Blessed is the man who perseveres under trial, because when he has stood the test, he will receive the crown of life that God has promised to those who love him."

Second paragraph (1:19-27). "Do not merely listen to the word, and so deceive yourselves. Do what it says. Anyone who listens to the word but does not do what it says is like a man who looks at his face in a mirror and, after looking at himself, goes away and immediately forgets what he looks like." As illustrated here, James' use of metaphor and simile is strikingly apt. "Religion that God our Father accepts as pure and faultless is this: to look after orphans and widows in their distress and to keep oneself from being polluted by the world."

Third paragraph (2:1-13). "My brothers, as believers in our glorious Lord Jesus Christ, don't show favoritism." Suppose that a man comes in wearing a gold ring and fine clothes and you show him special attention, and a shabbily dressed man comes in and you treat him abruptly, you have discriminated between them. "Listen, my dear brothers: Has not God chosen those who are poor in the eyes of the world to be rich in faith and to inherit the kingdom? Is it not the rich who are exploiting you? Are they not the ones who are dragging you into court?"

Fourth paragraph (2:14-26). "What good is it, my brothers, if a man claims to have faith but has not deeds?" "Show me your faith without deeds, and I will show you my faith by what I do. You believe that there is one God. Good! Even the demons believe that--and shudder." "James writes this part of his letter in an *argumentative* style, sometimes called a *diatribe*. He introduces an *imaginative objector* who states his own viewpoint as a foil for James' argument."[196] He attacks such as if they were present, and he appeals directly to his readers to judge the cogency of what he is saying.

Fifth paragraph (3:1-12). "Consider what a great forest is set on fire by a small spark. The tongue also is a fire, a world of evil among the parts of the body. It corrupts the whole person, sets the whole course of his life on fire, and is itself set on fire by hell." "With the tongue we praise our Lord and Father, and with it we curse men, who have been made in God's likeness. Out of the same mouth come praise and cursing. My brothers, this should not be."

Sixth paragraph (3:13-18). There are two kinds of wisdom: that which comes from below and above. As for the former, it harbors bitter envy and selfish ambition. As for the latter, it "is first of all pure; then peace-loving, considerate, submissive, full of mercy and good fruit, impartial and sincere. Peacemakers who sow in peace raise a harvest of righteousness."

Seventh paragraph (4:1-12). "Submit yourselves, then, to God. Resist the devil, and he will flee from you. Come near to God and he will come near to you." "Humble yourselves before the Lord, and he will lift you up." To *humble oneself before the Lord* means to recognize our spiritual poverty, leading to realizing our sufficiency in Christ.

Eighth paragraph (4:13-17). There is a saying: "Don't put off to tomorrow what you can do today." James would seem to elaborate: "Why, you do not even know what will happen tomorrow. What is your life? You are a mist that appears for a little while and then vanishes." Instead, if the Lord allows, we will do this or that. "Anyone, then, who knows the good he ought to do and doesn't do it, sins."

Ninth paragraph (5:1-6). "Now listen, you rich people.... The wages you failed to pay the workmen who mowed your fields are crying out against you. The cries of the harvesters have reached the ears of the Lord Almighty." To what end? "You have fattened yourselves in the day of slaughter." As the farmer fattens his animal for slaughter, so the rich indulge themselves at the expense of others and thereby invite judgment.

Tenth paragraph (5:7-12). "Be patient, then, brothers, until the Lord's coming. See how the farmer waits for the land to yield its valuable crop and how patient he is for the autumn and spring rains. You, too, be patient and stand firm, because the Lord's coming is near." Remember Job: how God rewarded his long-suffering.

James draws his correspondence to a conclusion. "Is anyone of you in trouble? He should pray. Is anyone happy? Let him sing songs of praise. Is any one of you sick? He should call the elders of the church to pray over him and anoint him with oil in the name of the Lord." The use of *oil* is either as a medical remedy, or as a religious ritual. If the former, which seems the more likely alternative, James means to encourage prayer coupled with medical assistance. As for his rationale, "The prayer of a righteous man is powerful and effective." Finally, remember your responsibility to admonish those who stray from the faith.

TRANSITION

Those scattered by persecution, *preached the word wherever they went* (8:4). "The story begins by showing how the persecution of the church in Jerusalem was turned to good effect. ...It is interesting that this particular movement is not attributed to any specific guidance from the Spirit."[197] Instead, it appears as it were the natural thing for wandering Christians to spread the gospel. Perhaps it was on occasion primed by those who inquired as to why they had fled in haste.

Philip went down to a city in Samaria, and proclaimed the Christ there. When the crowds heard what Philip said and saw the miraculous signs he did, they listened carefully. Now a man named *Simon* practiced sorcery in the city. He boasted of his own importance, and the people allowed that he was endowed with *the Great Power*, most likely a designation for God. Then, when others believed, he also believed and was baptized. After this, he followed Philip everywhere, and was astonished by the miracles he observed.

When the apostles in Jerusalem heard that Samaria had accepted the word of God, they dispatched Peter and John. Once the apostles arrived, they prayed that these might receive the Holy Spirit, since they were simply baptized into the name of the Lord Jesus. Then Peter and John placed their hands on them, and they received the Holy Spirit. This is perhaps the most puzzling episode recorded in Acts, even though various explanations have been set forth. David Williams proposes: "The Samaritans needed to be shown that they were fully incorporated into the Christian community. Without a clear link between the church in Samaria and that in Jerusalem, the schism that had for so long plagued Jewish-Samaritan relations might well have been carried over into the church."[198]

When Simon saw that the Holy Spirit was given at the laying on of the apostles' hands, he offered them money and said: "Give me also this ability so that everyone on whom I lay my hands may receive the Holy Spirit." Peter answered: "May your money perish with you, because you thought you could buy the gift of God with money! ...Repent of this wickedness and pray to the Lord. Perhaps he will forgive you for having such a thought in your heart." Then Simon pled: "Pray to the Lord for me so that nothing you have said may happen to me." When the apostles had witnessed and proclaimed God's word, they returned to Jerusalem, preaching the gospel in many Samaritan villages on the way.

Now an angel of the Lord said to Philip: "Go south to the road--the desert road--that goes down from Jerusalem to Gaza." So he started out and on the way met an Ethiopian eunuch, an important official in charge of the national treasury. This man had gone to Jerusalem to worship and was reading from the Isaiah scroll. Such would imply that he was a God-fearing Gentile. When Philip heard him, he asked: "Do you understand what your are reading?" "How can I," the latter responded, "unless someone explains it to me?" The text in question was: "He was led like a sheep to the slaughter, and as a lamb before the shearer is silent, so he did not open his mouth. In his humiliation he was deprived of justice. Who can speak of his descendants? For his life was taken from the earth" (8:32-33; cf. Isa. 53:7-8). "Tell me," the official requested, "who is the prophet talking about, himself or someone else?" Then Philip began with that passage and shared with him the good news concerning Jesus.

As they traveled along the road, they came to some water. The eunuch observed: "Look, here is water. Why shouldn't I be baptized?" Then both of them went down into the water, and Philip baptized him. When they came up out of the water, the Spirit directed Philip elsewhere. The eunuch didn't see him again, but went on his way rejoicing. Philip showed up at Azotus (Ashdod), and traveled about, preaching the gospel in all the towns until he reached Caesarea--the seat of Roman power in the province.

Meanwhile, Saul obtained from the high priest authorization to bring any of the Way he might discover in Damascus, whether men or women, as prisoners to Jerusalem. The term *way* was used in general terms of some distinctive mode of behavior. In this instance, it lent itself to both positive and negative assessment. If positive, then followers of the Righteous One. If negative, then deviants from the religious establishment.

As Saul neared Damascus, suddenly a light from heaven flashed around him. He fell to the ground and heard voice addressing him: "Saul, Saul, why do you persecute me?" (9:4) Saul responded: "Who are you, Lord?" "I am Jesus, whom you are persecuting," the voice continued. "Now get up and go into the city, and you will be told what you must do." Those with him had seen the light and heard a sound, but not the words.

Saul got up from the ground, but when he opened his eyes he could see nothing. So they led him by the hand into Damascus.

Saul was blind for three days, and refused to eat or drink. There was in Damascus at the time a man called *Ananias*. The Lord appeared to him in a vision and instructed him: "Go to the house of Judas on Straight Street and ask for a man from Tarsus named Saul, for he is praying. In a vision he has seen a man named Ananias come and place his hands on him to restore his sight." "Lord," Ananias protested, "I have heard many reports about this man and all the harm he has done to your saints in Jerusalem. And he has come here with authority from the chief priests to arrest all who call on your name." But the Lord insisted: "Go! This man is my chosen instrument to carry my name before the Gentiles and their kings and before the people of Israel. I will show him how much he must suffer for my name."

Then Ananias went as directed. Placing his hands on Saul, he said: "Brother Saul, the Lord--Jesus, who appeared to you on the road as you were coming here--has sent me so that you may see again and be filled with the Holy Spirit." Immediately, something resembling scales fell from Saul's eyes, and he could see again. He got up and was baptized, and after taking some food, regained his strength.

Saul spent several days with the disciples in Damascus. At once he began to preach in the synagogues that Jesus is the Son of God. All those who heard him were astonished and asked: "Isn't he the man who raised havoc in Jerusalem among those who call on this name? And hasn't he come here to take them as prisoners to the chief priests?" Saul continued to mature spiritually, and confounded those who opposed him. So it was that they conspired to kill him, and watched the city gates day and night so that he would not escape. Then his associates took him by night and lowered him in a basket though an opening in the wall.

When he had come to Jerusalem, Saul attempted to join the disciples there, but they were afraid of him--supposing that he was not a genuine believer. Barnabas nonetheless interceded, telling the apostles of Saul's experience on the Damascus road, and how he had preached fearlessly in the name of Jesus. So Saul stayed with them and moved freely about Jerusalem, speaking boldly concerning Jesus. Then when his life appeared in danger, the disciples brought him to Caesarea, and sent him to Tarsus.

This brings Luke again to characterize the early church (9:31). First, it enjoyed a time of peace throughout the region. Second, it was strengthened by the Holy Spirit. Third, it grew in numbers. Finally, it lived in awe of the Lord. While the *time of peace* would seem linked to the conversion of Saul, there were other factors involved. First, there had been a change of high priests. "In A.D. 37 Caiaphas had been deposed, and in his place Vitellius had installed first Jonathan, then his brother Theophilus. Second, there had been a change of emperor the same year, with Caligula succeeding Tiberius. The new emperor was far less sympathetic to the Jews than Tiberius had been."[199] Such would seem to assure the disciples that God was ultimately in control of circumstances.

Luke next turns our attention to the exploits of Peter. In Lydda, the apostle found a man named *Aeneas*, a paralytic who was bed-ridden for eight years. "Aeneas," he said, "Jesus Christ heals you. Get up and take care of your mat" (9:34). Immediately Aeneas got up, and when this was made known those in the region turned to the Lord.

In Joppa, there was a disciple named *Tabitha*, who was always doing good and helping the poor. About that time she became sick and died, and her body was washed and placed in an upstairs room. Lydda was near Joppa, so when the disciples heard that Peter was in Lydda, they sent for him. Peter went with them, and upon arrival they were ushered into the upstairs room. All the widows stood around crying, and showing him the clothing that Tabitha had made while she was still with them. Peter sent them out of the room, and knelt down in prayer. Turning toward the dead woman, he said: "Tabitha, get up." She opened her eyes and seeing Peter sat up. He took her by the hand and helped her to her feet. Then he called the others and presented her to them alive. Many more people consequently believed on the Lord.

At Caesarea, there was a man named *Cornelius*, a centurion. He and his family were God-fearing Gentiles. One day at about three in the afternoon he had a vision. He distinctly saw an angel of God, who greeted him. Cornelius stared at him in fear. "What is it, Lord?" he asked (10:4). The angel replied: "Your prayers and gifts to the poor have come up as a memorial offering before God. Now send men to Joppa to bring back a man named Simon who is called Peter." When the angel was gone, Cornelius summoned attendants and sent them to bring the apostle.

About noon the following day, Peter went up on the roof to pray. He became hungry and while food was being prepared, he fell into a trance. He saw heaven opened and something like a large sheet being let down to earth by its four corners. It contained all kinds of four-footed animals, as well as reptiles and birds. He likewise heard a voice saying: "Get up, Peter. Kill and eat." "Surely not, Lord!" Peter exclaimed. "I have never eaten anything impure or unclean." The voice spoke a second time: "Do not call anything impure that God has made clean." This happened three times, and the sheet was taken back into heaven. While Peter was still thinking about the vision, the delegation from Cornelius arrived. They said to him: "We have come from Cornelius the centurion. He is a righteous and God-fearing man, who is respected by all the Jewish people. A holy angel told him to have you come to his house so that he could hear what you have to say."

The next day Peter and those with him arrived in Caesarea. Cornelius was expecting them, and had called together his relatives and close friends. As Peter entered the house, Cornelius fell at his feet. "Stand up," Peter said, "I am only a man myself." After this, he addressed those who had gathered. "You are well aware that it is against our law for a Jew to associate with a Gentile or visit him," he began. "But God has shown me that I should not call any man impure or unclean. So when I was sent for, I came without raising any objection. May I ask why you sent for me?"

Since Peter was not aware of Cornelius' vision, the centurion shared his experience. Whereupon, the apostle commented: "I now realize how true it is that God does not show favoritism but accepts men from every nation who fear him and do what is right." He, in turn, heralded the gospel. They, in turn, received the Holy Spirit. The Jews, in turn, were astonished that Gentiles were recipients of the gift. This speech is the first recorded preaching of the gospel to the Gentile world. "It must be assumed, of course, that these were almost entirely *devout* people like Cornelius himself and that they were familiar, therefore, with the Jewish Scriptures. It must also be assumed that they knew something of the story of Jesus."[200] They were decidedly not a typical Gentile audience.

As for the Jews, they were told that "the cherished expectations of their race had been gratified, though in an unexpected way, that God has not waited for the perfection of Israel before sending the Messiah but had already sent Him, the Messiah had died, had risen, and would come again in glory and that...they were called to a new life."[201] As for the Gentiles, the disciples faced a world which did not know Judaism or which hated and despised it, "a world which was unacquainted with the prophets and familiar with cults not pretending to exclusiveness, with mysteries not requiring a moral standard of their devotees, with an unchangeable and immoral order of destiny determined, or at least indicated, by the stars, and magic of various kinds."[202] As for God-fearing Gentiles, they worshiped the God revealed in Scripture but were not disposed to become Jewish proselytes. In Jewish perspective, they were considered *righteous Gentiles*--in that they were thought to observe God's covenant with Noah.

"Can anyone keep these people from being baptized?" Peter inquired. "They have received the Holy Spirit just as we have." So they were baptized. So also Peter was asked to give an accounting for his actions. Now when Peter went up to Jerusalem, the Jewish disciples criticized him and said: "You went into the house of uncircumcised men and ate with them." But after Peter explained to them what had happened, they had no further objections and praised God, saying: "So then, God has granted even the Gentiles repentance into life."

Now those who had been scattered by the persecution in connection with Stephen traveled as far as Phoenicia, Cyprus and Antioch, typically ministering to Jews. Some of them, however, men from Cyprus and Cyrene, went to Antioch and began to speak to Greeks also, telling them the good news about the Lord Jesus. The Lord's hand was with them, and a great number of people believed and turned to the Lord. When news of this reached the church at Jerusalem, Barnabas was sent to Antioch. When he arrived and saw the evidence of God's grace at work, he encouraged the disciples and set out for Tarsus in search for Saul. Once he had found him, they returned to Antioch and ministered there for an entire year.

About that time, Herod (Agrippa I) arrested some of the disciples (12:1). He had James, the brother of John, executed. When he saw that this pleased the Jewish opposition, he seized Peter as well. Since it was the time of the Feast of Unleavened Bread, Herod put Peter in prison with the intent of a public trial after the celebration had run its course. Meanwhile, the church interceded with prayer on the apostle's behalf.

The night before Herod was to bring him to trial, Peter was sleeping between two soldiers, bound with two chains, and sentries stood guard at the entrance. Suddenly an angel of the Lord appeared and a light shone in the cell. "Quick, get up!" he said, and the chains fell off Peter's wrists. Then the angel said to him: "Put on your clothes and sandals." Peter did as instructed. "Wrap your cloak around you and follow me," the angel continued. The apostle followed him out of the prison, supposing he was seeing a vision. They passed the first and second guards and came to the iron gate leading to the city. It opened for them, and they passed through. When they had walked the length of one street, the angel left him. Then Peter came to himself, and said: "Now I know without a doubt that the Lord sent his angel and rescued me from Herod's clutches and from everything the Jewish people were anticipating."

When this dawned on him, he went to the house of Mary the mother of John, also called *Mark*, where many people had gathered and were praying. Peter knocked at the outer entrance, and a servant girl named *Rhoda* came to answer the door. When she recognized Peter's voice, she was so overjoyed she ran back without opening it and exclaimed: "Peter is at the door!" "You're out of your mind," they told her. When she kept insisting that it was so, they concluded: "It must be his angel." The ironic detail is especially striking. Peter meanwhile continued his knocking. When at last they opened the door and saw Peter, they were astonished. Peter, motioning with his hand for them to be quiet, described how the Lord delivered him from prison. "Tell James and the brothers about this," he said, and left for another place--presumably to go into hiding.

In the morning, there was no small commotion among the soldiers as to what had become of Peter. After Herod had a thorough search made and could not find him, he cross-examined the guards and ordered that they be executed. "Given the soldier's precautions (chains, doors and different guards posted for each), it was humanly impossible for Peter to have escaped without all the guards having aided him. ...Under Roman law, a guard whose prisoner escaped would pay for it with the penalty due the prisoner--in this case, his own life."[203]

Luke adds what resembles a footnote to the above episode, concerning the death of Herod. It seems that he went from Judea to Casearea and stayed there for a while. Since he had been quarreling with the people of Tyre and Sidon, they joined together and sought an audience with him. Having secured the support of Blastus, a trusted personal servant of the king, they petitioned for peace, because they depended on his territory for their food supply.

On the appointed day, Herod wearing his royal robes sat upon his throne and delivered a public address to the people. The populace shouted: "This is a voice of a god not a man." Immediately, because Herod did not give the honor to God, an angel of the Lord struck him down, and eaten with worms he died. Josephus reports that he was carried to the palace, where he died at the age of fifty-four, after five days of excruciating suffering.

But the word of God continued to increase and spread. That is, it was not only heard by more people, but its impact was increasingly felt. The disciples' nemesis Herod was dead, but the sustaining word of God was alive and active.

All things considered, this was a time of transition. The *Way* had taken root in Jewish soil. It had prospered, but not without persecution. Scattered by persecution, the disciples preached the word wherever they went. They ministered primarily to Jews, but some at Antioch shared the gospel with Gentiles as well. In particular, there appears to be a favorable response from among the God-fearing Gentiles. They, like the Jews, had the law and prophets to prepare them for the proclamation of the gospel. They, unlike the Jews, were not inhibited by ethnic restraint.

CONTROVERSY

In the church at Antioch, there were prophets and teachers: Simeon called Niger, Lucius of Cyrene, Manaen--raised in the household of Herod the tetrarch, and Saul (13:1). It is not clear whether *prophets* and *teachers* are meant to be taken as two groups or a twofold description of them all. In any case, it is a far more cosmopolitan group than the original twelve. While they were worshiping and fasting, the Holy Spirit instructed them to set apart Barnabas and Saul for the work to which they were called. So after they had fasted and prayed, they placed their hands on them and sent them on their way. Whereas the *laying on of hands* as a rule conveys the idea of blessing, here it takes the more distinctive meaning of setting them apart for a particular work.

The two of them, accompanied by John Mark, went down to Seleucia and sailed from there to Cyprus. When they arrived at Salamis, they proclaimed the word of God in the Jewish synagogues. They subsequently traveled through the whole island until they came to Paphos. There they encountered a Jewish sorcerer and false prophet named *Bar-Jesus*, who was an attendant of the proconsul, Sergius Paulus. The proconsul, who was an intelligent man, sent for Barnabas and Saul because he wanted to hear the word of God. But the sorcerer opposed them, and tried to turn the proconsul from the faith. Then Saul, filled with the Holy Spirt, looked straight at the antagonist and said: "You are a child of the devil and an enemy of everything that is right! You are full of all kinds of deceit and trickery. Will you never stop perverting the right ways of the Lord? Now the hand of the Lord is against you. You are going to be blind, and for a time you will be unable to see the light of the sun" (13:10-11). Immediately mist and darkness came upon him, and he groped about, seeking someone to lead him by the hand. When the proconsul saw what had happened, he believed--not for this reason alone but as if a confirmation of Paul's fervent teaching.

From Paphos, Paul and his companions sailed to Perga in Pamphylia, where John left them to return to Jerusalem. Luke here introduces three incidental observations. First, Paul replaces Barnabas in order of prominence. Second, he from this point on is referred to as *Paul* (associated with his Roman citizenship) rather than *Saul* (his Hebrew name). Third, John Mark leaves, perhaps in protest of a shift in leadership.

From Perga they made their way to Pisidian Antioch (13:14). On the Sabbath, they entered the synagogue and sat down. After the reading from the Law and the Prophets, the synagogue officials asked if they had a message of encouragement for the people. Standing up, Paul motioned with his hand, and said: "Men of Israel and you Gentiles who worship God, listen to me!" After this, he provided a brief resume of Jewish history from the time of bondage to the preaching of John the Baptist. "Brothers, children of Abraham, and you God-fearing Gentiles," the apostle continued, "it is to us that this message of salvation has been sent." With this and other words, he would persuade them to believe.

As Paul and Barnabas were leaving the synagogue, the people invited them to speak further about these things on the next Sabbath. So it was a week later that almost the whole city gathered to hear the word of the Lord. When the Jews saw the crowds and were moved by jealousy, they attacked what Paul had said. Then Paul and Barnabas answered them boldly: "We had to speak the word of God to you first. Since you reject it and do not consider yourselves worthy of eternal life, we now turn to the Gentiles." When the Gentiles heard this, they were glad and honored the word of the Lord, and those appointed to eternal life believed. So the word of the Lord spread through the whole region. But when persecution intensified, Paul and Barnabas pressed on to Iconium.

Upon their arrival, they went as usual to the synagogue. They spoke so persuasively that many Jews and Gentiles believed. However, the unbelieving Jews stirred up the Gentiles against them. As a result, the people of the city were divided. Then when it was learned that the opposition proposed to stone them, Paul and Barnabas fled to the cities of Lystra and Derbe.

Arriving in Lystra, they encountered a man crippled from birth and never able to walk. He listened to Paul as he talked. Paul, fixing his gaze on the man, perceived that he had faith to be healed. Calling out to the man, he commanded: "Stand up on your feet!" (14:10). At that, the man jumped to his feet and began to walk. When the people observed this, they cried out: "The gods have come down to us in human form!" Luke comments: "Barnabas they called Zeus, and Paul they called Hermes because he was the chief speaker." One would gather from this that

Barnabas was the more reserved, and Paul the more articulate. The priest of Zeus, whose temple was outside the city, brought bulls and wreaths to the city gates because he and the people wanted to offer sacrifices to the supposed gods. When Paul and Barnabas heard of this, they rent their clothes and rushed out into the crowd, shouting: "We too are only men, human like you. We are bringing you good news, telling you to turn from these worthless things to the living God, who made heaven and earth and sea and everything in them." Even with these words, they had difficulty keeping the people from sacrificing to them.

Events took a surprising turn. When certain Jews arrived from Antioch and Iconium, they won the crowd over. Paul, in turn, was stoned and dragged out of the city by those supposing that he was dead. When the disciples had gathered around him, he got up and went back into the city. The next day he and Barnabas left for Derbe. Luke does not represent this as a miracle of restoration to life. Conversely, we may see the hand of God in his survival. "Paul showed great courage in going back to the town, though it is unlikely that the magistrates had been involved, so he had nothing to fear at that level. Indeed, as a Roman citizen he had a strong case to put before them against his assailants had he wished to do so."[204] Choosing not to do so, he went on his way.

After a successful ministry in Derbe, the two retraced their steps to Lystra, Iconium, and Antioch. There they strengthened the believers, and encouraged them to remain true to the faith. "We must go through many hardships to enter the kingdom of God," they allowed (14:22). Paul and Barnabas also appointed elders for each of the churches, and commended them to the Lord in prayer and with fasting. After this, they returned to Antioch of Syria. Upon their arrival, they gathered the church together, and reported how God had opened the door of faith to the Gentiles. They subsequently stayed there for an extended time.

Now certain men came down from Judea to Antioch and were teaching: "Unless you are circumcised, according to the custom taught by Moses, you cannot be saved" (15:1). Paul and Barnabas took vigorous issue with them. Consequently, they along with others were appointed to go up to Jerusalem to consult with the apostles and elders on this critical matter. This development alerts us to break away Luke's narrative to consider Paul's epistle to the Galatians. After this, we will return to consider what transpired in Jerusalem.

Two theories compete for dating *Galatians*. Whereas the *South Galatian Theory* places it after Paul's first missionary journey and before the Jerusalem Council, the *North Galatain Theory* puts it after his second missionary journey. For our present purpose, I assume the former. All things considered, this seems best to fit the story line.

Salutation. First, we have the *sender* identified: "Paul, an apostle--sent not from men nor by man, but by Jesus Christ and God the Father, who raised him from the dead--and all the brothers with me." Next we have the *addressee*: "To the churches in Galatia." Finally, we have the *greeting*: "Grace and peace to you from God our Father and the Lord Jesus Christ, who gave himself for our sins to rescue us from the present evil age, according to the will of our God and Father, to whom be glory for ever and ever. Amen." While the expression *Paul, an apostle* is shared by a number of his epistles, it is employed here to make a point. In particular, he insists that he was commissioned to speak on behalf of *Jesus Christ and God the Father*, and contrary to what others may say.

Thanksgiving. The *thanksgiving* is notable for its absence. Instead, Paul writes: "I am astonished that you are so quickly deserting the one who called you by the grace of Christ and are turning to a different gospel--which is no gospel at all" (1:6). By way of contrast, he comments in *Philippians*: "I thank my God every time I remember you. In all my prayers for all of you, I always pray with joy because of your partnership in the gospel from the first day until now, being confident of this, that he who began a good work in you will carry it on to completion until the day of Christ Jesus" (1:3-6).

Body of the letter. Paul launches without hesitation into the topic. Some are preaching *a different gospel*, which is *no gospel at all.* Such assert that it is necessary to be circumcised in order to be saved, i.e., become Jewish proselytes. In doing so, they disallow that we are saved by grace through faith in Jesus Christ. "But even if we or an angel from heaven should preach a gospel other than the one we preached to you, let him be eternally condemned!"

Paul proceeds to draw from his own experience. "For you have heard of my previous way of life in Judaism," he recalls, "how intensely I persecuted the church of God and tried to destroy it. I was advancing in Judaism beyond many Jews of my own age and was extremely zealous for the traditions of my father. But when God...was pleased to reveal his Son in me so that I might preach him among the Gentiles, I did not consult any man" (1:13-16). As a matter of fact, he was faithful to his heavenly calling.

Then, when Peter came to Antioch, "I opposed him to his face, because he was clearly in the wrong. Before certain men came from James, he used to eat with the Gentiles. But when they arrived, he began to draw back and separate himself from the Gentiles because he was afraid of those who belonged to the circumcision group" (2:11-12). "The other Jews joined him in his hypocrisy," Paul continues, "so that by their hypocrisy even Barnabas was led astray. When I saw that they were not acting in line with the truth of the gospel, I said to Peter in front of them all: 'You are a Jew, yet you live like a Gentile and not like a Jew. How is it, then, that you force Gentiles to follow Jewish customs?'"

Moreover, the apostle inquires: "Did you receive the Spirit by observing the law, or by believing what you heard? ...After beginning with the Spirit, are you now trying to attain your goal by human effort? ...Does God give you his Spirit and work miracles among you because you observe the law, or because you believe what you heard?" (3:2-3, 5).

Consider Abraham. "He believed God, and it was credited to him as righteousness" (3:6; cf. Gen. 15:6). Understand then "that those who believe are children of Abraham. The Scripture foresaw that God would justify the Gentiles by faith, and announced the gospel in advance to Abraham: 'All nations will be blessed through you.' So those who have faith are blessed along with Abraham, the man of faith." "He redeemed us in order that the blessing given to Abraham might come to the Gentiles through Christ Jesus, so that by faith we might receive the promise of the Spirit."

What purpose then does the law serve? Paul has attempted to set aside one problem: that faith must be perfected through works. He doesn't want to fall prey to another: that we are free to sin. "So the law was put in charge to lead us to Christ that we might be justified by faith," he explains. "Now that faith has come, we are no longer under the supervision of the law." The coming of faith is thus expressed in terms of the coming of age. At such time, one takes on the obligations associated with maturity.

Paul extends the metaphor. "What I am saying is that as long as the heir is a child, he is no different from a slave, although he owns the whole estate. He is subject to guardians and trustees until the time set by his father" (4:1-2). "But when the time had fully come, God sent his Son, born of a woman, born under law, to redeem those under law, that we might receive the full rights of sons." "Jewish texts often speak of God's perfect wisdom in and sovereignty over history. (Some commentators have compared *the fullness of the time* to how ripe Greco-Roman culture was for the spread of Christianity; yet others could counter by citing the almost insurmountable obstacles that this culture presented... .)"[205]

After another appeal to his readers, Paul launches into a typical rabbinic argument perhaps as a means of rebutting his opposition. "For it is written that Abraham had two sons, one by the slave woman and the other by the free woman. Her son by the slave woman was born in the ordinary way; but his son by the free woman was born as the result of a promise" (4:22-23). So far none of Paul's opposition would disagree. The critical question however remains: "What do these two woman represent?" "These things may be taken figuratively, for the women represent two covenants," Paul concludes. Hagar represents the Torah and Jerusalem below, and Sarah represents Promise and Jerusalem that is above.

"It is for freedom that Christ has set us free," the apostle enthusiastically exclaims. "Stand firm, then, and do not let yourselves be burdened again by a yoke of slavery" (5:1-2). "For in Christ neither circumcision nor uncircumcision has any value. The only thing that counts is faith expressing itself through love." To Paul's credit, he is not one-sided even in the midst of controversy. He readily admits that uncircumcision is equally valueless, "a point often forgotten by those filled with reforming zeal, as it was probably forgotten by many a Gentile Christian. He will not allow the Gentile to boast of his uncircumcised state, any more than he will allow the Jew to boast of *the sign of the covenant.*"[206]

Paraenesis (*moral exhortations*). "So I say, live by the Spirit, and you will not gratify the desires of the sinful nature" (5:16). "The acts of the sinful nature are obvious: sexual immorality, impurity and debauchery; idolatry and witch-craft; hatred, discord, jealousy, fits of rage, selfish ambition, dissensions, fractions and envy; drunkenness, orgies, and the like. ...But the fruit of the Spirit is love, joy, peace, patience, kindness, goodness, faithfulness, gentleness and self-control."

"Brothers, if someone is caught in a sin, you who are spiritual should restore him gently. Watch yourself, or you also may be tempted" (6:1). "Carry each other's burdens, and in this way you fulfill the law of Christ." "Anyone who receives instruction in the word must share all good things with his instructor." "Do not be deceived: A man reaps what he sows." "Let us not become weary in doing good, for at the proper time we will reap a harvest if we do not give up. Therefore, as we have opportunity, let us do good to all people, especially to those who belong to the family of believers."

Closing. "See what large letters I use as I write to you with my own hand!" (6:11). "*With what large letters* probably refers to the sprawling untidy letters of one not a scribe by trade, and who was, perhaps, more used to writing Semitic letters than Greek. ...Those who see Paul's recurrent illness as ophthalmia will point to the large letters often written by the half-blind."[207] "Neither circumcision nor uncircumcision means anything; what counts is a new creation. Peace and mercy to all who follow this rule, even to the Israel of God. Finally, let no one cause me trouble, for I bear in my body the marks of Jesus. The grace of our Lord Jesus Christ be with your spirit, brothers. Amen." Such was Paul's sentiments in contending for the faith he had proclaimed, and to which he was committed.

So it was that as he, Barnabas, and the others traveled toward Jerusalem. Along the way, they told how the Gentiles were converted, causing the believers to rejoice. Then, when they arrived at Jerusalem, they reported all that God was doing through them. In response, certain of the believers who belonged to the sect of the Pharisees stood up and insisted: "The Gentiles must be circumcised and required to obey the law of Moses" (Acts 15:5).

The apostles and elders convened to consider the matter. After much discussion, Peter stood and addressed them: "God, who knows the heart, showed that he accepted them by giving the Holy Spirit to them, just as he did to us. He made no distinction between us and them, for he purified their hearts by faith." Then when Paul and Barnabas told about the miraculous signs and wonders God had done among the Gentiles through them, the council members were silent. When they were finished, James said: "It is my judgment, therefore, that we should not make it difficult for the Gentiles who are turning to God. Instead we should write to them, telling them to abstain from food polluted by idols, from sexual immorality, from the meat of strangled animals and from blood. For Moses has been preached in every city from the earliest times and is read in the synagogues on every Sabbath."

Such prohibitions would reflect the Jewish tradition in regard to the covenant with Noah, and was thought binding on righteous Gentiles. For instance, a later commentary clarifies an obscure point: "If something has been prepared to be offered to an idol, but has not yet been offered, it is permitted for personal use. One should be strict, however, and not use anything found in the house of idol worship. Therefore, one should never take candles from the place of idol worship."[208]

Then the apostles and elders, with the entire church, chose Judas and Silas to accompany the delegation from Antioch with a letter expressing the decision agreed upon. When the letter was read, the people rejoiced in its encouraging contents. Judas and Silas remained on for the present to minister to the people, and subsequently returned to Jerusalem. Paul and Barnabas remained in Antioch, where they and others taught and preached the word of the Lord. While the issue was not resolved to the satisfaction of some, the work was able to continue without concerted opposition.

FAR HORIZONS

Some time later, Paul suggested to Barnabas: "Let us go back and visit the brothers in all the towns where we preached the word of the Lord and see how they are doing" (Acts 15:36). Barnabas wanted to take John Mark with them, but Paul refused--since he had left them on an earlier occasion. So sharp was their disagreement that they parted company. Barnabas took Mark and sailed for Cyprus, while Paul chose Silas to share in his ministry.

There was in Derbe a disciple named *Timothy*, whose mother was a Jewish believer and father an apparently unbelieving Greek now demised. Timothy was well thought of. Since Paul wanted him to accompany them, he circumcised him. From Hebrew perspective, the son of a Jewish mother should be circumcised, and for whatever reason this had not been attended to. Paul therefore seems concerned not to cause any unnecessary offense. After this, they traveled from town to town, delivering the decision reached at the Jerusalem Council. So the churches were strengthened in the faith and grew in numbers.

Paul and his companions traveled extensively, guided by the Holy Spirit. At Troas, Paul had a vision of a man of Macedonia standing and pleading with him: "Come over to Macedonia and help us" (16:9). Since Luke reports that *we* got ready to leave, one would assume that he was present at the time. They consequently made their way to Philippi, a Roman colony and the leading city in that district. On the Sabbath, *we* went outside the city gate to the river where *we* supposed there would be a place of prayer. *We* sat down and began to speak with the women gathered there. One of them, named *Lydia*, was a merchant and a God-fearing Gentile. She believed and was baptized along with the members of her household. "If you consider me a believer in the Lord," she said, "come and stay at my house." So she persuaded *us*.

Once when they were going to a place of prayer, they were met by a slave girl who predicted the future, and thereby earned considerable money for her owners. This girl followed after them, shouting: "These men are servants of the Most High God, who are telling you the way to be saved." She continued to do so for several days. Finally, Paul became so troubled that he turned around and said to the spirit: "In the name of Jesus Christ I command you to come out of her!" At that moment the spirit left her, as did her profit as fortune teller. When her owners realized this, they seized Paul and Silas and dragged them before the authorities. "These men are Jews," they explained, "and are throwing our city into an uproar by advocating customs unlawful for us Romans to accept or practice."

The two were subsequently beaten and thrown into prison. About midnight, Paul and Silas were praying and singing hymns, while the other prisoners were listening to them. Suddenly there was such a violent earthquake that the foundations of the prison were shaken, all the prison doors flew open, and everyone's chains came loose. Not surprising, the jailor awoke. When he saw the doors open, he drew his sword and was about to kill himself since he thought the prisoners had escaped and he would be held accountable. But Paul shouted: "Don't harm yourself! We are all here!" The jailor then brought them out and asked: "Sirs, what must I do to be saved?" They replied: "Believe in the Lord Jesus, and you will be saved--you and your household." This "should be interpreted not that by the jailer's belief everyone would be saved, but rather that everyone in his house that believed would be saved. ...As a result of the proclamation, those in the jailer's house were baptized."[209]

When it was daylight, the jailor told Paul: "The magistrates have ordered that you and Silas be released. Now you can leave. Go in peace." But Paul responded: "They beat us publicly without a trial, even though we are Roman citizens, and threw us into prison. And now do they want to get rid of us quietly? No! Let them come themselves and escort us out." When the magistrates learned that they were Roman citizens, they were alarmed. "Reports of their deed could even disqualify them from office and (in theory, at least) deprive Philippi of its status as a Roman colony. This strategy would help secure the future safety of the fledgling Christian community."[210] The magistrates wasted no time in coming to appease the two, escorted them from the prison, and asked them to leave the city.

They subsequently made their way to Thessalonica, where there was a Jewish synagogue. As was his custom, Paul went to the synagogue and on three successive Sabbath days reasoned from the Scriptures how Christ must suffer and rise from the dead (17:2). But certain Jews rounded up some of the bad characters from the marketplace, formed a mob, and started a riot in the city. They rushed to Jason's house in search of Paul and Silas, but when they could not find them, they dragged Jason and others before the authorities. "These men who have caused trouble all over the world have come here," they complained, "and Jason has welcomed them into his house. They are all defying Caesar's decrees, saying that there is another king, one called Jesus." The magistrates caused Jason and the others to post bond, and let them go.

As soon as it was night, the brothers sent Paul and Silas away to Berea. "Now the Bereans were of more noble character than the Thessalonians, for they received the message with great eagerness and examined the Scriptures every day to see if what Paul said was true." As a result, many of the Jews believed, as did also a number of prominent Greek women and many Greek men." When the Jews in Thessalonica learned that Paul was preaching in Berea, they followed him there, agitating the crowds to oppose him. The brothers sent him off to Athens, where Silas and Timothy would join him as soon as possible.

While awaiting the arrival of his companions, Paul was greatly distressed to see that the city was full of idols (17:16). So he reasoned in the synagogue with the Jews and God-fearing Gentiles, and in the marketplace with whoever happened to be there. So it was that a group of Epicurean and Stoic philosophers began to dispute with them. The *Epicurean* was more likely to be from the privileged class, and the *Stoic* from the general populace. The former held that if God existed, he was not involved in the affairs of men, and life's chief goal was to find pleasure. The latter professed to believe in the gods, and led a self-disciplined life. Paul would discover more common ground with the Stoic.

Some of them asked: "What is this babbler trying to say?" Others remarked: "He seems to be advocating foreign gods." Then they brought him before a meeting of the Areopagus, where they inquired of him: "May we know what this new teaching is that you are presenting?" Luke observes: "All the Athenians and the foreigners who lived there spent their time doing nothing but talking about and listening to the latest ideas." Socrates had also been *led* or *brought* to the Areopagus many centuries before, as was well known. "Socrates was the ideal philosopher, and Luke may portray Paul as a new Socrates for his Greek audience; given the outcome of Socrates' speech (which, like Stephen's, provoked his hearers to martyr him), this allusion builds suspense."[211]

Paul then stood up in the meeting of the Aeropagus, and said: "Men of Athens! I see that in every way you are very religious. For as I walked around and looked carefully at your objects of worship, I even found an altar with the inscription: TO AN UNKNOWN GOD. Now what you worship as something unknown I am going to proclaim to you." Having done so, he concludes: "In the past God overlooked such ignorance, but now he commands all people everywhere to repent. For he has set a day when he will judge the world with justice by the man he has appointed. He has given proof of this to all men by raising him from the dead." Until now Paul had probably carried most of his audience with him. "But as soon as he started talking about repentance (which implies sin) and judgment (which implies moral responsibility) and the resurrection and return of Jesus (which ran counter to all their ideas of death and immortality, he had lost them--or at least most of them."[212] Some derided him, others deferred judgment, and a few believed.

After this, Paul left Athens for Corinth. There he met Aquila and Priscilla, who had recently come from Rome, because Claudias had ordered all Jews to leave the city. Since Paul was a tentmaker by trade, he worked and lived with them, and every Sabbath reasoned in the synagogue concerning Christ. When Silas and Timothy arrived, he devoted himself exclusively to proclaiming the gospel. But when the Jews opposed him and became abusive, he said to them: "Your blood be on your own heads! I am clear of my responsibility. From now on I will go to the Gentiles." Then Paul left the synagogue and went next door to the house of Titius Justus, a God-fearing Gentile. There he continued to minister for a year and a half, teaching the word of God, and seeing it bear fruit.

While at Corinth, Paul is thought to have written *First* and *Second Thessalonians.* What he develops in the first of his epistles would seem relevant to a fledgling church, enthusiastic but in need of instruction, attempting to live out its faith. It would appear that, on the whole, the apostle was well satisfied with the progress the Thessalonians had made. " But he was never the man to dwell on past achievements, whether his own or those of his converts. So he applies himself at once to the task of meeting the needs that had become apparent."[213]

One of the problems revolved around Paul himself. It appears that the Jewish opposition continued to discredit the apostle in every way they could conceive. Paul responds: "You are witnesses, and so is God, of how holy, righteous and blameless we were among you who believed. For you know that we dealt with each of you as a father deals with his own children, encouraging, comforting and urging you to live lives worthy of God, who calls you into his kingdom and glory" (2:10-12).

Another involved persecution by the pagans. Paul comments: "For you, brothers, became imitators of God's churches in Judea, which are in Christ Jesus; you suffered from your own countrymen the same things those churches suffered from the Jews, who killed the Lord Jesus and the prophets and also drove us out" (2:14). So by implication, they ought to rejoice in that they are found worthy to suffer persecution for Christ's sake.

For this and other reasons, they were tempted to return to a less demanding pagan lifestyle. Paul responds: "It is God's will that you should be sanctified--that you should avoid sexual immorality; that each of you should learn to control his own body in a way that is holy and honorable, not in passionate lust like the heathen, who do not know God" (4:3-5). In this regard, we are reminded of Paul's admonition to the Romans: "Do not conform any longer to the pattern of this world, but be transformed by the renewing of your mind" (12:2).

Some appear content not to work, but live off the charity of others. Paul enjoins them: "Make it your ambition to lead a quiet life, to mind your own business and to work with your hands, just as we told you, so that your daily life may win the respect of outsiders and so that you will not be dependent on anybody" (4:11). In this connection, the Hebrew work ethic consisted of *industry*, coupled with *generosity*.

There seems to have been a misunderstanding as to what Paul had to say about the return of Christ. Paul clarifies: "Brothers, we do not want you to be ignorant about those who fall asleep, or to grieve like the rest of men, who have no hope. We believe that Jesus died and rose again and so we believe that God will bring with Jesus those who have fallen asleep in him. ...After that, we who are still alive and are left will be caught up together with them in the clouds to meet the Lord in the air" (4:13-15, 17). "So we will be with the Lord forever," the apostle adds. "Therefore encourage each other with these words."

Some seem to have assumed a lax attitude toward the *parousia*. Paul admonishes them: "Now, brothers, ...you know very well that the day of the Lord will come like a thief in the night. While people are saying, 'Peace and safety,' destruction will come on them suddenly, as labor pains on a pregnant woman, and they will escape" (5:1-3). *But you*, "brothers, are not in darkness, so that this day should surprise you." You ought rather to encourage one another, as in fact you are doing.

Tension seems to have arisen between those in leadership and the congregation. Paul appeals: "Now we ask you, brothers, to respect those who work hard among you, who are over you in the Lord and who admonish you. Hold them in the highest regard in love because of their work. Live in peace with each other" (5:12-13). So it is that the apostle describes their leaders as working hard among them, being over them in the Lord, and admonishing them. The qualifying phrase *in the Lord* suggests that the leaders were in turn accountable to the Lord for their service. The bottom line is that the people should regard their leaders for what they do, and not for personal qualities--which may be lacking.

There appears to have been some disagreement concerning the exercise of spiritual gifts. Paul counsels: "Do not put out the Spirit's fire; do not treat prophecies with contempt. Test everything. Hold on to the good. Avoid every kind of evil" (5:19-22). In more general terms, "Be joyful always, pray continually, give thanks in all circumstances, for this is God's will for you in Christ Jesus."

Paul's second epistle was probably written within months of his first. In particular, there are two matters that Paul deals with in the second epistle. "The first is doctrinal. Evidently a report was circulating in the church that 'the day of the Lord had already come.' ...The second matter is of more practical nature and something addressed in the earlier letter: namely, the problem of 'those who are idle.'"[214] As for the former, "Don't let anyone deceive you in any way, for that day will not come until the rebellion occurs and the man of lawlessness is revealed. ...The coming of the lawless one will be in accordance with the work of Satan displayed in all kinds of counterfeit miracles, signs and wonders" (2:3, 9). While the notion of *rebellion* often conveys a political event, it can be used in connection with apostasy. Perhaps both are implicated in the apostle's comment.

As for the latter concern, "In the name of the Lord Jesus Christ, we command you, brothers, to keep away from every brother who is idle and does not live according to the teaching you received from us. ...For even when we were with you, we gave you this rule: 'If a man will not work, he shall not eat'" (3:6, 10). "As for you brothers," the apostle concludes, "never tire of doing what is right."

Paul's travels eventually brought him to Ephesus. There he found certain who had been baptized by John. "Johns' baptism was a baptism of repentance," Paul explained. "He told the people to believe in the one coming after him, that is, in Jesus" (19:4). On hearing this, they were baptized into the name of the Lord Jesus. Then, when Paul placed his hands on them, the Holy Spirit came on them, and they spoke in tongues and prophesied.

Paul entered the synagogue and spoke boldly there for three months.

But some became obstinate, refused to believe, and publically maligned the Way. So Paul left them, and held discussions daily in the lecture hall of Tyrannus. This went on for two years so that many in the region heard the gospel proclaimed. God also did extraordinary miracles through Paul, so that many of those who believed came and openly confessed their evil deeds. A number who had practiced sorcery brought their scrolls together and burned them publically. In this manner, the word of the Lord spread widely and grew in power.

About this time, there arose a great disturbance about the Way. A silversmith named *Demetrius*, who made shrines to Artemis, called together those of his trade and associated trades, and said: "Men, ...you see and hear how this fellow Paul has convinced and led astray large numbers of people here in Ephesus, and in practically the whole province of Asia. He says that man-made gods are no gods at all. There is danger not only that our trade will lose its good name, but also that the temple of the great goddess Artemis will be discredited." When they heard this, they were furious and began shouting: "Great is Artemis of the Ephesians!" Soon the whole city was in an uproar. The people seized certain of Paul's companions and rushed them into the theater. Paul wanted to appear before the crowd, but the disciples restrained him.

The city clerk quieted the crowd. "You have brought these men here, though they have neither robbed temples nor blasphemed our goddess," he observed. "If, then, Demetrius and his fellow craftsmen have a grievance against anybody, the courts are open and there are proconsuls. ...As it is, we are in danger of being charged with rioting because of today's events." If there was one thing the Romans would not tolerate, it was that things get out of hand. After this, the official dismissed the assembly. When the uproar had ended, Paul left on a journey that would eventually bring him to Jerusalem.

At Troas, Paul extended his message until after midnight, because he intended to leave the next day. There were many lamps in the upstairs room where they were meeting. Seated in a window was a young man named *Eutychus*, who was sinking into a deep sleep as Paul talked on and on. When he was sound asleep, he fell to the ground from the third story and was picked up for dead. Paul went down and threw himself on the young man. "Don't be alarmed," he declared. "He is alive!" (20:10). The people took Eutychus home alive, and were greatly comforted.

At Melitus, Paul sent to Ephesus for the elders to join him. When they arrived, he said to them: "And now, compelled by the Spirit, I am going to Jerusalem, not knowing what will happen to me there. ...Keep watch over yourselves and all the flock of which the Holy Spirit has made you overseers. Be shepherds of the church of God, which he bought with his own blood" (20:22, 28). Then when he had spoken along this line, he knelt down with them and prayed. He didn't tarry longer, for he hoped to reach Jerusalem in time for Pentecost.

IMPRISONED

Once again Luke introduces *we* into the narrative. "After *we* had torn ourselves away from them (the Ephesian elders), *we* put out to sea and sailed straight to Cos. *We* found a ship crossing over to Phoenicia, went on board and set sail. After sighting Cyprus and passing to the south of it, *we* sailed to Syria. *We* landed at Tyre, where our ship was to unload its cargo" (21:1-3). Finding disciples there, they stayed with them seven days. During this time, the Spirit warned Paul through them of the danger awaiting him in Jerusalem. He, however, was determined to press on, believing this to be God's will for him.

They continued their journey first to Ptolemais and then to Caesarea. In the latter instance, a prophet named *Agabus* took Paul's belt, tied his own hands and feet with it and warned: "In this way the Jews of Jerusalem will bind the owner of this belt and will hand him over to the Gentiles." When the disciples heard this, they pled with the apostle not to go up to Jerusalem. Then Paul inquired: "Why are you weeping and breaking my heart? I am ready not only to be bound, but also to die in Jerusalem for the name of the Lord Jesus." Luke would seem intent on pointing out the similarity between the passion accounts of Jesus and Paul.

When they arrived in Jerusalem, they received a warm welcome from the brothers there. The next day, they went to see James and all of the elders present. Paul greeted them, and reported in detail of his labors and God's blessing. Then they said to him: "You see, brother, how many thousands of Jews have believed, and all of them are zealous for the Law. They have been informed that you teach all the Jews who live among the Gentiles to turn away from Moses, telling them not to circumcise their children or live according to our customs." To correct this misunderstanding, they suggested that Paul sponsor the purification rites of four young men. This would in no way compromise the decision reached earlier concerning Gentile believers.

So it was that the next day Paul took the men and purified himself along with them. Then they went to the temple to give notice of the date when the days of purification would end, and the offering would be made for each of them. When the seven days were nearly over, some Jews from the province of Asia saw Paul at the temple. They stirred up the people, shouting: "Men of Israel, help us! This is the man who teaches all men everywhere against our people and our law and this place. And besides, he has brought Greeks into the temple area and defiled this holy place." Luke explains: "They had previously seen Trophimus the Ephesian in the city with Paul and assumed that Paul had brought him into the temple area."

The whole city was aroused, and people came running from all directions. Seizing Paul, they dragged him from the temple, and shut the gates behind him. While they were bent on killing him, news reached the commander of the Roman troops in the city. He immediately took some of his officers and soldiers and forced their way into the crowd. When the people saw the Romans, they stopped beating Paul. The commander had the apostle chained, and asked what he had done. Some in the crowd shouted one thing, and some another. When the commander could not get at the truth because of the uproar, he ordered the prisoner taken into the barracks. When Paul reached the steps, the violence of the mob was so great that he had to be carried by the soldiers. The crowd that followed kept shouting: "Away with him!"

As the soldiers were about to take Paul into the barracks, he asked permission to speak to the people. The commander allowed him to do so. Paul, in turn, launched into an account of his experience on the Damascus' road. The crowed listened until he recalled Jesus' commission to him: "Go, I will send you far away to the Gentiles." Then they raised their voices, shouting: "Rid the earth of him! He's not fit to live." At this, the commander ordered that Paul be taken back into the barracks and flogged.

"Even had Paul not been a Roman citizen, the tribune would have no authority to try a provincial belonging to another jurisdiction... . But it was legal to scourge slaves or aliens to extort confession or to determining the truth concerning a situation."[215] While the apostle had previously been beaten with rods, this was with the *flagellum*--leather thongs into which pieces of metal or stone were woven. It could easily lead to the victim's death. As they stretched him out to flog him, Paul inquired of the centurion in charge: "Is it legal for you to flog a Roman citizen who hasn't even been found guilty?" Those who were about to question him withdrew immediately. The commander himself was alarmed when he realized that he had put a Roman citizen in chains.

Since the commander wanted to know precisely why Paul was being accused, he ordered him released from his chains and brought before the Sanhedrin. The apostle, looking straight at the council, declared: "My brothers, I have fulfilled my duty to God in all good conscience to this day" (23:1). At this, the high priest ordered those nearby to strike him on the mouth. Then Paul responded: "God will strike you, you whitewashed wall! You sit there to judge me according to the law, yet you yourself violate the law by commanding that I be struck!" Those standing near the apostle asked: "You dare to insult God's high priest?" "Brothers, I did not realize that he was the high priest," Paul replied, "for is written: 'Do not speak evil about the ruler of your people'" (cf. Exod. 22:28). "This has sometimes been taken to mean that Paul had literally failed to recognize Ananias, either through weakness of sight or because he did not know him by sight. But more likely he resorted to irony, as much to say, 'I did not recognize the high priest in the behavior and speech of this man.'"[216]

Then Paul, knowing that some of the council members were Sadducees and others Pharisees, asserted: "My brothers, I am a Pharisee, the son of a Pharisee. I stand on trial because of my hope in the resurrection of the dead." When they heard this, a dispute broke out between the two opposing sects. It became so violent that the commander had Paul removed and returned to the barracks. When news reached him of a conspiracy to have the prisoner killed, he sent him on to Caesarea, along with an account of what had happened.

Five days later, the high priest Ananias, some of the elders, and the lawyer Tertullus presented their case against the apostle before the governor Felix. Paul's defense was along this line: "My accusers did not find me arguing with anyone at the temple, or stirring up a crowd in the synagogue or anywhere else in the city. ...However, I admit that I worship the God of our fathers as a follower of the Way, which they call a sect." Then Felix, who was well acquainted with the Way, adjourned the proceedings. "When Lysias the commander comes," he said, "I will decide your case."

When two years had passed, Felix was succeeded by Porcius Festus. Paul was still in prison, as a favor to the Jews. Festus, likewise intent on doing the Jews a favor, inquired of Paul: "Are you willing to go up to Jerusalem and stand trial before me there on these charges?" He answered: "I am now standing before Caesar's court, where I ought to be tried." After conferring with his council, Festus responded: "You have appealed to Caesar. To Caesar you will go!"

A few days later King Agrippa II and Bernice (his sister) arrived to pay their respects to Festus. Since they were spending some time there, he discussed Paul's case with the king. Then Agrippa said to Festus: "I would like to hear this man myself" (25:22). Agrippa replied: "Tomorrow you will hear him." Once more, Paul takes this opportunity to share his experience. At one point, Festus breaks in: "You are out of your mind, Paul! Your great learning is driving you insane." "I am not insane, most excellent Festus," Paul protested. "What I am saying is reasonable and true."

Turning his attention to Agrippa, Paul continued: "King Agrippa, do you believe the prophets? I know you do." Agrippa responded: "Do you think that in such a short time you can persuade me to be a Christian?" Some have taken this as a rather superficial comment made to hide the kings' embarrassment. "Others have found in the words a gentle irony, as if...pointing out that it was not so simple a matter to become a Christian even if one did believe the prophets. Others again regard Agrippa as expressing cold disdain, adopting the tone...of Jewish orthodoxy in response to this Christian enthusiast."[217] In any case, Paul replies: "Short time or long--I pray God that not only you but all who are listening to me today may become what I am, except for these chains." When they had left the room, Agrippa confided in Festus: "This man could have been set free if he had not appealed to Caesar."

Since *Romans* is thought to be written in anticipation of a visit to Rome, probably from Corinth (cf. 20:3), we touch on it in passing before taking up the account of Paul's journey to the Imperial City. The epistle is divided into doctrinal and practical sections, the latter beginning with chapter 12. F.F. Bruce develops Paul's argument in the first section in five connections.[218] First, Paul declares: "I am not ashamed of the gospel, because it is the power of God for the salvation of everyone who believes; first for the Jew, then for the Gentile. For in the gospel a righteousness from God is revealed, a righteousness that is by faith first to last" (1:16-17). "The expression, *faith from first to last*, is an agreeable rendering, which literally reads, *from faith to faith*. ...God's righteousness both awakens faith and produces faith. ...Faith is less a quantum of something possessed than an orientation in which one participates actively and freely."[219]

Second, the need of such a message becomes clear as we contemplate the world in which we live. "For although they knew God, they neither glorified him as God nor gave thanks to him, but their thinking became futile and their foolish hearts were darkened" (1:21). "What shall we say then? Are we any better? Not at all! We have already made it clear that

Jews and Gentiles alike are all under sin" (3:8).

Third, if persons are to be pronounced righteous before God it must be by his grace rather than our merit. "But now a righteousness from God, apart from law, has been made known to which the Law and the Prophets testify. This righteousness from God comes through faith in Jesus Christ to all who believe. There is no difference, for all have sinned and fall short of the glory of God, and are justified freely by his grace through the redemption that came by Christ Jesus" (3:21-24).

Fourth, in Christ we are raised to a life freed from the bondage of sin. "What then? Shall we sin because we are not under law but under grace? By no means! ...You have been set free from sin and have become slaves to righteousness" (6:15, 18). "Therefore, there is now no condemnation for those who are in Christ Jesus, because through Christ Jesus the law of the Spirit of life set me free from the law of sin and death" (8:1-2).

Fifth, there remains a faithful remnant within Israel. "I ask then: Did God reject his people? By no means! I am an Israelite myself, a descendant of Abraham, from the tribe of Benjamin" (11:1). "Again I ask: Did they stumble so as to fall beyond recovery? Not at all! Rather, because of their transgression, salvation has come to the Gentiles to make Israel envious. But if their transgression means riches for the world, and their loss means riches for the Gentiles, how much greater riches will their fullness bring!" (11:11-12).

"Therefore, I urge you, brothers, in view of God's mercy, to offer your bodies as living sacrifices, holy and pleasing to God--this is your spiritual act of worship" (12:1). So originates "the most aesthetic formulation of Christian ethics in Scripture. Earlier buds of ethics (6:12-23; 8:12-13) now come to full flower. The issue concerns not religious renewal or increased spiritual consciousness, but the transformation of bodily existence as an expression of spiritual worship."[220]

The circumstances under which Paul would sail for Rome had changed, but not his message. He and other prisoners were handed over to a centurion named *Julius*, who belonged to the Imperial Regiment. This, in turn, has been identified with the"Cohors I Augusta, a regiment of auxiliaries attested by inscriptions to have been in Syria after A.D. 6 and in Batanea (Bashan, east of Galilee) in the time of Herod Agrippa II. A detachment of the cohort may have been stationed at Caesarea. The duty assigned to Julius normally fell to centurions."[221]

"*We* boarded a ship from Adramyttium about to sail for ports along the coast of the province of Asia," Luke reports, "and *we* put out to sea" (27:2). The next day, they landed at Sidon, and Julius out of kindness to

Paul allowed him to go to his friends so that they might provide for his needs. From there, they put out to sea again and sailed in the lee of Cyprus, because the prevailing winds were against them. In such manner, Luke continues to describe the voyage in some detail.

As they were sailing along the shore of Crete, a wind of hurricane force bore down upon them. When the men had hoisted the lifeboat aboard, they passed ropes under the ship itself to hold it together. Fearing that they would run aground on the sandbars of Syrtis, they lowered the sea anchor and let the ship be driven along. "*We* took such a violent battering from the storm that the next day they began to throw the cargo overboard. On the third day, they threw the ship's tackle overboard with their own hands. When neither sun nor stars appeared for many days and the storm continued raging, *we* finally gave up all hope of being saved."

After the men had gone a long time without food, Paul stood up before them and said: "Last night and angel of the God whose I am and whom I serve stood beside me and said, 'Do not be afraid, Paul. You must stand trial before Caesar; and God has graciously given you the lives of all who sail with you.' So keep up your courage, men, for I have faith in God that it will happen just as he told me."

Time which must have seemed an eternity passed. About midnight, the sailors sensed that they were approaching land. They took soundings and found that the water was a hundred and twenty feet deep. A short time later they took soundings, and found it was ninety feet deep. Fearing they would be dashed against the rocks, they dropped four anchors from the stern, and prayed for daylight. When daylight came, they didn't recognize the land, but they saw a bay with a sandy beach--where they decided to run the ship aground. Cutting loose the anchors, they untied the ropes that held the rudders. Then they hoisted the foresail to the wind and made for the beach. However, the bow stuck fast in a sandbar, and the stern was broken to pieces by the pounding of the surf. The soldiers planned to kill the prisoners, so none would escape, but the Centurion intervened out of deference to Paul. He ordered those who could swim to jump overboard first and get to land. The rest were to get there on planks or other pieces of the ship. In this manner, everyone reached land safely.

Their landfall was Malta. Its inhabitants showed great kindness, and built a fire--since it was raining and cold. Paul gathered a pile of brushwood, and as he was putting it on the fire a viper fastened itself on his hand. When the native people saw this, they supposed that he must be a murderer, for though he escaped from the sea *Justice* would not allow him to live. But when he showed no ill effects, they changed their minds, and decided that he was a god.

After three months, they again set sail. At Puteoli (a sea-coast town on the Bay of Naples), they found believers, who invited them to stay for the week. After this, they pressed on toward Rome. Along the way, they met others from Rome who had heard of their coming and had come to meet them. At the sight of these men, Paul thanked God and was encouraged. When they got to Rome, Paul was allowed to live by himself, with a soldier to guard him. "For two whole years Paul stayed there in his own rented house and welcomed all who came to see him. Boldly and without hindrance he preached the kingdom of God and taught about the Lord Jesus Christ" (18:30-31).

This also allowed him to correspond with the congregations he had spawned and ministered to. *Philippians* provides a prime case in point. After the salutation and the assurance of his profound thanksgiving and prayer for this friends at Philippi, "Paul tells them how his present situation, despite the restrictions of imprisonment, has promoted the spread of the gospel among the officials in whose care he is and has encouraged many of the local Christians to be more uninhibited in witnessing to their faith."[222] He concludes: "For to me, to live is Christ and to die is gain" (1:21).

He then makes an appeal for harmony among the brothers. "If you have any encouragement from being united with Christ, if any comfort from his love, if any fellowship with the Spirit, if any tenderness and compassion, then make my joy complete by being like-minded, having the same love, being one in spirit and purpose" (2:1-2). "Do nothing out of selfish ambition or vain conceit," the apostle continues, "but in humility consider others better than yourselves. Each of you should look not only to your own interests, but also to the interests of others."

Then, as if an afterthought, Paul warns them about subversive intruders. "Watch out for those dogs, those men who do evil, those mutilators of the flesh" (3:2). He has one group in mind, described in three ways: as *dogs, men who do evil,* and *mutilators of the flesh.* All things considered, it seems best to identify these reprobate persons as Jewish believers, who insist on enforcing Gentile Christians to be circumcised.

Paul exhorts his readers: "Rejoice in the Lord always. I will say it again: Rejoice! Let your gentleness be evident to all. The Lord is near. Do not be anxious about anything, but in everything, by prayer and petition, with thanksgiving, present your requests to God. And the peace of God, which transcends all understanding, will guard your hearts and your minds in Christ Jesus" (4:4-7). "Finally, brothers," for the second time he would conclude (cf. 3:1), "whatever is true, whatever is noble, whatever is right, whatever is pure, whatever is lovely, excellent or praiseworthy--think about such things."

ACTS 29

Acts 29 represents the continuing story line, picking up where Luke left off. We will explore this expanded narrative in two connections: with the *Pastoral Epistles*, and *Revelation.* As for the former, they would seem to indicate that Paul secured release from prison, only to return at a later date to face execution. As for the latter, it peers down the dim corridors of time toward eternity. In this regard, it completes the comprehensive narrative begun with *Genesis*, and sometimes designated as *Salvation History.*

The picture of Paul emerging from 1 Timothy and Titus portrays him traveling freely in the East. "He and Titus have evangelized Crete (Titus 1:5); he has apparently traveled to Ephesus with Timothy and hopes to return (1 Tim. 1:3; 3:14); at some point in all of this he intends to winter in Nicopolis, on the southern Adriatic (Titus 3:12)."[223] However, in 2 Timothy he is again in prison, this time in close confinement, anticipating death. None of this can be realistically reconciled with Luke's narrative, unless it describes a subsequent period in Paul's life. This traditional resolution is by far the best that has been proposed.

"Paul, an apostle of Christ Jesus by the command of God our Savior and of Christ Jesus our hope, to Timothy my true son in the faith: grace, mercy and peace from God the Father and Jesus our Lord" (1:1-2). So reads the salutation. So also we are alerted to the author and addressee.

"As I urged you when I went into Macedonia," Paul writes, "stay here in Ephesus so that you may command certain men not to teach false doctrines any longer nor to devote themselves to myths and endless genealogies" (1:3). The apostle further explains: "These promote controversies rather than God's work--which is by faith. The goal of this command is love, which comes from a pure heart and a good conscience and a sincere faith. Some have wandered away from these and turned to meaningless talk. They want to be teachers of the law, but they do not know what they are talking about."

Such would vividly contrast to Paul's disposition. He consequently writes: "Here is a trustworthy saying that deserves full acceptance: Christ Jesus came into the world to save sinners--of whom I am the worst. But for that very reason I was shown mercy so that in me, the worst of sinners, Christ Jesus might display his unlimited patience as an example for those who would believe on him and receive eternal life" (1:15-16).

The apostle proceeds to instruct Timothy in his duties (1:18). As for worship, intercede for those in authority, and observe proper decorum in the services. As for leaders in the church, they must be exemplary and diligent. As for older persons, treat them as parents. As for younger persons, treat them as brothers and sisters. As for widows devoted to the church, see to it that they are worthy of such recognition. As for masters and slaves, let them respect one another. As for possessions, be content with life's necessities.

"But you, man of God, flee from all this (the acquisition of wealth), and pursue righteousness, godliness, faith, love, endurance and gentleness. Fight the good fight of the faith. Take hold of the eternal life to which you were called when you made your good confession in the presence of many witnesses" (6:11-12). *Fight the good fight* "may by this time have become stereotyped as an athletic metaphor, or it may still have retained its military meaning. Whether in contest or in conflict, the verb implies a disciplined struggle already begun."[224]

While 1 Timothy and Titus have much in common, there are notable differences. "Like Timothy (1 Tim. 1:3), Titus has been *left* on Crete, but unlike Timothy, who was left to reform an established church, Titus has been left behind to set in order what had not yet been accomplished, namely, the *appointing* of elders in the various churches over the whole island (1:5)."[225] Consequently, Titus appears to have been written at a later time, when there was less urgency.

"The reason I left you in Crete," Paul writes, "was that you might straighten out what was left unfinished and appoint elders in every town" (1:5). "Since an overseer is entrusted with God's work, he must be blameless--not overbearing, not quick-tempered, not given to drunkenness, not violent, not pursuing dishonest gain. Rather he must be hospitable, one who loves what is good, who is self-controlled, upright, holy and disciplined." He must also hold firmly to what he has received, encourage others to embrace sound doctrine, and refute those who would oppose it.

"Remind the people to be subject to rulers and authorities, to be obedient, to be ready to do whatever is good, to slander no one, to be peaceable and considerate, and to show true humility toward all men"

(3:1). Avoid foolish controversies. "Warn a divisive person, once, and then warn him a second time. After that, have nothing to do with him" (3:10). By his intransigence, he condemns himself.

The key to understanding 2 Timothy is to recognize Paul's altered circumstances. He is no longer free to pursue his itinerant ministry. "Arrested once again (probably in Troas), he is now in confined imprisonment in Rome (1:16-17; 2:9). He has already undergone a preliminary hearing (4:16-18) and is awaiting his final trial, from which he has little hope of anything except death (4:6-8)."[226] Meanwhile, the situation at Ephesus has worsened. Some, from whom the apostle would have expected better things, have deserted him and the gospel (1:15), and despite his prior excommunication, Hymenaeus is still creating havoc (2:17-18).

"You then, my son, be strong in the grace that is in Christ Jesus. And the things you have heard me say in the presence of many witnesses entrust to reliable men who will also be qualified to teach others. Endure hardship with us like a good soldier of Christ Jesus" (2:1-3). "Do your best to be approved, a workman who does not need to be ashamed and who correctly handles the word of truth." In this connection, "All Scripture is God-breathed and is useful for teaching, rebuking, correcting and training in righteousness, so that the man of God may be thoroughly equipped for every good work" (3:16).

As for Paul, he writes: "For I am already being poured out like a drink offering, and the time has come for my departure. I have fought the good fight, I have finished the course, I have kept the faith. Now there is in store for me the crown of righteousness, which the Lord, the righteous Judge, will award to me on that day--and not only to me, but also to all who have longed for his appearing" (4:6-8). *For I* contrasts to *but you* (v. 5). Whereas Paul's ministry is coming to a triumphant conclusion, others will now have to carry on the gospel ministry.

With such in mind, we turn our attention to *Revelation.* The text begins: "The revelation of Jesus Christ which God gave him to show his servants what must soon take place" (1:1). The term *revelation* (*apokalypsis*) provides a key to what will follow. The primary intent of such literature is to reveal the mysteries of God "to believers presently experiencing oppression and suffering. ...Further, I suspect that John has an evangelistic purpose for writing Revelation: his desire is that even the non-believer respond to his message of God's triumph over the anti-Christian kingdom and be converted."[227] While the latter may be true, it perhaps reflects a more cautious and considered approach to those who might otherwise resort to opposition and persecution.

Visionary literature is what its name implies: imagined pictures, "frequently symbolic rather than literal, of events that have not yet happened at the time of writing, or of realities such as heaven that transcend ordinary reality. Such writing requires that readers be ready to use their imagination--to let it fly beyond the stars."[228] It is also as a rule revolutionary in character, since it announces the conclusion of things as they now are, and the advent of new, exciting opportunities.

Revelation is a qualified apocalypse, written to encourage those who have or may put their faith in God's sovereign purpose for mankind as revealed in Christ's exaltation. It is God and not Satan "who sits on heaven's throne, it is God who exercises judgment against the enemies of the Lord's reign; it is God who can make good on the Bible's promise of salvation; and it is God who dispenses the blessings of salvation to the community of those who faithfully follow the Lamb."[229]

Consistent with this purpose, John addresses seven churches of Asia Minor, congregations with which he was personally familiar. As a case in point (concerning Ephesus), "I (Christ) know your deeds, your hard work and your perseverance. I know that you cannot tolerate wicked men, that you have tested those who claim to be apostles, but are not, and have found them false. You have persevered and have endured hardships for my name, and have not grown weary" (2:2-3). "Yet I hold this against you: You have forsaken your first love. Remember the height from which you have fallen! Repent and do the things you did at first." It is not clear whether this pertains to love for Christ, or for one another, or for mankind at large. "It may be that a general attitude is meant which included all three. ...They had yielded to the temptation, ever present to Christians, to put all their emphasis on sound teaching. In the process they lost love, without which all else is nothing."[230]

As another case in point (concerning Laodicea), "I know your deeds, that you are neither cold nor hot. I wish you were either one or the other! So, because you are lukewarm...I am about to spit you out of my mouth" (3:15-16). "The imagery may be derived from the water-supply of the city which appears to have been drawn from hot springs at some distance, so that it arrived at the city lukewarm. This forms a contrast with the hot springs at nearby Hierapolis and the cold, refreshing water at Colosse."[231] Hot water has healing properties and cold water refreshes, but lukewarm water serves neither purpose.

After this, John sees a door standing open in heaven, and a voice invites him: "Come up here, and I will show you what must take place after this" (4:1). "At once I was in the Spirit, and there before me was a throne in heaven with someone sitting on it." God's *throne* is mentioned in virtually every chapter, as a continuing testimony to his sovereign character and encouragement to those who trust their ways to him. A rainbow encircled the throne, which was surrounded by twenty-four other thrones on which were seated elders. They were dressed in white, and had crowns of gold on their heads. From the throne came flashes of lightning, rumblings and peals of thunder. Before the throne were seven blazing lamps, representing the seven spirits of God--an apparent reference to the Holy Spirit. Also before the throne was what looked like a sea of glass, clear as crystal. In the center, around the throne, were four living creatures. Day and night, they never stopped declaring: "Holy, holy, holy is the Lord God Almighty, who was, and is, and is to come." At which the elders would fall down before him who sat upon the throne to worship him.

Then John saw in the right hand of him who sat on the throne a scroll with seven seals. After this, he saw an angel inquiring in a loud voice: "Who is worthy to break the seals and open the scroll?" (5:2). Since there was not one who could do so, John wept. Then one of the angels encouraged him: "Do not weep! See, the Lion of the tribe of Judah, the Root of David, has triumphed. He is able to open the scroll and its seven seals." John saw a Lamb, looking as if it had been slain, standing in the center of the throne, encircled by the four living creatures and the elders. When he took the scroll, they sang: "You are worthy to take the scroll and to open its seals, because you were slain, and with your blood you purchased men for God from every tribe and language and people and nation. You have made them to be a kingdom and priests to serve our God, and they will reign on the earth." Angels likewise responded, as did every creature in heaven and earth.

John watched as the Lamb opened the first of the seals, the second, and so on until it had opened all seven. This is the first of a series of sevens: *seven* seals (5:1-8:5), *seven* trumpets (8:6-11:19), *seven* signs (12:1-14:20), and *seven* plagues (15:1-16:21). Each symbolize divine judgment. Legal documents were sealed with the attestation of witnesses. They were to be opened only by those authorized to do so. As the Lamb opened the first seal, John looked and there was a white horse! Its rider held a bow, was given a crown, and "rode out as a conqueror bent on conquest." After the sixth seal was open, there was a great earthquake. Then people called for the rocks to fall on them, and shield them from God's wrath.

After this and before the seventh seal was opened, John sees 144,000 redeemed of Israel (7:3-4). These were joined by a great multitude that no one could count, "from every nation, tribe, people and language, standing before the throne and in front of the Lamb. They were wearing white robes and holding palm branches in their hands." They likewise cried out in a loud voice: "Salvation belongs to our God, who sits on the throne, and to the Lamb." "These are they who have come out of the great tribulation; they have washed their robes and made them white in the blood of the Lamb."

John now returns to the seals. The final seal is opened. There is an impressive silence, which portends the end and serves to build suspense. "But instead it begins a new series of visions heralded by angels with trumpets. This is typical of John's method. He goes over the ground again and again, each time teaching us something new."[232] So he relentlessly pursues his topic, with the conclusion not yet in sight.

When at last the series is completed, one of the angels who had the seven bowls invited John: "Come, I will show you the punishment of the great prostitute, who sits on many waters. With her the kings of the earth committed adultery and the inhabitants of the earth were intoxicated with the wine of her adulteries" (17:1). "I saw that the woman was drunk with the blood of the saints," John reports, "the blood of those who bore testimony to Jesus." Imperial Rome is clearly the culprit.

After this, John sees another angel coming down from heaven. He was given great authority, and the earth was illuminated by his splendor. With a mighty voice, he shouted; "Fallen, Fallen is Babylon the Great" (18:2). Then he heard another voice, saying: "Come out of her, my people, so that you will not share in her sins, so that you will not share any of her plagues." Such brings to mind God's instruction to Lot to leave Sodom so as not to perish in her devastation.

John next hears what sounded like the roar of a great multitude in heaven, shouting: "Hallelujah! Salvation and glory and power belong to our God, for true and just are his judgments" (19:1-2). At this, the twenty-four elders and four living creatures prostrated themselves in worship. Then a voice from the throne urged: "Praise our God all you his servants, you who fear him, both small and great!" At this, John heard what sounded like a great multitude, like the roar of rushing waters and like loud peals of thunder, shouting: "Hallelujah! For our Lord God Almighty reigns. Let us rejoice and be glad and give him glory! For the wedding of the Lamb has come, and his bride has made herself ready." These rejoice not over those who perish, but who reap a reward from righteousness.

Shortly, John saw an angel coming down out of heaven, having the key to the Abyss and having in his hand a great chain (20:1). He seized the dragon, that ancient serpent, who is the devil, or Satan, and bound him for a thousand years. When the thousand years are over, Satan will be released to again deceive people, and gather his associates for a final, desperate engagement. "They marched across the breadth of the earth and surrounded the camp of God's people, the city he loves. But fire came down from heaven and devoured them." Then Satan was thrown into the fire to be tormented day and night for ever.

John subsequently saw a great white throne and him who was seated on it. "And I saw the dead, great and small, standing before the throne, and books were opened. Another book was opened, which is the book of life. The dead were judged according to what they had done as recorded in the books. ...If anyone's name was not found written in the book of life, he was thrown into the lake of fire" (20:12, 15). All would be judged according to their deeds, but any would be forgiven if they repented and embraced God's offer of redemption.

John moreover saw a new heaven and a new earth. "I saw the Holy City, the new Jerusalem, coming down out of heaven from God... . And I heard a loud voice from the throne saying, 'Now the dwelling of God is with men, and he will live with them. They will be his people, and God himself will be with them and be their God. ...There will be no more death or mourning or crying or pain, for the old order of things has passed away" (21:2-4).

The angel also showed John the river of the water of life, as clear as crystal, flowing from the throne of God and the Lamb down the middle of the great street of the city. On each side of the river stood the tree of life, bearing twelve crops of fruit, one for each month of the year. "The throne of God and of the Lamb will be in the city, and his servants will serve him. They will see his face, and his name will be on their foreheads" (22:3-4). There will be no need for a lamp or the light of the sun, because the Lord God will give them light. The ultimate privilege is to *see* and *serve* God, and be acknowledged as his own.

"Behold, I am coming soon! Blessed is he who keeps the words of the prophecy in this book" (22:7). "Behold, I am coming soon! My reward is with me, and I will give to everyone according to what he has done." "The Spirit and the bride say, 'Come!' And let him who hears say, 'Come!' Whosoever is thirsty, let him come, and whoever wishes, let him take the free gift of the water of life." In context, this appears to be a two-edged invitation: for Christ to return and for unbelievers to respond. John has given us a glimpse of the future, but it remains for us to seize the opportunity life affords. In so doing, we add our personal chapter to salvation history.

ENDNOTES

1. Jacob Licht, *Storytelling in the Bible*, p. 14.
2. William Stegner, *Narrative Theology in Early Jewish Christianity*, p. 4.
3. Leland Ryken, *How to Read the Bible as Literature*, p. 52.
4. Annemarie de Waal Malefit, *Religion and Culture*, pp. 151-152.
5. Robert Wall, *Revelation*, p. 272.
6. Gordon Wenham, *Genesis 1-15*, p. 318.
7. David Williams, *Acts*, pp. 308-309.
8. Ryken, *op. cit.*, p. 43.
9. Licht, *op. cit.*, p. 118.
10. Ibid., p. 9.
11. Ryken, *op. cit.*, p. 40.
12. James Mays, *Psalms*, p. 42.
13. Ryken, *op. cit.*, p. 51.
14. Edgar Peters, *Chaos and Order in the Capital Markets*, p. 204.
15. Douglas Hare, *Matthew*, p. 71.
16. Ryken, *op. cit.*, p. 40.
17. Licht, *op. cit.*, p. 96.
18. Herbert Wolf, *An Introduction to the Old Testament Pentateuch*, p. 44.
19. Ibid., p. 78.
20. Morris Inch, *Saga of the Spirit*, p. 14.
21. R. Alan Cole, *Exodus*, p. 56.
22. Licht, *op. cit.*, p. 96.
23. David Griffen, et. al., *Founders of Constructive Postmodern Philosophy*, p. viii.
24. Wolf, *op. cit.*, p. 132.
25. Ibid.
26. Cole, *op. cit.*, p. 219.
27. Samuel Schultz, *Deuteronomy: The Gospel of Love*, p. 116.
28. Frank Eakin, Jr., *The Religion and Culture of Israel*, p. 123.

29. Ryken, *op. cit.*, p. 181.
30. John Polkinghorne, *Quarks, Chaos & Christianity*, p. 37.
31. Glen Tinder, *The Political Meaning of Christianity*, p. 163.
32. Wenham, *op. cit.*, pp. 15-16.
33. Milton Steinberg, *Basic Judaism*, p. 19.
34. Ryken, *op. cit.*, p. 178.
35. Robert Seltzer, *Jewish People, Jewish Thought*, p. 197.
36. Derek Kidner, *Genesis*, p. 78.
37. Victor Hamilton, *The Book of Genesis 1-17*, p. 276.
38. Chaim Clorfene and Yakov Rogalsky, *The Path of the Righteous Gentile*, p. 103.
39. Kidner, *op. cit.*, p. 109.
40. Ryken, *op. cit.*, p. 75.
41. Kidner, *op. cit.*, p. 132.
42. E.A. Speiser, *Genesis*, p. 196.
43. V. Paul Flint, *Strangers & Pilgrims*, p. 166.
44. Ryken, *op. cit.*, p. 165.
45. Ibid., p. 172.
46. Kidner, *op. cit.*, pp. 168-169.
47. Ryken, *op. cit.*, p. 78.
48. John Walton and Victor Matthews, *Bible BackgroundCommentary: Genesis-Deuteronomy*, p. 48.
49. Cole, *op. cit.*, pp. 150-151.
50. Walter Kaiser, Jr., *Toward Old Testament Ethics*, p. 85.
51. Cole, *op. cit.*, p. 158.
52. Ibid., p. 161.
53. R.K. Harrison, *Leviticus*, p. 13.
54. Walton and Matthews, *op. cit.*, p. 177.
55. Ryken, *op. cit.*, pp. 159-161.
56. Meredith Kline, *Treaty of the Great King*, p. 52.
57. J. Carl Laney, *Baker's Concise Bible Atlas*, p. 89.
58. Ryken, *op. cit.*, p. 37.
59. Charles Pfeiffer, *Old Testament History*, p. 219.
60. Arthur Hertzberg (ed.), *Judaism*, p. 148.
61. Leviticus Rabbah, 34; Kiddushin, 49; Genesis Rabbah, 59.
62. E. John Hamlin, *Joshua: Inheriting the Land*, p. 5.
63. Ibid., p. 17.
64. Ibid., p. 45.
65. Kaiser, *op. cit.*, pp. 267-268.
66. Hamlin, *op. cit.*, p. 87.

67. Laney, *op. cit.*, p. 97.
68. Hamlin, *op. cit.*, p. 110.
69. E. John Hamlin, *Judges: At Risk in the Promised Land*, p. 2.
70. Arthur Cundall and Leon Morris, *Judges & Ruth*, p. 17.
71. E. John Hamlin, *Judges*, p. 82.
72. Cundall and Morris, *op. cit.*, p. 155.
73. A. Berkely Mickelsen, *Interpreting the Bible*, pp. 199-200.
74. Ryken, *op. cit.*, p. 83.
75. Cundall and Morris, *op. cit.*, p. p. 213.
76. Ibid., p. 241.
77. Ryken, *op. cit.*, pp. 81-82.
78. Mickelsen, *op. cit.*, pp. 281-282.
79. Gnana Robinson, *1 & 2 Samuel: Let Us Be Like the Nations*, p. 23.
80. Ibid., p. 30.
81. Joyce Baldwin, *1 & 2 Samuel*, p. 80.
82. Ibid., p. 85.
83. Ryken, *op. cit.*, pp. 41-42.
84. Baldwin, *op. cit.*, p. 123.
85. Ibid., pp. 194-195.
86. Mickelsen, *op. cit.*, pp. 265-266.
87. Walter Kaiser, Jr., *Toward an Old Testament Theology*, p. 154.
88. Pfeiffer, *op. cit.*, p. 237.
89. Ibid., p. 306.
90. Helmer Ringgren, *Israelite Religion*, p. 59.
91. Eakin, *op. cit.*, pp. 264-265.
92. Johannes Lindblom, *Prophecy in Ancient Israel*, p. 11.
93. Pfeiffer, *op. cit.*, p. 306.
94. Ibid., p. 309.
95. Walter Kaiser, Jr., *Toward an Exegetical Theology*, p. 197.
96. Pfeiffer, *op. cit.*, p. 310.
97. David Hubbard, *Hosea*, p. 62.
98. Gleason Archer, *Encyclopaedia of Biblical Difficulties*, p. 170.
99. Ringgren, *op. cit.*, p. 59.
100. Pfeiffer, *op. cit.*, pp. 357-358.
101. Samuel Schultz, *The Prophets Speak*, p. 61.
102. R.K. Harrison, *Jeremiah & Lamentations*, p. 137.
103. Pfeiffer, *op. cit.*, pp. 373-374.
104. Ralph Klein, *Israel in Exile: A Theological Interpretation*, p. 3.
105. Robert Anderson, *David: Signs and Wonders*, p. 31.
106. Ibid., p. 37.

107. John Goldingay, *Daniel*, p. 96.

108. Ibid., p. 168.

109. Anderson, *op. cit.*, p. 153.

110. John Taylor, *Ezekiel*, pp. 21-22.

111. Ibid., p. 62.

112. Bruce Vawter and Leslie Hoppe, *Ezekiel: A New Heart*, p. 42.

113. Ibid., p. 186.

114. Derek Kidner, *Ezra & Nehemiah*, p. 47.

115. Ibid., p. 77.

116. Ibid., p. 83.

117. Joyce Baldwin, *Esther*, p. 17.

118. Ibid., p. 79.

119. Gleason Archer, *A Survey of Old Testament Introduction*, p. 360.

120. Robinson, *op. cit.*, p. 279.

121. Ryken, *op. cit.*, p. 87.

122. Mickelsen, *op. cit.*, pp. 418-419.

123. Mays, *op. cit.*, p. 7.

124. *Constitutions of the Apostles*, lix.

125. James Crenshaw, *Old Testament Wisdom*, p. 19.

126. Morris Inch, *Understanding Bible Prophecy*, pp. 69-70.

127. Francis Anderson, *Job*, p. 15.

128. Morris Inch, *My Servant Job*, p. 41.

129. Derek Kidner, *Proverbs*, p. 129.

130. Archer, *A Survey of Old Testament Introduction*, p. 459.

131. G. Lloyd Carr, *The Song of Solomon*, p. 37.

132. Josephus, *Contra Apion*, I, pp. 209-210.

133. John Bright, *A History of Israel*, p. 414.

134. Ibid., p. 417.

135. Pfeiffer, *op. cit.*, p. 564.

136. Ibid., p. 586.

137. Bruce Metzger (ed.), *The Apocrypha of the Old Testament*, p. 63.

138. Ibid., p. 128.

139. Bright, *op. cit.*, p. 430.

140. Ryken, *op. cit.*, p. 131.

141. Ibid., p. 132.

142. Scott McKnight, *Interpreting the Synoptic Gospels,* p. 14.

143. Ibid., p. 109.

144. Ibid., p. 112.

145. Morris Inch, *Exhortations of Jesus According to Matthew* and *Up From the Depths: Mark as Tragedy*, p. 121.

146. Fred Craddock, *Luke*, p. 27.
147. Ethelbert Stauffer, *Jesus and His Story*, p. 33.
148. Craddock, *op. cit.*, p. 42.
149. Oscar Brooks, *The Drama of Decision: Baptism in the New Testament*, p. 32.
150. Douglas Hare, *op. cit.*, p. 20.
151. Craddock, *op. cit.*, p. 54.
152. Ibid., p. 56.
153. Craig Evans, *Luke*, pp. 106-107.
154. Ryken, *op. cit.*, p. 152.
155. Craddock, *op. cit.*, p. 112.
156. Lamar Williamson, Jr., *Mark*, p. 151.
157. Leon Morris, *Luke*, p. 206.
158. Evans, *op. cit.*, p. 180.
159. Morris, *op. cit.*, p. 241.
160. Craddock, *op. cit.*, p. 227.
161. Morris, *op. cit.*, p. 308.
162. Donald Hagner, *Matthew 14-28*, p. 651.
163. Marvin Wilson, *Our Father Abraham: Jewish Roots of the Christian Faith*, pp. 246-247.
164. Evans, *op. cit.*, p. 325.
165. Robert Stein, *Luke*, p. 566.
166. Morris, *op. cit.*, p. 356.
167. David Gooding, *According to Luke*, p. 345.
168. J. Ramsey Michaels, *John*, p. 21.
169. R.V.G. Tasker, *John*, p. 49.
170. Michaels, *op. cit.*, pp. 70-71.
171. Tasker, *op. cit.*, pp. 122-123.
172. Michaels, *op. cit.*, p. 196.
173. Morris Inch, "The Apologetic Use of *Sign* in the Fourth Gospel," *Man: The Perennial Question* (Inch, ed.), p. 7.
174. Tasker, *op. cit.*, pp. 212-213.
175. Craig Keener, *Bible Background Commentary: New Testament*, p. 316.
176. Tasker, *op. cit.*, p. 233.
177. Morris Inch, "Interpreting Luke-Acts," *The Literature and Meaning of Scripture* (Inch & Bullock, eds.), p. 173.
178. Ibid., p. 177.
179. Craddock, *op. cit.*, p. 273.

180. Morris Inch, "Salvation Formulae in Luke-Acts," *Man: The Perennial Question* (Inch, ed.), p. 116.
181. Inch, "Interpreting Luke-Acts," p. 183.
182. Bellarmino Bagatti, *The Church of the Circumcision*, p. 118.
183. I. Howard Marshall, *Acts*, p. 68.
184. Ibid., pp. 68-69.
185. Williams, *op. cit.*, p. 41.
186. Nils Holm, "Sunden's Role Theory and Glossolalia," *Psychology of Religion* (Molony, ed.), p. 218.
187. Williams, *op. cit.*, p. 59.
188. Ibid., p. 61.
189. Marshall, *op. cit.*, p. 98.
190. Williams, *op. cit.*, p. 83.
191. Ibid., p. 112.
192. Keener, *op. cit., pp. 338-339.*
193. *Ryken, op. cit.*, p. 155.
194. Ibid., p. 158.
195. Peter Davids, *James*, p. 10.
186. Douglas Moo, *James*, p. 99.
197. Marshall, *op. cit.*, pp. 153-154.
198. Williams, *op. cit.*, p. 157.
199. Ibid., p. 178.
200. Ibid., p. 191.
201. Arthur Nock, *Early Gentile Christianity and Its Hellenistic Background*, p. 2.
202. Ibid., p. 3.
203. Keener, *op. cit.*, pp. 356-357.
204. Williams, *op. cit.*, p. 252.
205. Keener, *op. cit.*, p. 529.
206. R. Alan Cole, *Galatians*, p. 193.
207. Ibid., p. 233.
208. Clorfene and Rogalsky, *op. cit.*, p. 51.
209. Brooks, *op. cit.*, p. 62.
210. Keener, *op. cit.*, p. 371.
211. Ibid., p. 373.
212. Williams, *op. cit.*, p. 309.
213. Leon Morris, *1 & 2 Thessalonians*, p. 26.
214. David Williams, *1 & 2 Thessalonians*, pp. 10-11.
215. Keener, *op. cit.*, p. 390.
216. Williams, *Acts*, p. 385.

217. Ibid., p. 425.
218. F.F. Bruce, *Romans*, pp. 59-62.
219. James Edwards, *Romans*, pp. 42-43.
220. Ibid., p. 282.
221. Williams, *Acts*, p. 427.
222. F.F. Bruce, *Philippians*, p. 8.
223. Gordon Fee, *1 and 2 Timothy, Titus*, p. 3.
224. Donald Guthrie, *The Pastoral Epistles*, p. 127.
225. Fee, *op. cit.*, p. 11.
226. Ibid., p. 12.
227. Wall, *op. cit.*, p. 14.
228. Ryken, *op. cit.*, p. 174.
229. Wall, *op. cit.*, p. 39.
230. Leon Morris, *Revelation*, p. 60.
231. Ibid., p. 81.
232. Ibid., p. 116.

BIBLIOGRAPHY

Anderson, Francis. *Job*. Downers Grove: Inter-Varsity, 1974.

Anderson, Robert. *Daniel: Signs and Wonders*. Grand Rapids: Eerdmans, 1984.

Archer, Gleason. *Encyclopaedia of Biblical Difficulties*. Grand Rapids: Zondervan, 1982.

_____. *A Survey of Old Testament Introduction*. Chicago: Moody, 1964.

Bogatti, Bellarmino. *The Church from the Circumcision*. Jerusalem: Franciscan, 1984.

Baldwin, Joyce. *Esther*. Downers Grove: Inter-Varsity, 1984.

_____. *1 & 2 Samuel*. Downers Grove: Inter-Varsity, 1988.

Bright, John. *A History of Israel*. Philadelphia: Westminster, 1981.

Brooks, Oscar. *The Drama of Decision: Baptism in the New Testament*. Peabody: Hendrickson, 1987.

Bruce, F.F. *Philippians*. Peabody: Hendrickson, 1993.

_____. *Romans*. Grand Rapids: Eerdmans, 1992.

Carr, G. Lloyd. *The Song of Solomon*. Downers Grove: Inter-Varsity, 1984.

Clorfene, Chaim and Yakov Rogalsky. *The Path of the Righteous Gentile*. Southfield: Targum, 1987.

Cole, R. Alan. *Exodus*. Downers Grove: Inter-Varsity, 1973.

_____. *Galatians*. Grand Rapids: Eerdmans, 1991.

Constitutions of the Apostles.

Craddock, Fred. *Luke*. Louisville: John Knox, 1990.

Crenshaw, James. *Old Testament Wisdom*. Atlanta: John Knox, 1981.

Cundall, Arthur and Leon Morris. *Judges and Ruth*. Downers Grove: Inter-Varsity, 1968.

Davids, Peter. *James*. Peabody: Hendrickson, 1993.

Eakin, Frank, Jr. *The Religion and Culture of Israel*. Washington, D.C.: University Press of America, 1977.

Edwards, James. *Romans*. Peabody: Hendrickson, 1993.

Evans, Craig. *Luke.* Peabody: Hendrickson, 1990.

Fee, Gordon. *1& 2 Timothy, Titus.* Peabody: Hendrickson, 1993.

Flint, V. Paul. *Strangers & Pilgrims: A Study of Genesis.* Neptune: Loizeaux, 1988.

Goldingay, John. *Daniel.* Dallas: Word, 1991.

Gooding, David. *According to Luke.* Grand Rapids: Eerdmans, 1987.

Griffen, David, et. al. *Founders of Constructive Postmodern Philosophy.* Albany: State University of New York, 1993.

Guthrie, Donald. *The Pastoral Epistles.* Grand Rapids: Eerdmans, 1992.

Hagner, Donald. *Matthew 14-28.* Dallas: Word, 1995.

Hamilton, Victor. *The Book of Genesis: Chapters 1-17.* Grand Rapids: Eerdmans, 1990.

Hamlin, E. John. *Joshua: Inheriting the Land.* Grand Rapids: Eerdmans, 1983.

_____. *Judges: At Risk in the Promised Land.* Grand Rapids: Eerdmans, 1990.

Hare, Douglas. *Matthew.* Louisville: John Knox, 1993.

Harrison, R.K. *Jeremiah and Lamentations.* Downers Grove: Inter-Varsity, 1973.

_____. *Leviticus.* Downers Grove: Inter-Varsity, 1980.

Hertzberg, Arthur (ed.). *Judaism.* New York: Barziller, 1961.

Holm, Nils. "Sunden's Role Theory and Glossolalia," *Psychology of Religion* (Malony, ed.), 213-230.

Hubbard, David. *Hosea.* Downers Grove: Inter-Varsity, 1989.

Inch, Morris. "The Apologetic Use of *Sign* in the Fourth Gospel," *Man: The Perennial Question* (Inch, ed.), 3-11.

_____. *Exhortations of Jesus According to Matthew* and *Up From the Depths: Mark as Tragedy.* Lanham: University Press of America, 1997.

_____. "Interpreting Luke-Acts," *The Literature and Meaning of Scripture* (Inch & Bullock, eds.), 173-189.

_____ and C. Hassell Bullock (eds). *The Literature and Meaning of Scripture.* Grand Rapids: Baker, 1981.

_____. *Man: The Perennial Question.* Lanham: University Press of America, 1999.

_____. *My Servant Job.* Grand Rapids: Baker, 1979.

_____. *Saga of the Spirit: A Biblical, Systematic, and Historical Theology of the Holy Spirit.* Grand Rapids: Baker, 1985.

_____. "Salvation Formulae in Luke-Acts," *Man: The Perennial Question* (Inch, ed.), 111-125.

_____. *Understanding Bible Prophecy.* New York: Harper & Row, 1977.

Josephus. *Contra Apion*

Kaiser, Walter, Jr. *Toward an Exegetical Theology.* Grand Rapids: Baker, 1981.

_____. *Toward Old Testament Ethics.* Grand Rapids: Academia Books, 1983.

_____. *Toward an Old Testament Theology.* Grand Rapids: Zondervan, 1978.

Keener, Craig. *Bible Background Commentary: New Testament.* Downers Grove: InterVarsity, 1993.

Kidner, Derek. *Ezra & Nehemiah.* Downers Grove: Inter-Varsity, 1979.

_____. *Genesis.* Downers Grove: Inter-Varsity, 1967.

_____. *Proverbs.* Downers Grove: Inter-Varsity, 1964.

Klein, Ralph. *Israel in Exile: A Theological Interpretation.* Philadelphia: Westminster, 1979.

Kline, Meredith. *Treaty of the Great King.* Grand Rapids: Eerdmans, 1963.

Laney, J. Carl. *Baker's Concise Bible Atlas.* Grand Rapids: Baker, 1988.

Licht, Jacob. *Storytelling in the Bible.* Jerusalem: Magnes, 1986.

Lindblom, Johannes. *Prophecy in Ancient Israel.* Philadelphia: Muhlenberg, 1962.

Malefijt, Annemarie de Waal. *Religion and Culture.* New York: Macmillan, 1968.

Malony, H. Newton (ed.). *Psychology of Religion.* Grand Rapids: Baker, 1991.

Marshall, I. Howard. *Acts.* Grand Rapids: Eerdmans, 1991.

Mays, James. *Psalms.* Louisville: John Knox, 1994.

McKnight, Scot. *Interpreting the Synoptic Gospels.* Grand Rapids: Baker, 1988.

Metzger, Bruce (ed.). *The Apocrypha of the Old Testament.* New York: Oxford University, 1965.

Michaels, J. Ramsey. *John.* Peabody: Hendrickson, 1993.

Mickelsen, A. Berkeley. *Interpreting the Bible.* Grand Rapids: Eerdmans, 1963.

Moo, Douglas. *James.* Grand Rapids: Eerdmans, 1985.

Morris, Leon. *1 & 2 Thessalonians*. Grand Rapids: Eerdmans, 1984.

_____. *Luke*. Grand Rapids: Eerdmans, 1990.

_____. *Revelation*. Grand Rapids: Eerdmans, 1990.

Nock, Arthur. *Early Gentile Christianity and Its Hellenistic Background*. New York: Harper,1964.

Peters, Edgar. *Chaos and Order in the Capital Markets*. New York: Wiley, 1991.

Pfeiffer, Charles. *Old Testament History*. Grand Rapids: Baker, 1973.

Polkinghorne, John. *Quarks, Chaos & Christianity*. New York: Crossroad, 1997.

Ringgren, Helmer. *Israelite Religion*. Philadelphia: Fortress, 1966.

Robinson, Gnana. *1 & 2 Samuel: Let Us Be Like the Nations*. Grand Rapids: Eerdmans, 1993.

Ryken, Leland. *How to Read the Bible as Literature*. Grand Rapids: Zondervan, 1984.

Schultz, Samuel. *Deuteronomy: The Gospel of Love*. Chicago: Moody, 1971.

_____. *The Prophets Speak*. New York: Harper & Row, 1968.

Seltzer, Robert. *Jewish People, Jewish Thought*. New York: Macmillan, 1980.

Speiser, E.A. *Genesis*. Garden City: Doubleday, 1982.

Stauffer, Ethelbert. *Jesus and His Story*. New York: Knopf, 1960.

Stegner, William. *Narrative Theology in Early Jewish Christianity*. Louisville: Westminster/John Knox, 1989.

Stein, Robert. *Luke*. Nashville: Broadman, 1992.

Steinberg, Milton. *Basic Judaism*. New York: Harcourt, Brace & World, 1947.

Tasker, R.V.G. *John*. Grand Rapids: Eerdmans, 1992.

Taylor, John. *Ezekiel*. Downers Grove: Inter-Varsity, 1969.

Tinder, Glen. *The Political Meaning of Christianity*. New York: HarperCollins, 1991.

Vowter, Bruce and Leslie Hoppe. *Ezekiel: A New Heart*. Grand Rapids: Eerdmans, 1991.

Wall, Robert. *Revelation*. Peabody: Hendrickson, 1991.

Walton, John and Victor Matthews, *Bible Background Commentary: Genesis-Deuteronomy*. Downers Grove: InterVarsity, 1997.

Wenham, Gordon. *Genesis 1-15*. Dallas: Word, 1991.

Williams, David. *Acts*. Peabody: Hendrickson, 1993.

_____. *1 & 2 Thessalonians*. Peabody: Hendrickson, 1994.

Williamson, Lamar, Jr. *Mark*. Louisville: John Knox, 1983.

Wilson, Marvin. *Our Father Abraham: Jewish Roots of the Christian Faith.* Grand Rapids: Eerdmans, 1989.

Wolf, Herbert. *An Introduction to the Old Testament Pentateuch.* Chicago: Moody, 1991.

INDEX